Joe Saward's 2022 Green Notebook

Joe Saward is a British-born journalist, who works in
Formula 1 motor racing. He travels the world to
all the Grands Prix, and has done so for 35 years.
When not on the road, he lives in France

Also by Joe Saward

Jaguar V12 Race Cars (with Ian Bamsey)

The World Atlas of Motor Racing

Brock and Moffat on the road to Spa

The Grand Prix Saboteurs

The Man who caught Crippen

Fascinating F1 Facts Vol 1

Fascinating F1 Facts Vol 2

Fascinating F1 Facts Vol 3

Fascinating F1 Facts Vol 4

To the little girl who
called me "Papi d'amour"

First published in 2023 by Flat Out Publishing

3 5 7 9 8 6 4 1

All rights reserved

Copyright © Joe Saward 2023

The right of Joe Saward to be identified as the author of this work has asserted his right under the Copyright, Designs and Patents Act 1988.

www.flatoutpublishing.com

This book is sold subject to the conditions that it shall not, by way of trade or otherwise, be lent, re-sold, hired out, or otherwise circulated without the publisher's prior consent in any form of binding or cover other than that in which it is published and without a similar condition including this condition being imposed on the subsequent purchaser.

ISBN 0-9554868-7-4

Introduction

When I first started writing for Autosport, in the early 1980s, it seemed to me that no motor racing magazine ever picked up its readers and carried them away on a magic carpet to the places where international races were taking place. Reports began with "Such-and-such was quick away from his pole position", and there almost never any suggestion of scene-setting. No-one thought that race fans wanted more than facts.

I started writing reports with a few opening paragraphs providing some local colour and within a couple of years I had a column in the magazine called "Globetrotter". I have no idea who came up with the name, but it fitted well. I was always on the road, going from one race to the next, and I rarely spent much time in the office.

For five years Globetrotter appeared in Autosport but then, as electronic communication began, I transferred my life to France and worked for anyone who was willing to pay me. The column reappeared in a publication called Formula 1 News.

The goal was always to amuse and inform, but primarily to transport to exotic places all over the world, and give them a sense of what it is like to part of Grand Prix racing, and to take them out of their day-to-day lives, even if it was just for a few minutes.

Globetrotter disappeared at some point along the way, but the spirit of the original idea remains unchanged, even if today it is published on the Internet, under the "Green Notebook from..." banner. If you are looking for it, you can simple Google joeblogsf1.com.

The Green Notebook name comes from the fact that I use notebooks, manufactured by Moleskine and green in colour. These suit my purpose perfectly, although finding them is harder than ever as the company has gone off into a world of pastel shades, rather than sticking with solid old-fashioned colours. I live in hope that I have sufficient supplies to get me through to the end of my career, or that I will be able to find more by visiting book shops around the world.

The notes within these books are usually just scrawls, often one word, reminding me of a story that I must write, as the Green Notebook is not just about travelling, but also about what is happening in the Formula 1 world at any given moment.

– Joe Saward's 2022 Green Notebook –

From a quiet forest in Normandy

14 December 2021

These last days have been tumultuous times for Formula 1, with the extraordinary World Championship showdown in Abu Dhabi. But one needs perspective in these matters and sitting at home, watching the activity on the marsh which my home overlooks, provides a good opportunity to think clearly about things. The ragondin (coypu) swimming in the pond and the silly scuttling moorhens remind one that outside the world of F1, rivers still flow to the sea and the seasons still change, despite what happened in Yas Marina.

Social media has become a battleground between supporters of one side or the other and everyone is throwing things at Michael Masi, a man who had to make difficult decisions, which turned out to be controversial. That's the problem with being a race director. You don't ever get praise when things go right. You only get mentioned when things go wrong. It's like being an F1 spark plug...

After Nicholas Latifi crashed (and those who blame the Canadian for causing this really do need to have their heads examined by professional medical staff) there was a problem. There was a lot of debris on the track, more than one could deal with using a Virtual Safety Car, but not really enough for a Red Flag. It was a Safety Car moment. This was the Mercedes nightmare because Lewis Hamilton's lead was effectively wiped out, which was unfair, but the way the rules are. Hamilton was not far from the pit lane entrance and so the strategists had to make a quick call. Stay out. To have come in and get new tyres would perhaps have led Red Bull to leave Verstappen out and that would have given him track position that could have handed him victory at the restart. Logically the race was going to end under caution, so Lewis was safe. But Red Bull stopped Max, put him on soft tyres and sent him out again. That put him behind some backmarkers in the queue behind the Safety Car. Normally the lapped cars would be allowed to pass the Safety Car when the wreckage was cleaned up and then the race could start again. In that case, Hamilton was screwed, except that there were not enough laps to do that. The race would have ended under caution. And what a damp squib that would have been, with Lewis and Max driving around the last lap, unable to fight. An initial message from Race Control said that the lapped cars should remain in place. That was normal because there was still clean-up work going on and the safety of the track workers was still a question.

Then Masi gave the instruction that only the cars between Hamilton and Verstappen should unlap themselves. Before that we heard Max explaining that it was typical of the FIA to leave the lapped cars in place to screw him (he and Red Bull both have a persecution complex in this respect). Masi's instruction was logical in that the cars behind Max were irrelevant and there was no time to clear them all. They did not matter. The ones between Lewis and Max would get in the way of the title fight. But with Max on new tyres and Lewis on old tyres this effectively gave Max a chance to snatch the title. Max took it. Lewis tried to stop it.

It wasn't fair perhaps, but it was within the rules. Live sport has a habit of creating such insane situations and referees have to deal with them. Masi did nothing wrong. He used the powers he has to do what he felt was best was the World Championship. What happened was no-one's fault. Max was lucky. Lewis was not. I never want to hear Max complain again that the FIA has got it in for him, and I want Christian Horner to learn a lot about stewarding when he attends the FIA Stewards event later this winter. Lewis took his defeat with grace and style. Toto and his cohorts reacted as one would expect them to react, but is appealing the various decisions going to help F1? No, probably not. It was the sporting gods having their say. Losing with grace is better than losing with lawyers. But I feel their pain. It wasn't fair and it wasn't right, but it was the way the rules are.

Are there better ways? Perhaps, and I hope that the FIA will spend some time looking at the Safety Car rules and asking whether this is the right way to run things. Masi's only fault, if you call it that, was to try to make sure there was a race at the end. And he did that for the fans and for the good of the sport.. NASCAR has some complicated rules which can extend races when there is a late caution. Perhaps F1 should have the same. But perhaps not.

Anyway, the subsequent mess and the celebrations, mixed with Mercedes's pain and sense of outrage, combined to create a bitter-sweet evening, with work delayed and plans blown apart. We did not get the official race result until 00.05. Five and a half hours after the chequered flag fell. There is only so much one can do when the F1 balloon goes up. And thus it was that at 02.30 having put together GP+ and sent it into the world, I left the Media Centre in Abu Dhabi to the last of the scribblers (there were still a few left) and I walked through the deserted car parks of Yas Island to the Media Parking (the shuttles had stopped). It was cool and quiet. It had been quite a day. And Saturday night had involved only a couple of hours of sleep so I was feeling weary.

But it had also been a long, long season and it was time to go home. But that is not always easy. I drove through the night and the desert for the next two hours, up to Dubai, passing the Expo site on the way, and arriving at Dubai International Airport still in darkness with the first wave of morning flyers heading into the airport to fly away in different directions. I tried to work as I waited for the flight. The story of the race was the lead item on the international news being piped into the lounge but I could barely keep my eyes open by then. I was writing words that were all jumbled up. At some point I heard the muezzin calling the faithful with his salat al fajr, the pre-dawn call to prayer. The start of a new day. On the plane I was asleep long before we left the tarmac.

We had struggled to find the right tone for the GP+ cover. We didn't want it to be too this or too that, but we wanted it to be positive and memorable. In the end we chose "A Night to Remember" and a picture of Lewis and Max chinking bottles on the podium. In the end it was perfect, although as someone pointed out there was film called A Night to Remember about the sinking of Titanic. Did we choose the title for that reason? No, it was just a coincidence...

The green notebook was filled with scribbles during the weekend. Including such notes as "Piastri = champion" and "French govt EXPO delegation". I had the words "Philip Morris" circled and various scrawls about races: "USA 2026", "Bahrain + I week" and "Monaco ?" there was also "RB dept moving in-house FIA" and "Raducano/Bolt/Larson", "Vegas 23" and "BWT-Alpine".

French Government EXPO meant that in the days before the Grand Prix French GP promoter Eric Boullier (who heads the promotions company that runs the race) was invited to join a delegation with the French Sports Minister to the EXPO in Dubai, to tell the world about France's sporting achievement and about a rumour that Eric was recently spotted visiting the Elysée Palace, where President Emmanuel Macron hangs out. On Monday night, the French motorsport federation (FFSA) had a prize-giving to which Macron sent a video message, underlining the importance of French motorsport and saying that the government would help to save the French GP. Great news.

"Philip Morris" meant that the Abu Dhabi Grand Prix was the last race in which the tobacco company Philip Morris International (PMI) was involved in an official capacity. The firm, which owns Marlboro, has been the biggest F1 sponsor in history, dating back to 1971 when Marlboro first sponsored the BRM team. The deal lasted for three years but without much success and in the final year Marlboro was also involved with Frank Williams's Iso team. In 1974 Marlboro did a new deal with McLaren, starting a

relationship that lasted until 1996 and then Ferrari. It was still a significant sponsor of Ferrari this year, with the Mission Winnow concept. But that has not been renewed. PMI may still have some hospitality packages in the years ahead but it looks like all sponsorships are finished – which is something that should not pass unnoticed...
The word is that Ferrari will up its links with Amazon in the future.

The note "USA 2026" is fairly self-explicit. There is a deal in place between F1 and Austin for another five years. It will be announced soon. The "Bahrain + one week" note meant that Bahrain is about to announced an extension for its deal with F1 and this will either go to 2032, or possibly to 2037.

The news that Abu Dhabi has signed a new contract to be last race of the Formula 1 season until 2030 was no real surprise, following the announcements in recent weeks about 10 year deals for Qatar (2023-2032) and Saudi Arabia (2021-2030) and it is entirely logical that Bahrain too will protect its investment in the sport. The kingdom never gave details of how long the current deal is. It was signed in 2016 and at the time there was talk of a 15 year deal. The truth is that it was a 10-year contract covering 2017-2026, with an option to continue beyond that. That option can be for either five or 10 years. Thus, F1 will have at least four races in the Middle East from 2023 until 2030, although it is unlikely to increase from that.

The "Monaco ?" note is perhaps the most interesting because it indicates that the future of the Monaco GP is not yet sorted out – and no-one wants to talk about it. Monaco and Formula 1 are like an old marriage. It is hard to imagine one without the other, but they don't always get on. Prince Albert of Monaco said not so long ago that the Grand Prix was worth $1 billion for Monaco – just for the weekend. That did not include the value it has pulling in tourists for the rest of the year. Or to put it in another way, Monaco needs F1. And F1 really needs Monaco because a World Championship without Monaco is hard to imagine. The last deal, signed in 2010, was for 10 years to cover the period between 2011 to 2020.
As the final race was cancelled because of the global pandemic ,the F1 group offered an additional race for 2021 and a one-year deal has been cobbled together for 2022 – on the basis that Monaco would give up its four-day format.

The last deal was negotiated by Bernie Ecclestone and the President of the Automobile Club de Monaco (ACM), Michel Boeri. Ecclestone is now 92 and out of the picture, but Boeri at 82 has recently been re-elected for another five-year term. He has held the office since 1972 and has some strong views about the importance of his race. His dad Etienne was President of the ACM between 1965 and 1968 and so it's rather a personal thing. But Monaco has some significant problems in relation to F1 that need sorting. There is no overtaking and so the races are generally dull, despite the race being a great spectacle. The fee Monaco pays is fair smaller than any other race. TV coverage is also not controlled by F1 as Monaco insisted on keeping control of its role as host broadcaster. In recent years this has been well below the modern standards. The club also retains some of the trackside signage, but this is also troublesome as the ACM slots are muddled and do not follow F1's usual one sponsor per corner philosophy. It's a jumble of names. It also has a big deal with TAG-Heuer, which does not sit well with F1's partner Rolex. There are problems over hospitality as the ACM controls much of it and F1 is not cashing in on the potential value of the event. And the quality of the offering may not be up to F1's usual standards. So there is a lot to discuss and negotiation is difficult because neither side wishes to change its demands. Monaco's unique status has weakened somewhat in recent years with the Singapore night race and more recently with the arrival of Saudi Arabia and Miami, both of which are paying far more than Monaco. Thus Monaco's status may not have quite the same power that it had under Bernie Ecclestone and it is clear that the ACM's attitude, which filters through the whole organisation, seems to be that no-one in the world knows how to organise a race as well as Monaco does, which is patently not the case any longer, if indeed it ever was. It is not a favourite for those who work in F1. Not even close. And the arrogance grates on the nerves.

There is no question that F1 would be poorer without Monaco, at least in some respects, but it is also fair to say that F1 gives the Principality a huge amount and gets relatively little in return, except the intangible value of association... It's a tough one to negotiate.

The note "RB dept moving in-house to FIA" means that there will be changes within the Formula 1 group during 2022 with the company's managing director of motorsport Ross Brawn (67) expected to retire and the chief technical officer Pat Symonds (68) also standing down. The F1 technical group in London is out of place and so will soon come under the control of the FIA, with the remaining engineers reporting to FIA chief technology officer

Nikolas Tombazis. This is entirely logical as the idea of the commercial rights holder running a technical operation to work on car design regulations and to help with circuit design, never really made much sense. It is a little known fact that before he joined the FIA Tombazis spent some months working as a consultant with the Formula 1 team of engineers in London, and so he knows them well. The principal members of the group are the F1 head of aerodynamics Jason Somerville and the head of vehicle performance, who also plays a big role in circuit work, is Craig Wilson.

The FIA operation is located at the FIA Logistics and Technical Centre, in Valleiry, in the Haute-Savoie region of France, close to the Swiss border and the FIA offices in Geneva. It is not clear whether the London-based engineers will be based in Europe, or whether they will work remotely, or will leave. The FIA already has a number of engineers working at Valleiry, including Tim Goss, who works as Tombazis's deputy. However, not all of the FIA engineers are there as Dominic Harlow, the head of F1 technical audit, operates from the UK. This will not impact on the sporting side of the organisation, which is headed by Steve Nielsen, which will continue to operate from London.

The note about VIPs in Abu Dhabi was self-explanatory with the most interesting for racing folks being that NASCAR champion Kyle Larson was in the F1 house. And he was drooling. I was fortunate enough to spend some time with him, showing him around and introducing him to a few people. Nothing shows the blinkered nature of F1 better than the NASCAR champion walking into the paddock and not being recognised by photographers (who are usually good at this stuff) or journalists. Anyway, Larson was loving it. And wanted to have a go in an F1 car… There was an interesting conversation too between Kyle and Daniil Kvyat, who wants to go to race in NASCAR…

Larson said that he hadn't been into F1 much before the started watching Drive to Survive on Netflix. Boom! That shows you the kind of impact that the series has had and the future impact it will have with F1 growing in the US markets. After Abu Dhabi most folks went home, but some went off to Nevada where a number of F1 execs went to work on closing a deal with the city and to plan exactly where the race track could be…

The recent months has seen a scramble in F1 circles as race promoters begin to realise that the growth of F1 is causing more demand for Grands Prix and so it is best to get new long-term contracts done quickly, so as to avoid losing out in what will become a game of musical chairs in the future.

F1 remains big news around the world but, as I wrote in my GP+ column, it is not the only thing in the world.

"They say that people on islands tend to have less of a global view than those who live on the mainland," I wrote. "It certainly felt that way on Yas Island over the weekend, where a lot of the Formula 1 circus believed that there was nothing in the world apart from the World Championship showdown between Lewis Hamilton and Max Verstappen; and the fight for the Constructors' title between Red Bull Racing and Mercedes. In the heat of a battle one can lose perspective about what is important and one does things which later on, when things have calmed down and there are cooler heads, seem to have been a little excessive.

"The 2021 Abu Dhabi Grand Prix was a strange affair, a story so bizarre that no-one could have imagined such an outcome. If it was a film script it would have been thrown out as being unrealistic. For some, it was a fabulous story, for others it was unfair.

Was it luck? Was it a situation where the Race Director, trying to do the right thing, created something very wrong? These are the kind of questions that will be asked in the days ahead. The sport did not want to end an epic F1 season with the cars crossing the finish line running line astern – under caution – unable to fight. Did Mercedes get it wrong by not pitting Hamilton? Was Michael Masi right to call the race as he did? What we got in the end seemed unfair.

"What is important now, unsatisfactory though it may be, is to protect the World Championship. One cannot overturn the result. It happened. You cannot take a World Championship away after the event. It would make a mockery of the sport and would, inevitably lead to endless law suits flying about that no-one wants and nobody needs. It's just sport. Will Mercedes sell more cars if they win another title? Will Red Bull become cooler to its target audience because it won another title?

"The sport should be treated with respect. I detest the Verstappen fans who boo Lewis, the greatest Formula 1 driver we have ever seen. He deserves more respect. He is one of the cleanest racers there has ever been. I dislike people who suggested that Max would settle the title by driving into Lewis. He too deserves more respect.

"I have enormous respect for both men and I think what we are seeing at the moment is epic stuff and we will be talking about it years from now, remembering a time when the old lion Lewis Hamilton battled with the rising star Max Verstappen to be the leader of the pride.

"Formula 1 is about passion but it should never be treated as something other than that. Yes, winning and losing are important but the world outside the Yas Marina Circuit did not stop because of what happened on the island on Sunday evening.

"Perhaps this was a pivotal moment in Formula 1 history, but elsewhere babies were born, old folks passed on, people still fell in and out of love.

"The world turned ever onwards. On Monday, Abu Dhabi moves on to the next event: the FINA World Swimming Championships, in which another group of elite athletes would be battling for titles. As Kimi Raikkonen would say, it is what it is. It's happened. It's gone. The sport should learn the lessons, if there are lessons that need to be learned, but that should be the end of it. It should not become a court room battle."

From a lounge at DXB

21 March 2022

DXB is Dubai International Airport and while a lot of Formula 1 folk went from Bahrain for a few days before moving on to Jeddah, I decided not to, on the basis that I really don't need any more probes stuck up my nose after two years of endless testing, and while it really does no bother me any longer, I just cannot be bothered to do it unless I have to. And one can fly through Dubai without needing to test, but one cannot enter without a negative result. So I stayed in Bahrain for a day and a bit, catching up on work, and then headed off and will be in Jeddah tomorrow. DXB at night is one of the places where F1 people tend to meet up. The lounges are wonderful. It's a good place to get a last glass of wine before heading into Saudi Arabia, where one has to cope with Prohibition-like rules.

I went to Bahrain after two weeks without Internet, thanks to our Russian friends messing up the satellite that I need in order to get on to the Web, having made the wise decision a few years ago that living in the wilds of France between races was really a wonderful thing to do. I have no regrets, but then no-one really considered that there was someone like Putin, who might want to take the world back in time and fight wars that no-one needs. Judging by what one can read, he's probably regretting that now given that the war was not over in a few days and Russia has been dumped on massively by the international community.

Anyway, I did meet one Russian F1 regular in Bahrain and commiserated with him. He said he was not having an easy time, living in the West, but was glad that to take his mind off the serious stuff, he had got in his car and driven to Warsaw to collect refugees from Ukraine, who needed help.

People think that F1 is filled with selfish and unpleasant individuals (there are a few truly horrible examples) but most F1 people are actually remarkably human and more than a few are truly remarkable. I met a long time pal at accreditation in Bahrain on the day before the action began. He has been an F1 wheeler-dealer for a LOT of years and such people are not always known for their humanity.

When I asked how he was keeping, he replied that he was fine and that he had 18 children more than he had had when I last saw him. I was somewhat taken aback by this declaration as I was pretty sure I'd seen him at some point in 2021. "I run an orphanage," he smiled. "We have 18 new children from Ukraine. Now I have 43 children."

It is nice to be able to report on such things… rather than just the usual dog-eat-dog politics of the sport. It warms the heart.

The weekend was filled with catch-ups because there were a lot of people who I have not seen in F1 for the last two years and it was fun to have some of the old faces back in action again. There was precious real news beyond the dregs of the dreadful

Abu Dhabi story from last year, with a report that is going to cost the FIA a pile of money because it appears to have dismissed a man who did nothing wrong and there is no reason why Michael Masi would want to stay with an organisation that threw him under the bus, but has no real explanation of what he did wrong to deserve it. Of course, those who are following in his wake now feel that they don't want to be exposed to the same sort of things and I did hear that one race director was looking for some guarantees that the same thing won't happen again. I don't know who one should blame for this caving in to external pressures but the FIA did itself no favours.

Still, perhaps we should give the new folk a chance to prove that they can do the job properly, although the last few months have not been stellar. The FIA does not need to be loved as an organisation, but it helps if it is understood and respected and so there is a lot of work to do... I'm not sure that having two race directors and some kind of eye in the sky in Geneva will really help as there are bound to be differences of opinion and so there will be more inconsistency than was the case with one man. Still, it probably won't hurt the place to get shaken up a bit after 12 years of Jean Todt.

If the award existed, then Jean would have been "Micromanager of the Year" for most of that time and now there needs to be a new structure because the new President does not give the impression that he is a man given to all-nighters.

Anyway, the notes in the green notebook in Bahrain were very limited. A lot is happening in racing terms and yet at the same time not a lot is happening in F1 news and politics. There will be an announcement soon that Qatar will step in to replace the Russian Grand Prix, which is as dead as a Norwegian Blue parrot. We will be in Doha on the Russian date and if you are reading this and have not yet booked a hotel room, it is too late...

There will also soon be an announcement about a Grand Prix on the streets of Las Vegas from 2023 until at least 2032. This will be a night race and part of the track will be a section of The Strip. It sounds amazing and will give the US three races for the next three years before the Austin date goes up for auction again.

If F1 growth rates in the US continue as they are now, that could be a fascinating battle, as there will likely be other contenders who could outspend Austin.

The Bahrain race marked the first appearance of a new managing director of commercial activities in F1, who takes up the same sort of role that Sean Bratches had. Brandon Snow in an American marketer with a background in advertising, both in the US and in Europe, specifically in Poland, Austria and Germany. He then spent some time with the NBA before moving to the games publishing firm Activision Blizzard as its head of esports. At F1 he will be responsible for sponsorship, licensing, esports and marketing.

I had a rather odd experience when I met Gilles Villeneuve in the paddock in Bahrain. Well, I met a Gilles Villeneuve, the grandson of the late, great Ferrari driver, who was killed at Zolder in 1982. Gilles II seemed to be a sweet little chap, about three months old, and was there with his father Jacques, the 1997 World Champion. JV is still commentating about F1 for France's Canal+, while also racing NASCAR stock cars in the US as and when he can. He did a commendable job in the recent Daytona 500 and hopes to be back in action again soon. He was also showing interest in the recently-announced plan for NASCAR to run a car in the Le Mans 24 Hours in 2023, which will be the 100th anniversary of the famous event. It seems that NASCAR is keen to promote itself in Europe and Le Mans wants higher profile in the United States, so it sounds a little like love at first sight. The car will be entered in the Garage 56 category, which means that it would not have any opposition, but must comply with the safety rules.

It all sounds very interesting and Jacques would be the perfect driver, although it sounds like multiple NASCAR champion Jimmie Johnson, who is now racing IndyCars, will be involved as well.

Bahrain showed that the new F1 regulations seem to work pretty well and so there is great excitement about what we can expect for the rest of the year. With a Ferrari 1-2 – and no questions about whether or not the cars are legal – F1 is in a healthy place. Ferrari needs some success as it has not won a World Championship since 2008, which is an unimpressive 14 years ago. Mind you, between 1983 and 1999 it was a similar – but longer – story.

The last note that I have scrawled in the notebook related to the war in Ukraine (Sorry, Vlad, but a "special military operation" is the kind of thing when shadowy figures in dark combat fatigues arrive in the night in Black Hawk choppers and slot away bad guys in an efficient manner). This has impacted the F1 world to some extent with the departure of the Russian GP, Nikita Mazepin and a few sponsors, but is likely to cause further disruption in ways that might not be immediately obvious. Last year Formula 1 had a couple of near-misses with the delivery of freight at the Brazilian and Qatar Grands Prix and during the pre-season testing Haas ran into trouble when a freight plane had technical problems.

F1 logistics is one of the most impressive things about the sport, but it involves an enormous effort to get the entire circus from one track to another in just a few days. Formula 1 needs seven Boeing 747 freighters to go to each flyaway event and seven more to take the equipment on to the next destination. This means that there are around 160 planes needing to be booked each year. The war in Ukraine has significantly reduced the world's air freight capacity with one of the biggest freight operators being the Volga-Dnepr Group's AirBridgeCargo (ABC) operation, which has a fleet of 17 Jumbos. They have all been withdrawn from international operation.

There are still about 250 others but there is huge pressure in the market and so prices are rising. Other airlines have been forced to reroute to avoid flying over Russian air space and so fuel costs have gone up and delays have increased. Added to this the price of fuel has increased so it's a double whammy. Freight prices have gone through the roof. Will this make a difference for Formula 1? Not immediately, unless freight was booked to go on Russian planes, but the danger for the sport lies ahead if planes "go technical" because replacements are hard to find. And, of course, it will add to the team costs…

Mind you, the traditional European races, which require a fleet of around 300 trucks criss-crossing Europe, is going to cause trouble as well because of the escalation of fuel costs. Not to mention all the Brexit paperwork and, of course, the issue of the environment.

My notebook is rather greener than F1 in this respect.

From another airport lounge

28 March 2022

The Jeddah weekend was dominated by the explosion that occurred on Friday evening, five miles to the east of the circuit, at the Saudi Aramco North Jeddah Bulk Plant, close to the King Abdulaziz International Airport. This happened a few minutes before the first F1 practice session began and a huge dark cloud of oil smoke was visible, although this had no impact on the circuit, as strong winds were blowing from the north. So you can safely assume that any report you may have read about smoke blowing across the circuit was written by someone who was not there.

The other amusing giveaway were the reports that this had all happened 10 miles from the circuit. These probably derived from people using Google Directions to figure out the distance and not bothering to look at how far it was as the crow flies, rather than in a car. Figuring out what was happening was not that hard. One found a street that lined up with the source of the smoke and then used Google Earth and simply followed the direction of the street until one found an oil facility. Readers of this blog may remember back in December that I accidentally dropped by the "fuel farm" at the airport in Jeddah – on my way home – so when things went bang on Friday, I had a pretty good idea of what had happened and where.

The Houthi movement in Yemen has been firing missiles and drones at Saudi Arabia for months… and they soon claimed responsibility for their strike.

To be honest I was not overly bothered by all this. Having grown up in London in the 1970s and 1980s, one was used to bomb attacks caused by the IRA. One day, if I ever write the story of my life, I might relate adventures that I had as a result of this, but today is not really the moment.

Anyway, when I stopped to think about it, by far the scariest thing in Jeddah were the driving standards, which offered a much more immediate threat to life and limb than any explosive device. I am not kidding. After years travelling the world, watching drivers in action, I have reached the conclusion that while some drive too quickly, and some drive without sufficient competence, the two elements are rarely combined.

In Saudi Arabia every journey to and from the circuit (and it was not any great distance) seemed to include seeing at least one shunt – and a number of near-misses. The statistics bear this out. In 2010 there were only 250,000 drivers in Saudi Arabia, today there are three million, so in 12 years the number of people with driving licences has multiplied by 12. According to a recent survey by MDPI (whoever they are) Saudi Arabia has one of the highest death rates caused by road accidents, with about 130,000 people each year popping their expensive clogs and not coming home from missions to the supermarket. It really is quite shocking. I decided at one point that I might have finally found a plan for how to get rich. I shall write a book called "How to use Indicators" and have it translated into Arabic, so that the drivers of Saudi Arabia, of which there are believed to be around three million of the 35 million people in the country, will be able to spend more time on Earth before disappearing off to some garden in the sky.

If you check out the website Expatica.com, which is designed for foreigners who want to settle abroad, there are some useful tips about driving in Saudi, the first of which is: "grow a pair of eyes in the back of your head". I guess that if chameleons could get driving licences, they would be safe in Saudi Arabia, as each of their eyes can pivot and focus independently, allowing them to observe two different objects simultaneously. I cannot say I saw any chameleons driving in Jeddah, but I did see an awful lot of absolutely hopeless driving, most of it at very high speed and often with the driver squinting into a mobile phone, adjusting his dishdash, or preening his beard. It seems to be a society in which bearded men show off their masculinity by driving with a machismo that would cause even Spanish bull fighters to blanch. The Saudis tailgate, undertake, text at 100 mph and never (ever) use indicators.

Expatica also warned that one should watch out for camels at night, although I cannot say I ever saw one, probably because they have all become roadkill. The civic planners of Jeddah have adopted the roundabout for some junctions, but the locals have not yet grasped the concept of priority and assume that this is dictated by the size of your vehicle. The bigger you are, the bigger your priority.

Weirdly, they have also adopted the Brazilian ritorno concept, where in order to turn across a major road one has to go past the junction you want and then hang a Uey to go back to turn. This means that after your Uey you have to cross four or five lanes with cars barrelling along at daft speeds, the drivers in whichever lane they fancy. They say that safety standards are improving rapidly, but I didn't see much evidence of this.

However, one has to say that most Saudis are very friendly, although some of the ruling classes seem a little haughty and arrogant, with a sense of entitlement that one often sees in pay-drivers in the motorsport world. Because they have tons of money, they seem to think that this somehow transforms them into masters of the universe. Perhaps it does…

F1 is in Saudi Arabia for one reason alone. We can pretend otherwise, if we wish to be delusional, but the truth is that we are in Jeddah because the Saudis pay more than other places. A lot more. A shed-load more. F1 doesn't talk about who pays what, but the biggest paying races each year are in the Middle East and Asia, and Saudi seems to pay the biggest fee these days, although perhaps Qatar has gone beyond that. There is also a major global partnership with Saudi Aramco. Ultimately, the actual numbers are not important, but one must understand that most of the decisions made are liable to be swayed by the impressive number of noughts on the F1 bank statements. F1 needs to deny this, of course, because these days everyone wants to ride the band wagon of social awareness, to please the younger generations, who seem to think that companies ought to have a broader purpose, rather than existing solely in pursuit of profit. This is a concept born from the global financial crisis of 2007-2008, which demonstrated that there are drawbacks to the pursuit of profit for its own sake. Today companies are supposed to achieve more if they are seen to be a positive force for good in society.

The inclusion of Saudi Arabia in the FIA Formula 1 World Championship was always a risk, but the powers-that-be believed that the financial returns from such a relationship would outweigh the potential damage of the association with a country often portrayed as being authoritarian and ultra-conservative, which has long attracted criticism for its strict interpretation of Sharia law, its excessive use of capital punishment, its poor human rights record and its role in the Yemeni civil war. One must say that there is some evidence that change is happening and the younger people in Saudi are keen to move forwards, but not everyone is broad-minded.

And changing the image of a country is not helped by mass executions or doing away with critics in medieval style. This is why F1 had to consider its position after a drone attack. You can call it a coincidence if you like, but coming a few months after a bomb attack on the Dakar Rally, which some misguided folk have tried to pass off as an exploding compressed air canister, one must ask the question whether it is sensible for the sport to go to such a place.

It is quite hard to describe the Houthi movement in Yemen. The Saudis call them terrorists, the Houthis say the same about the Saudis. In the West, where oil is important (more so since Vlad the Invader decided to send his armies into Ukraine), governments tend to stick their fingers in their ears and go "la-la-la-la" when Yemen is mentioned. This is why the Houthis have been sending missiles and bomb-laden drones into Saudi on a regular basis for the last few years. They want people in Saudi to feel uncomfortable and they want to highlight their arguments.

The British proved with the IRA that the solution is to talk and try to address grievances. Today we walk the streets of London without fear that we will be blown into pieces by explosive devices.

Formula 1 has always risked being a target for terrorism, because of the high profile it enjoys around the world and if you read shareholder information about the sport, you can find this listed as one of the risk factors involved.

"The general risk of a terror attack has increased recently in a number of the countries in which events are held," the F1 group advises, without naming names. In other words. We are going to dodgier places. The proximity of the explosion, which was clearly not a coincidence, led to uncomfortable feelings and lots of folk saying: "What if?" Terrorists are (usually) quite clever people, who do what they do because they have a cause they believe in. Their attacks are designed to deliver a message. When they use sophisticated equipment, such a mercury tilt switches, they are telling the authorities what they can do. They do not usually embark on indiscriminate killing, as this usually does more harm than good.

News of the Dakar attack was suppressed by all those concerned, except by the people who were blown up. They were French and the French government decided that if no-one else would take action, it would investigate. So the Parquet National Anti-Terroriste (PNAT) sent a team to Jeddah to examine the events and the machines. No report has yet been published in France, but leaks to the media indicate that the investigation concluded with 100 percent certainty that the explosion had been caused by a bomb. The fact that the report has not been published suggests that the government is now in "la-la-la-la" mode and so the policemen leaked the details to the media.

The Houthis clearly want to attract attention but, at the same time, they want to avoid international outrage and so an attack in the proximity of a big event makes more sense than blowing up the event itself. The goal of both attacks was probably to try to get the events cancelled and thus create a bigger story that would hurt Saudi's programme of using sport to forge better links with the world. When that did not happen, the Houthis did a clever thing and declared a three-day ceasefire to take advantage of the publicity generated from F1 by the attack. This ensured that the racing teams did not need to worry about further attacks. It was a very neat piece of propaganda. Very few F1 people ran off to the airport, with the notable exception of German TV.

The real question now is whether F1 feels it is worth continuing the relationship, hoping that Saudi Arabia will be able to provide a safe and secure venue for motorsport in a short space of time, or whether it might be better to pause and come back to Saudi when the country has sorted out more of these problems.

Stefano Domenicali has made much of late about the demand that exists for F1 races and so replacing the Saudi race will not be an issue, although perhaps the F1 bank account would have a few fewer noughts.

In any case, the majority of people in the sport think that F1's expansion has gone far enough and it would now be wiser to expand the audiences at every event, rather than expanding the number of events. There are still too many races which have small crowds, because they don't need to promote, because the governments pay for the races to happen.

Having too many races creates a lot of problems, both with scheduling and with logistics. As I mentioned last week, F1 is already dancing on the rim of the volcano when it comes to freight and the war is going to cause more trouble as freight-handlers are under pressure. F1 might be wise to do a deal with one company, rather than shopping around, and that way it will become a valued customer, as opposed to an occasional user. I did hear at some point last year that there could be a deal in the pipeline with Qatar Airlines, as part of the agreement to have a Grand Prix in Qatar. Qatar Airlines has an enormous cargo fleet including 83 Boeing 777s, the plane that will become F1's preferred choice in a world of declining Jumbos. It seems also that the teams now all have freight containers that has been designed for 777 freighters.

The other thing that needs sorting, both from a scheduling and an environmental point of view is the calendar, which often makes no sense at all. F1 is keen to promote a green image and yet here we are this summer with a five-week period which will include the British, Austrian, French and Hungarian GPs in that order. It is incomprehensible because Britain-France and then Austria-Hungary is much more efficient, and when your fleet consists of close to 300 40ft trucks, all pumping out diesel fumes, going backwards and forwards across Europe, it really isn't very smart.

The big news for me in Jeddah, apart from things going bang, was the plans that will soon be announced for the new Grand Prix of Las Vegas. The first will take place on 24 November 2023, on America's Thanksgiving holiday weekend. If you look it up, you will find that this is a Saturday, the day after Black Friday, the first day of the Christmas shopping season.

This is not a mistake as the race, which will take place on Saturday night under lights on The Strip in Las Vegas, will hit the US television markets at peak hours – and will be broadcast at a sensible hour on Sunday morning in F1's traditional markets in Europe, and later on the Sunday in Asia.

The other big innovation is that the race will not have a local promoter, but will be organised by the Formula 1 group itself, working closely with the city of Las Vegas. Thus the race will not pay a race promotion fee, as other events do, but rather will contribute all of its revenues to the F1 coffers.

This has been done before by Bernie Ecclestone, the last time being in Austria, when he worked closely with Paddy McNally to run an event. It was not a great success. The problem with this is that while there is potential for big profits, there is also potential for losses, so there is a risk involved. But with F1's new popularity, the risks are significantly reduced, as a race in Las Vegas is bound to sell well. It is worth noting that a circuit design which has been circulating in the United States in recent days, is not at all what the track will look like. The F1 circuit will run down The Strip from Caesars Palace, crossing Flamingo Road and passing the celebrated Bellagio fountains and the Eiffel Tower, until it reaches the Cosmopolitan Casino, where it will go left on to Harmon Avenue. It will then work its way north, through the existing roads and empty land in that area and will end up looping around the soon-to-be-completed MSG Sphere and then run along Sands Avenue, passing The Venetian and rejoining The Strip near Wynn Las Vegas.

Meanwhile, down in Miami, the word is that the folk at the Hard Rock Stadium in Miami will create a small lake inside the circuit, in order to ensure that the track does not look like a facility laid out in car parks. Much work has gone into landscaping the new facility to give it character and the lake, complete with yachts that cannot go anywhere, will help this to happen.

While that might seem bizarre, it is not the first time it is happened in F1, as the lake in Albert Park in Australia features much the same idea, with yachts positioned to appear on camera during the races, to add a little of the Monaco-like glamour.

After the difficult times in Saudi Arabia, F1 returns to Australia in 10 days, the first visit since the Australian GP was cancelled at the start of the pandemic in March 2020.

Melbourne seems to be a complete sell-out and other races are enjoying similar surges in interest. There are also signs that China is beginning to show a bit more interest in the sport. This is usually the case when a country gets an F1 driver and it is why F1 is looking for an American racer at the moment. The Holy Grail, of course, is a woman racer, as that will attract the interest of around half the world population...

Anyway, Guanyu Zhou is already having an impact, although the fact that there will not be a Chinese GP this year will not help matters. Zhou's impressive debut in Bahrain, which resulted in him scoring a point for 10th place, was a very good start and, although he was promoted by the retirements of the two Red Bulls and Pierre Gasly's AlphaTauri, he is only going to improve. And it may not be long before he will be up to speed with team-mate Valtteri Bottas, who managed to finish sixth in Bahrain.

What is interesting is the reaction in China to Zhou's F1 debut. The race took place late at night in China, but within eight hours of the finish the Chinese social media platform Weibo, has registered 120 million people, reading about his achievement. China is F1's biggest TV audience these days, with around 73 million viewers every race, so we can expect to see that improve.

Otherwise F1 is quiet enough. Some of the drivers don't want to go back to Jeddah in the future, but if push comes to shove they will because they have contracts and they don't want to hand over their cars to reserve drivers.

No-one expects the FIA to do anything, particularly now the president is from the UAE, and so the only way things are going to change is if the F1 Group ignores all the noughts and concludes that the race there does them more harm than good. And that is about as likely as Greenland starting a space programme and putting a man on the Moon.

From Collins Street

13 April 2022

When in Melbourne, I stay always on Collins Street, in what they call "The Paris End", where the shops are fancy (and not places I frequent). But if you need a tie from Hermès or proper-looking macaroons, you can find them. It has an RM Williams store, so you can buy the best boots in the world. There is Armani and Prada, Cartier and Fendi, but also antiquarian bookshops and great little cafés, although a lot have closed down during the pandemic. They say that it was at the top end of Collins that they first had pavement cafés in Melbourne, now they are everywhere.

Collins Street is lined with old trees and heritage buildings. At the top is the imposing Old Treasury building and, in the hubbub, one can always hear the clang of trams. If you jump on the 96 tram, it goes door-to-door to Albert Park, although on race weekends, normal service is disrupted and you have to get off at Southern Cross and get on one of the special expresses that use the 96 route for the Grand Prix.

Sometimes, as a result, I take a cab and so meet the next generation of Australian entrepreneurs, immigrants who are working to build their futures, driving taxis. They come from India, Iraq and odd bits of Africa. It's been tough, they say, because Melbourne had the longest lockdown of anywhere in the world. For them – and for many of us – Australia is still a kind of paradise.

One thing that I have always found, going right back to when I first started visiting the country in the 1980s, is that Australians complain a lot more than British people and thus it seems ironic that they often talk of "whingeing Poms" when they are the ones complaining all the time. The truth is that British people don't like to make a fuss and will sit and smile politely, and then tell all their friends and family about the bad experience they had. Australians complain instantly and loudly, believing (probably correctly) that it will solve the problem and will improve the venue or service.

My great-grandfather arrived in Australia at the age of 16, back in 1890, after spending five and a half months on a sailing ship. The adventures he had included working a gold miner and with the pearling fleets on the Torres Strait. Perhaps if they had had more telephones he would have rung home and told his mum that he was fine and would have stayed forever, but instead returned to the Old World in Europe. When he departed on a voyage that would go round Cape Horn and take six and a half months, he wrote: "There are no better and finer people on this earth than the Australians: man, woman and child. It is the only country where true hospitality lives." Much has changed over the years, but by and large I think it is still true today. Australians have a funny way of asking for things because whereas a British person might say: "Could I have a beer please", and Australian will always say: "I'll have a beer thanks". They always say thank you first.

One of the things that I have always loved about Australians is that are forever inventing new words and expressions. Today half the world says "No worries" and that came from Down Under. When you think about it, there is a whole language that Australians speak: Bloody oath, bludger, bogan, chook, arvo, drongo, hoon and footy are all examples. Fantastic things are ripper, sausages are snags and if you're stuffed, it doesn't mean you have eaten too much. Things get complicated when you think about barbies in bathers and blokes in budgie-smugglers, and you don't get sick, you get crook.

This year I learned a new Australianism when reading in the local newspaper about how F1 now attracts a much bigger audience, with women and youngsters particularly having now joined the throng. It's not just blokes these days. The girls have embraced the sport in an unusual way and it seems that they see the sport as some sort of fashion show, or at least that is how it read. One local scribe, describing the VIP hospitality, said that it was filled with "glamazons", a splendid new word to describe well-dressed lady F1 fans.

There is one Australianism that I have never understood. They call people who have red hair "Blue" or "Bluey". I was going to use that to greet Alex Albon, when he arrived in the paddock with what looked like a head of hair that had been dyed slightly auburn, but decided against it. I asked him what was going on.

He had been in Thailand, he said, on the way to Australia, and had visited an orphanage run by the Iceman Charity, which was set up by a bloke called Volker Capito, following the 2004 tsunami. Volker is the brother of Williams team principal Jost Capito. Alex explained that many of the kids are now in their late teens and they are mad about the Liverpool football club. In fact they are so fanatical that some have dyed their hair red to show their support. They asked Alex if he wanted to do the same and he couldn't think of a good reason to say no... Most of it had washed out.

Anyway, for me Bluey Albon was the driver of the day on Sunday, taking his Williams from last on the grid to a World Championship point, completing all but one lap of the race on the same set of tyres. It was a mighty performance in a difficult car, and while Charles Leclerc won the Driver of the Day award for steering a dominant Ferrari to victory, I think Alex did a better job. Anyway, Leclerc's victory was popular in Melbourne where the second largest ethnic group (after those with English roots) comes from Italy. That is about seven percent of the local population. They have a neighbourhood known as Little Italy and, naturally, they are all Ferraris fans.

With Ferrari doing well (finally) and with the success of "Drive to Survive", F1 in Melbourne in booming and there was a huge crowd for the Grand Prix, with an official figure of 419,114 fans having gone through the turnstiles over the weekend. Everyone was busy trumpeting this as the highest F1 crowd of all time, which it definitely was not. No-one really knows the biggest crowd ever, because back in the 1950 and 1960s there were vast crowds in places like Monza and Mexico (when a large percentage of fans came over the walls). The race day crowd in Melbourne was 128,294, but this was not even close to the first Hungarian GP in 1986, when it was reckoned there were 200,000 on race day. The first United States GP at Indianapolis in 2000 had a crowd in the region of 225,000, while the last Australian GP in Adelaide had a race day figure of 210,000 and a four-day attendance figure of 525,000. If one discards the 74,000 who turned up that Thursday in Adelaide, that Grand Prix still had a three-day figure of 451,000. Still, it is all good for promotion to say that something is popular...

One of the odd things about Albert Park this year was that the grandstands had a lot of orange and it seemed amazing that Max Verstappen's army had travelled to Australia (or that Dutch-Australians are a big group). But, of course, when one looked closely it was not Dutch orange but rather papaya orange, in support of McLaren's Daniel Ricciardo (an Italian-Australian). There were loads of red hats for Ferrari and quite a lot of black ones, supporting Mercedes. There were not a huge number of Alpine blue hats, but the number will probably rise over time as the next big thing in Australian racing is Oscar Piastri (of Italian heritage, of course), who is now waiting for his chance to race F1 as Alpine's reserve driver.

The French team is doing quite well at the moment and that creates a bit of a problem because Fernando Alonso is still quick, despite his age, and Esteban Ocon is matching and beating Fernando on a regular basis. Ocon has a three-year deal with the team. Alonso's contract finishes this year, but he doesn't want to stop. At the same time the team wants to keep hold of Piastri.

Three into two doesn't go, so Alpine is already looking around for some way of putting Piastri elsewhere for a year or two, or putting Fernando out to grass in sports cars. It is a good problem to have, of course, but Alpine does not have any customer

teams and so needs to find a proper deal to place Oscar elsewhere. There are not many opportunities as other manufacturers are also trying to bring on their new talent. Piastri's options are a bit limited.

Alpine will let him go for a year or two, but not forever, and so probably Alpine needs to find him a job in 2023, and that depends on who might take him if an Alpine contract remains in place. The whisper is that Haas might like the idea as Ferrari protégé Mick Schumacher is clearly struggling to cope with the pace of Kevin Magnussen. And Kevin is not yet up to full speed. Mick's big crash in Saudi was the sign of a youngster driving beyond his talent, trying to match his team-mate...

So that's worth watching for.

However, it may be some time before such decisions are made and if Fernando or Esteban don't deliver the goods in 2022, it is still possible that Oscar will get a ride and turn the Melbourne grandstands blue. Another Italian-Australian who has been in the news of late is Michael Masi, and the whisper in Melbourne was that the FIA has now come up with a settlement with the former F1 Race Director, following his removal from the role as a result of the Abu Dhabi Grand Prix at the end of last season. The federation made a bit of a big's ear of its report on events, suggesting that Masi had not done anything wrong, as the FIA Stewards said at the time, but removed him from the role nonetheless. Why this happened is not entirely clear, although obviously there were a lot of people who didn't agree with what was done (mainly Lewis Hamilton fans). There have been suggestions that Masi's removal was the result of personality clashes between Michael and the FIA President Mohammed Ben Sulayem and the recently-appointed FIA's head of F1 – Peter Bayer – which came to a head after Abu Dhabi.

Anyway, whatever the reasons, Masi was ejected and soon a fairly substantial cheque will arrive in his bank account. This was necessary because the FIA could not reassign roles before it had cleared away the debris. Thus as soon as the whole thing is signed off, the federation will be able to announce some of its F1 plans with DAMS's managing director François Sicard expected to have some sort of FIA F1 sporting director role. The thing that does not quite make sense here is that Ben Sulayem says that he wants the federation to be more efficient and proactive and yet its structure seems to be becoming more and more bureaucratic. F1 now has to deal with the FIA President, the Deputy-President Sport Robert Reid, Bayer and soon a new sporting director as well. Efficient structures usually involve fewer people, in order to allow for swift decisions and to avoid politics.

The new FIA Race Directors were in the meantime much in evidence in Australia (except the virtual one, whoever that is). The new folks are trying to build relationships within F1 and there has been more than a little pushing and shoving over things like DRS zones in Albert Park, jewellery and fire-proof underwear. Sebastian Vettel was upset for being fined for riding a motor scooter on the track while returning to the pits after one of his many incidents during the weekend, while Lewis Hamilton said that they would have to cut his ear off to remove some of his jewellery. The need to change their underwear caused some amusement amongst the drivers about the checking process. All these rules exist for good reasons – mainly safety – but they have not been heavily-policed because Masi – and Charlie Whiting before him – were quite flexible.

If that sounds odd, one must remember that in a fire metal jewellery and watches conduct heat that will burn a driver while the fire retardant materials are meant to stop that happening. That is the logic and the science of the rule. I guess that if Hamilton wishes to risk having his ears burned and is willing to sign a suitable waiver then he can keep his bling, although creating paperwork to allow him to express himself is probably not the most efficient way of doing things.

F1's booming popularity is the reason for another of the big rumours over the Australian GP weekend: that the replacement for the Russian GP will be held in Singapore, a week before the Singapore GP. There are some very good reasons why this is a better choice than Qatar, which was originally rumoured to get the date.

– Joe Saward's 2022 Green Notebook –

Firstly, Qatar in December is hot and F1 teams don't want their cars to melt, their tyres to turn to gloop and the spectators to be toasted. The fact that there were almost no spectators for the first Qatar race is neither here nor there. The time to have a race in Doha is November and that cannot happen this year because of the World Cup soccer competition.

F1 does not want to have to rejig the calendar more than is absolutely necessary because of the freight crisis that is ongoing at the moment, having two races in the same place makes a lot of sense. It would also allow F1 to trial the idea of a two-day Grand Prix, and the word is that the folks in Singapore are confident that the demand for F1 at the moment means that they could sell tickets for two events.

The two could be differentiated by being run at different times: one in daylight, the other at night, and one must remember that the fees paid are largely met by a special hotel tax that exists in the city over Grands Prix weekends, so the actual cost to Singapore would not be huge; would bring in more people; and would thus generate additional revenues and more global coverage for the city, showing the world what Singapore looks like in daylight as well as in darkness.

It is probably not yet decided what the event would be called, but one can expect something like the Marina Bay GP or the Lion City GP. Both would do nicely.

F1's popularity is also causing media rights deals to go up in value, and with the US rights up for sale at the moment for 2023 and beyond, there seems to be quite an auction going on, with Liberty Media aiming for the stars, hoping for $75 million a year, compared to the current $5 million. The likely figure is probably somewhere in the $40-50 million bracket. ESPN (which is part of Disney) wants the rights, but NBC, Fox Sports and perhaps even some streaming services such as Amazon or Netflix, are all supposed to be in the bidding. The number of US viewers is growing fast, but there is still a lot of potential for growth – so it will be worth watching what happens.

The current growth of the sport and the rise in value of the F1 teams is also leading to chat about the 11th and 12th team slots that exist – in principle – in the commercial agreements of the sport. F1 is quite happy with 10 teams, all of which are now pretty solid and the sport does not need a couple of extra outfits which could become cannon-fodder, as has happened with almost all new teams in the sport in recent years.

There were three new teams in 2009: Campos Meta, Manor Grand Prix and USF1.

USF1 never materialised, but an entry was given to Lotus Grand Prix (later to become Caterham).

Manor became Virgin (and then Marussia).

Campos turned into Hispania (and then HRT), but disappeared at the end of 2012. Caterham died in 2014 and Virgin/Marussia/Manor ground to a halt in 2016.

Today there are at least four groups making noises about wanting an entry. There is Andretti, one from Monaco, one based around an existing Formula 2 team and another that I cannot discuss because I have agreed not to say anything, on the basis that I might get the story as and when it happens (I'll probably get screwed on that one).

There may be others I haven't heard about. The problem with all of this is that ambition is free, but to create an F1 team requires something in the region of $1 billion. You can do it in a different way (as Haas showed) but Gene Haas is a billionaire and so there is a safety net. The reality is that buying a team is still probably the best way to do it, but as the asking price has now risen to about $700 million, there are some folk who think that starting something new might have become a better option.

Andretti has been talking rather more than is good for such projects, as it is usually best not to say too much and keep things quiet until an entry has been secured.

This process is quite complicated, but the first step required is for Formula 1 and the FIA to agree that a new team is worth having. There are huge complications involved because one needs to consider the impact of new teams on all the stakeholders in the sport.

Race promoters, for example, might need to build new facilities because the existing garages/paddocks are insufficient to cope with a larger number of cars. There is a process, outlined in the commercial agreements, that allows for two new teams to get a share of revenues as soon as they start operating, but in order to access that one needs to buy your right to earn the money and so must commit to pay an anti-dilution payment of $200 million. This is then split between the existing stakeholders to make sure they do not lose money by allowing more competition.

If one has the money to pay that fee, and then the entry fee and the cost of creating a team, the numbers quickly add up and so buying a team has been a better option. However the new commercial agreements have pushed up the value of teams and made existing operations more stable, and so there are fewer opportunities to acquire "distressed" teams. The last opportunities were William and Force India. At the moment no-one looks like they need to sell and most of the teams are supported either by a car manufacturer, or by a billionaire.

The Haas business model is not a bad idea, but there are not many opportunities to do the same thing. Aston Martin is using the Mercedes F1 windtunnel in Brackley, Haas uses the Ferrari tunnel at Maranello and Scuderia AlphaTauri is using the Red Bull tunnel in Bedford. Haas uses Dallara to manufacture chassis and while there are chassis-making companies such as Multimatic, ORECA and Ligier, they would need big investment to embark on F1 programmes. Engines are not difficult. Alpine would like to have customers – but it doesn't need them.

For the moment no-one has convinced the FIA and F1 to start a bidding process. They could do it, I suppose, but the other thing to bear in mind is that there is no requirement to accept any project if the FIA does not think it is sensible. Which is why buying teams still makes more sense for those who have money to burn (and products to sell).

At the moment, there is much talk of Volkswagen having decided to enter Formula 1 in 2026, with the Audi and Porsche brands, although final official decisions on this will not be made until the rules are finally set in stone.

There continue to be reports that Audi will buy into McLaren, initially taking shares in the McLaren F1 team and then perhaps buying into the McLaren Group as well. But it seems that there is no agreement as yet regarding the price, although there has been speculation in Germany that Audi is willing to pay more than $700 million to buy the F1 team. McLaren wants more than that.

So there have been rumours that Audi is now shopping around, if only to get McLaren to negotiate downwards. The word is that Audi could buy Aston Martin or Sauber. The first is a complete long shot because the car company and the racing team both use Mercedes engines, and you are not going to get an Audi-Mercedes F1 car any time soon. An Aston-Mercedes, a McLaren-Mercedes and an Alfa Romeo-Ferrari are already daft enough concepts – but there are limits.

In addition, it is not entirely clear why Volkswagen would want to add a new supercar brand to its portfolio. Right now, it has Porsche and Lamborghini and has effectively sold Bugatti to Rimac. VW is planning to spin off Porsche soon to turn its value into cash, just as Fiat did a few years back with Ferrari.

Audi buying another supercar brand does not make a heap of sense and McLaren is something that BMW might want to pursue, because it does not own any supercar brands.

Stellantis (the company that grew from the Fiat-Peugeot merger) owns Alfa Romeo and is involved in F1 (in a cut-price kind of way), but needs to make its own engines in the future if it is going to be serious. It also owns Maserati, but wants to turn this into an electric-only business.

Renault has Alpine.

Aston Martin is currently chomping its way through vast prairies of cash belonging to Lawrence Stroll and folks who think he might make the brand successful. Maybe he will, but there is also a strong possibility that it could all flop horribly as Aston Martin as a brand has never been a great commercial success, even with the help of James Bond.

For the moment, Stroll is still pursuing the dream, hoping to turn the team into something that will allow Lance Stroll to win the World Championship. We are at the early stages of that programme and in Melbourne things were definitely not going well, with green bits of bodywork all over the shop and there were even complaints about how the Aston Martin Safety Car needed to be quicker.

The good thing was that the Safety Car did not collide with either of the Aston F1 cars, but it was all a bit of comedy store last weekend. Lawrence Stroll's management style may work in the fashion world, but there is no sign at the moment that it will build a great team for the future.

I did hear over the Melbourne weekend that Stroll, in an effort to find a way to build his own F1 engines, asked if he might buy part (or all) of the Mercedes AMG High Performance Powertrains company in Brixworth. The proposal was, by all accounts, politely declined. Mercedes is happy to have Aston Martin as a customer, but does not seem to be overly interested beyond that. Still, I suppose Stroll's logic was that Mercedes has recently reduced its involvement in the F1 team, has sold off its truck division and will soon announce that it is selling its Formula E team to McLaren...

The most logical choice for Audi would seem to be to acquire Sauber and turn that into an Audi F1 team, in much the same way as BMW did with the Swiss team 20 years ago. In many respects this might be a better deal than buying McLaren because of the Germanic approach that Audi and Sauber share. Audi has long been a major customer of the Sauber wind tunnel and so knows what it is buying, and the proximity of Sauber to Germany would obviously help. That would mean that Alfa Romeo would have to think again about F1, but at the moment the firm is getting a bit of a free ride off the sport and at some point needs to either get serious or to get out.

The possibility of a Porsche F1 project at the same time as Audi might seem strange, but there are going to be clear differences between the two and by the time it all happens, they will probably be part of different companies, as Porsche will be independent of VW.

In a normal situation, Porsche would always do its own thing and build everything in-house, but it looks like the F1 plan in 2022 is more to do with marketing than technology. Thus, badging the Red Bull Power Trains power units makes sense. Red Bull has spent a huge amount of money (rumoured to be $400 million) on its new engine facility at the Red Bull Technology Campus. This leaves the Austrian drinks company with lots of options. It can go on doing its own thing and not have to worry about partnerships with manufacturers; it can have partnerships and they can change over time; or it can sell the whole thing if the right manufacturer comes along. Red Bull founder Dietrich Mateschitz is now 77 and the future of the company is not clear. Mateschitz has an heir, but he also has partners in Thailand who probably have a say in who manages the business.

Perhaps the future will be for Red Bull to go public and all concerned take the money and leave the business to others. Who knows? Perhaps Porsche is thus positioned to get the whole racing business as and when things happen.

Porsche is also heavily involved in synthetic fuel, as a fuel manufacturer in addition to building super-efficient internal combustion engines/hybrid engines, and this will be part of the F1 rules of the future.

It is all fascinating stuff.

The other thing that should be considered is the rumours that South Africa will join the F1 calendar. This is not really big news because the intention has always been there.

I know this because, back in 1993, Bernie Ecclestone introduced me to an official from the African National Congress (ANC) – Nelson Mandela's party – who was there to represent the organisation. It was a long time ago, but the bloke was completely mad about F1, while also coming across as being very clever. I was impressed and so I wrote down his name in my notebook and then watched over the years to see what would become of him. His name was Cyril Ramaphosa and he has been President of South Africa since 2019. He wanted a Grand Prix as soon as he took office and F1's Chase Carey went to South Africa a couple of times in that era to discuss possibilities. The problem was that South Africa was gripped in a crisis over electricity supplies. Then came the pandemic and throughout all this Ramaphosa has been fighting to change the ANC and renew its image, which is not good.

National liberation movements in Africa tend to fade away as political parties as time passes. Ramaphosa has been trying to oust some of those in the party who want him out and that has meant that his reforms have had to be hesitant. It is all going to come to a head in December this year when the ANC holds a national elective conference, prior to the next general election in 2024.

Ramaphosa's popularity was once at 70 percent, but it has fallen although he remains the most popular leader in the country. And he is so popular that some think that the ANC is holding him back. This means that he can either reform the ANC and reverse its gradual decline (which is the first option) or perhaps set up his own new party in order to win power in 2024.

Holding a Grand Prix is not thus a primary priority for the President, but he knows that it is a good idea and that it will help boost the South African image and economy, although some might try to use it against him if he starts the project too early...

So, we will see. If he has control of the ANC by the end of this year then a race in 2024 is quite possible. If other scenarios play out, then things may be different.

Finally, there is just one point worth mentioning about Melbourne. The Media Centre was deserted. This is worrying, but also understandable. The written media in F1 took a huge hit in the pandemic and new processes developed to maintain coverage without writers travelling were introduced. The problem is that these processes remain in place and editors and publishers don't want to spend money sending their people halfway around the world for just a few days.

If Australia was twinned with a race in Asia, then perhaps it would have been more cost-effective. The fact that Melbourne was on its own this year was a problem. There were about 50 international journalists in total, down from the pre-Covid number of round 300. Hopefully, it will bounce back, but there are no guarantees. During the pandemic the press corps went down to a low point of nine in Russia in 2020. There were several races with less than 20 reporters.

While F1 thrives on TV, the sports still needs written journalists to weave the tapestry behind the coverage. Netflix tapped into this need but it too has limited available time.

OK, in the modern era, some people cannot read 5,000 words without their heads exploding, but those who are reading this sentence have done it...

It's not impossible if you love the sport and want to know more.

From Chickenville

27 April 2022

Motorway service areas – known as *aires* in France – are generally not very interesting. They are named after a nearby hamlet or sometimes a fancy local château. Some have wistful names, such as *Soleil Levant* (rising sun), some have odd names like *Chien Blanc* (white dog) while others act as promotional tools for their region: the *aire des Volcans d'Auvergne* is one.

And then there is the *Aire du Poulet de Bresse*, the rest area of the Bresse chicken. This features a very large monument to chickens. If that seems a little odd, one must remember that gastronomy is important to the French and they are immensely proud of their culinary reputation, prowess and traditions. And they are very protective and object to anyone trying to copy their products. There is an elaborate system of certification for authenticity, known as *appellation d'origine contrôlée* (AOC) and one cannot legally sell Champagne or Camembert unless it comes from the right place.

Back in 1957, the first animals to be granted AOC status were the chickens of Bresse, and it would be 50 years before they were joined by the salt marsh lamb of the Baie de Somme.

The chickens of Bresse are the gallinaceous version of Wagyu beef and they are spoiled rotten before they fly off to the great coop in the sky. Each one MUST have 10 square metres of land for their own use. They cannot be stuffed with corn and have to live off the land a bit. Most chickens can only ever dream of a future as a golden nugget, but the chickens of Bresse are royalty. They are quite nationalistic and must have blue feet, white feathers and red combs. They are small-breasted because of their energetic lifestyles make them lean and tasty, and not chubby like their boosted supermarket-ed colleagues. They are at the top of the pecking order. Michelin chefs get starry-eyed about them. Presidents wish to devour them.

The Bresse is a region to be found at the foot of the Jura mountains, where the plains of the Rhone begin. At the centre of this is Bourg-en-Bresse and, on the Monday evening after the horribly-named Made in Italy e dell'Emilia-Romagna GP, I found myself dining in the Bresse, where they even flavour their mayonnaise with chicken juices (...and very nice it is too).

I had a pleasant enough weekend in Imola, despite the poor weather, nervous Race Directors who seemed more besotted with red flags than Chairman Mao used to be, and some very muddy car parks. It had been a Red Bull rout in the end and the *tifosi* went home down in the mouth, rather than frothing. On Monday morning I set off to drive the 745 miles home. It had been a long night of work and I knew that I was not going to get home in one go, but I hoped that I might get to Avallon or Auxerre before night fell. I was steaming along and happy that the traffic was light when I approached the town of Novara, to the east of Milan, where a million years ago I spent a day or two at Novamotor, watching the engine wizard John Penistan rebuilding a Formula 3 engine, and asking intelligent questions such as "What does that bit do?"

I was thinking of John when there was a sudden odd vibration. A change of surface? No, it got worse and I knew it was time to get off the road as my left rear tyre was clearly falling apart. Fortunately I managed to do this before things got nasty and found myself on the hard shoulder. So I donned my *gilet jaune* and set about solving the problem, digging out the space-saver spare from deep in the bowels of the boot. Fortunately (or perhaps unfortunately) I have done this a few times as French rural living does cause occasional punctures. This was a pretty impressive failure, but despite keeping a wary eye on approaching vehicles, I was able to jack up the car and loosen the wheel nuts by jumping on the tyre wrench.

My plan was to drive into Novara, find a *gommista* (I learned a new word if nothing else) and then get back on the road again. It was then that I discovered that it was Italian Liberation Day, a national holiday,

which explained the empty roads. Everything was closed. I pondered holing up in a hotel until Tuesday morning and then driving home, but that meant I would lose a day at home. Time is precious in F1 and so I decided that the best option was to head for France with the spare, driving at 50 mph up to the Mont Blanc tunnel. It was about 120 miles away, which is a bit further than one wants to go on a space saver, but I knew if I drove gently it would not be a problem. France would be open for business and I could do a quick pit stop and be on my way again.

The upside of it being a national holiday was that I was able to potter along, with my flashers on whenever an Italian approached at vast speed (speed limits in Italy seem only ever to be consultative numbers) and after about two and a half hours and no major incidents, I got to Mont Blanc and popped out of the big bore near Chamonix. Fifteen minutes later I was at a tyre dealership which had the tyres required and 15 minutes after that I was en route again. It wasn't quite an F1 pit stop – and F1 drivers never have to show a credit card – but I was happy enough. The tyre fitter shrugged in the finest Gallic fashion when I asked why the tyre had failed. He didn't know and he didn't much care.

And so I ended up in Chickenville, as I reached a point at which it was unwise to go driving as I had worn myself out and the risks-versus-reward calculation made no sense. As I sat down to dinner I watched a McLaren transporter whizzing past. When I had breakfast the next morning there were a fleet (or at least a flotilla) of F1-branded trucks, lugging equipment home.

Risk assessment is a big part of Formula 1 these days, not just in terms of race strategies but in all decision-making and I suspect that some of the teams probably have chief risk officers, who sit in offices and worry about how things can go wrong. If I was CRO at Mercedes, I mulled while watching a coypu frolicking in the pond next to the hotel, I'd be worried now about Lewis Hamilton. It's a difficult thing to predict because it is based on emotions, but I would nibble my nails about Sir Lewis walking away. Just as Nico Rosberg famously did back in 2016, catching everyone on the hop. Lewis had been asked the question at Imola and said he was 100 percent committed to the team, and Toto Wolff had said the same to me when I asked if he was worried. I feel that Lewis would not dump the team in it because he is always banging on about everyone being responsible. It was hard to imagine him walking away mid-season, as some have done in the past. "It will be a painful year that we will have to ride out together," he said. That was an interesting comment, because it basically said that there is no real chance for the team to fight back. After Imola, Ferrari has 124 points and Mercedes 77, and that gap had been achieved without Carlos Sainz scoring in the last two races. In the Drivers' Championship, Chuck Le Cluck (nothing to do with chickens) had 86 points, with Lewis on 28, a gap of 58 points.

Given the normal levels of F1 reliability, where cars rarely break down and drivers are so good that they deliver week after week, closing big gaps is not easy. With the budget cap getting in the way of massive splurges, the CRO might argue that the best thing to do would be to give up on the W13 and focus the resources on the W14.

This new generation of cars are not yet fully understood, and that means that there is potential for big gains as the engineers get the hang of the 2022 cars. But that is true for all the teams, not just Mercedes. There is the added problem that there are several other teams ahead of Mercedes in terms of pace and so collecting big scores is slowed because others are getting those points, which helps Ferrari and Red Bull pull further away. If you put this into perspective, if Lewis starts dominating in Miami and Leclerc finishes second on all occasions, it will still take Lewis until the summer break before he can get back into contention – and it is pretty safe to say that this isn't going to happen.

So really the big question is whether Hamilton has faith that the team will do a better job in 2023 and give him the chance to win an eighth title, or whether the time has come to admit that at 37 he might call it a day and change his lifestyle and go do all those things other things he wants to do, like becoming a shareholder in a soccer team, fashion design, or whatever. I think it would annoy Lewis to have to leave the record-breaking eighth title on the table, having beaten all of the other F1 records, but there is the also the possibility that he might become a driver who stayed on too long, as Michael Schumacher did.

On the other hand, Lewis might look at his old rival Fernando Alonso and conclude that the Spaniard is competitive at 40 – so why not continue.

All the signs in the paddock are that Fernando will soon sign a new two-year deal with Alpine, which will mean that he stays until the end of 2024. After that the French firm may wish him to move into its LMDh sports car programme. Fernando is a smart cookie and knows that dumping him would be a negative thing for Alpine, but with Oscar Piastri sitting uncomfortably in the wings, Fernando needs not only to perform but also to get support. He has just announced a personal sponsorship deal with Castrol, Alpine's oil sponsor, which makes it harder for Alpine to move him on. A clever move.

So, with Esteban Ocon under contract until the end of 2024, Alpine needs to find Oscar a job, before some else does... The Australian has marked himself out as a major future talent in F1 with victories in the 2019 Formula Renault Eurocup, the 2020 FIA Formula 3 Championship and the 2021 Formula 2 Championship. These three titles (each in a rookie year) are mightily impressive, particularly when you compare them to Charles Leclerc (GP3 and F2 in 2016 and 2017) and George Russell (GP3 and F2 in 2017 and 2018). Neither managed three titles in three years – and now they are the future stars of the F1 game. So Alpine needs to find Oscar a home for a couple of years so that he can be trained up and then step into a top drive in 2025 (hoping that Alpine is a top drive by then).

The obvious choice would be a two-year deal for Piastri at Williams, which needs a stronger second driver than Nicholas Latifi. The team does not need funding these days and wants two competitive drivers as results will pay as much as the Canadian's sponsors will do. The team is happy to take young drivers who might go on to better things (a la Bottas and Russell), but it also wants to build up its own driver squad. In this respect Piastri does not fit in and the team would be better off going with Nyck de Vries, a Mercedes Formula E champion, who is looking for things to do in the future as Mercedes is leaving the all-electric series soon and will sell its team to McLaren. De Vries used to be a McLaren driver and was ditched by the current management in 2019 and so he would rather look for a job in F1, if there are any options available. Down at Williams, they quite like the look for the strong-jawed Dutch imp. The other problem is that, while getting Piastri for a couple of years might be possible, it is not much good for him if the Williams is not very competitive... and he might think that a stopover at Haas would be a better option.

Ferrari has some influence at Haas but does not have the right to nominate drivers, as once it did when it lumbered Sauber with the ageing Kimi Raikkonen. Mick Schumacher is a Ferrari future project and he looked half-decent last year but the arrival of the Viking Kevin Magnussen has been a shock for Mick and he now needs to prove that he can he play at the big table. The only way he can do that is to beat Kevin – and Magnussen has still some more preparation to do before he gets fully up the speed, as he jumped into the seat at the last minute and was not really fit enough. If Kevin shows Mick the way around this year, Ferrari might give up the dream of "Schumacher II – The Sequel" and look for a new idea.

Australians are pretty excited about F1 at the moment, although Daniel Ricciardo seems a little lost at McLaren and there continue to be rumours that in 2024 (if not earlier) Daniel will be replaced by Colton Herta, the American who Zak Brown believes could open the gates of Formula 1 to corporate America. We will have to see if Herta has everything needed to be an F1 star, but he seems to have the speed, whether he can go on being a drummer in a rock band called Zibs in his spare time remains to be seen, as F1 is a full-time job.

Anyway, Australia is excited about Piastri and having had a massive sell-out crowd a few weeks ago, the talks are now ongoing about where the race should be on the F1 calendar as a stand-alone intercontinental flyaway is not the best option for Formula 1, which wants to cut is costs by twinning Australia with an Asian race. That might be possible if China came back in the spring but the way things are going in Shanghai at the moment suggests that it may be a while before F1 goes racing in China again. The alternative would be to move the Australian GP to the end of the season, but that would require the Australian Motorcycle Grand Prix to move to earlier in the years, as both events are organised by the Australian Grand Prix Corporation and so a clash needs to be avoided. The days when Australia opened the season are gone as Bahrain is now believed to have a deal for years to come.

The calendar chat at the moment is largely related to which event will replace Russia in September and my understanding is that it will either be a second race in Singapore, or it will be nothing at all, as Qatar seems to have dropped from the equation. Still the Qatar race will be back in 2023. I did hear whispers that Saudi Arabia would like to throw its financial weight around a bit more and thinks that a Grand Prix at each end of the season would be a good thing: with one race in the spring in Jeddah and the other in the autumn up in Riyadh. The F1 group may not like the idea much as there are sufficient Middle Eastern races now and there are other priorities, but the Saudis do have an awful of money and, as the old song goes, this is what makes the world go around.

F1 fans in Europe are increasingly worried that the number of races in F1's traditional homelands is going to reduce. This is almost certainly true, but I am not sure it will go much lower than eight, even if Monaco gets put in the corner with a hat marked with a big D for one year, if the Monegasques fail to recognise the danger of not agreeing to a deal that is less dismissive of what F1 does for the Principality.

I have been hearing for some weeks that the Germans are getting more and more ambitious and want to get a 10-year deal for a race. This is probably only going to happen at Hockenheim as the Nürburgring finds itself in a troublesome situation as it is owned by a Russian oligarch and F1 is not about to do a deal with one of those folk. It is bad for the share price. It is also doubtful, by the way, that the Nürburgring will be able to get an international circuit licence as the FIA does not seem to be keen to dole these out to anyone with Russian connections. Russians can complain about that if they like, but sadly the actions of President Putin and the lack of opposition to his activities at home have meant that Russia is no longer a big player in international motorsport.

Germany has a few things in its favour, even if the German drivers are not setting the world on fire, and no-one in Germany sees Mercedes as being a German team. It is the home of Audi and Porsche and the word continues to be that they will both come wading into F1 in 2026 if the sport can get its act together and produce some rules. This needs to be done quickly because time is short. It is fairly clear that Porsche is going to come in alliance with Red Bull, while the Audi rumours flit about from week to week. Last week it was McLaren that Audi will buy, this week it was Sauber, next week it will be Aston Martin. Whatever the details, the word is that the Automobilclub von Deutschland (AvD) is very keen on putting Germany back on the F1 map and while there is some regional money for the track, the best hope may come from federal sources as the new finance minister is a fellow called Christian Lindner, who loves cars and I am told is a Porsche freak – with a competition licence.

The rumours about Audi buying Sauber seem to have come to the attention of Alfa Romeo, as Imola saw the appearance in the F1 paddock of Carlos Tavares, the president and CEO of Stellantis, which owns the Alfa Romeo brand, and Alfa's own CEO Jean-Philippe Imparato. They have been funnelling some money into Sauber in recent years, dressing the Sauber-Ferrari up as an Alfa Romeo but obviously no-one really believes the team is actually a factory Alfa Romeo programme.

This has made very little obvious difference to Alfa Romeo sales, which are pretty poor given that 2020 was a bad year for everyone and 2021 was supposed to be the year when things bounced back. Alfa Romeo sold 63,000 cars in 2020 and then bounced back to 55,000 in 2021...

This is not good. Imparato says that the brand will be selling 200,000 a year by 2027 and I'd love to see that but they need to find a way to make Alfa Romeo look like a sexy brand if that is going to happen. Dressing up Sauber-Ferraris is probably not the right answer. Alfa Romeo has a great history as a firm that was once known for its luxury, technology, Italian style, high performance and racing passion. It is an obvious brand to try to use in F1 but it looks like Tavares will need to be a big more serious about F1 if that is going to happen. The good news is that Swedish billionaire Finn Rausing would be happy to sell the team to someone with sensible plans in F1 and so there is potential for a proper Alfa Romeo team.

With new engine rules and budget caps in F1, there is an opportunity for all car manufacturers to get involved in F1 with technologies that are quite useful when one considers that the take up of electric cars is not going to meet predictions and F1's move to synthetic fuels is a good way for a car company to paint itself green.

F1 is a brilliant marketing tool, if you do it right, and the popularity of F1 and the development of new, younger and global fans, is something that is causing car companies to think about the idea. Tavares is (quietly) a racing nut and has competed in some pretty exotic machinery over the years, but he is always careful not to let his passion put him in a difficult situation within a car company, as he does not want accusations that his passion caused the company to lose money. There are plenty of clever engineers within the Stellantis motorsport ranks and the company has money if it wants to spend it. The company chairman, by the way, is also pretty keen on racing, as Jon Elkann's other job is as chairman of Ferrari. At Imola he was in Ferrari gear, Imparato and Tavares were wearing Alfa clothing (below). Rausing was in plain clothes as usual.

Passion is what drives the sport and if you want evidence that Tavares might do something with Alfa Romeo, you need only to look back to his days at Renault, before he left from Peugeot and then worked the deal to merge with Fiat Chrysler to form Stellantis. Tavares thought that a bloke called Tony Fernandes was manna from heaven when the Malaysian turned up in 2011 suggesting that Renault and Caterham create a joint venture to build road-going sports cars. The Caterham version never appeared but Renault decided to push ahead without Fernandes, to develop the Alpine... which is now a Formula 1 brand.

I was reminded of the importance of passion at Imola where I kept bumping into old friends from the days when I was a Formula 3 reporter back in the early 1980s. We went to Imola in 1983 and many of those who raced that day went on to big things in F1, or won big in other championships, or headed teams or manufacturer departments. As I walked through the paddock I met three of the top six from that European Formula 3 race at Imola in 1983 and we discussed who else might have been there. Stefano Domenicali seemed like a good bet. Imola is his home town and he started out young as a racing fan. I bumped into Stefano and asked him the question: "Yes, I was there," he said. "I was organising the parking in the paddock..."

From Route 66

10 May 2022

Yeah, I know. Route 66 does not go through Florida. In fact, if one is being 100 percent accurate Route 66 no longer exists. It was removed from the US Highway System in 1985, decommissioned because it had been replaced by new Interstates along its entire length.

It takes time for legends to die, a fact I was reminded of on Sunday, the 40th anniversary of the death of Gilles Villeneuve – in addition to being the first Formula 1 race in Miami. The latter was, of course, treated on social media as the sporting equivalent of the Red Sea parting and Moses putting a pass around his neck and leading his flock on to the grid...

It seems that every commentator from Boca Raton to Sausage Gully in Australia had overlooked the fact that there were 11 IMSA races that used the same name between 1983 and 1993, not to mention a string of GrandAm races in the Noughties which used the name. Never mind. Media inexactitude was in fashion in southern Florida, which might have been a good thing given Formula 1's pretty awful history in the United States.

The good news (I think) is that we are entering a new age. And while some of the Old School F1 types might hrmph at the idea that the Miami International Autodrome is not a patch on the old Nurburgring, or laugh at the idea that it made perfect sense to build a fake marina, the whole thing passed off pretty well. Southern Florida is flat as a (European) pancake and utterly featureless, it's only saving grace in physical terms is a string of beaches, and some (but not all) human bodies which appear on the sand to catch some rays.

Anyway, to return to the point, US Highway 66, known as Route 66, was an important road that linked Chicago to Los Angeles from 1926 until 1985 and became one of the great American symbols, meaning progress and optimism, not to mention the sense of freedom that came with the automobile. It was more than just another highway. It unified the US and symbolised the American Dream. What does it have to do with Miami? Not much, except that today there is a sense of optimism and excitement across the United States about another automotive activity... Formula 1, which is big news these days, thanks to "Drive to Survive". The race was held on the same weekend as the Kentucky Derby and that would not have got much coverage if it hadn't been won by an 80-to-1 outsider, which was the equivalent of the Haas team winning a Grand Prix.

I find myself on Route 66 because F1 lives are complicated. They leave relatives and friends strewn around the globe, although the sport also provides a means by which one can them from time to time, even if it means more time away from the homestead.

So, unlike most of the F1 circus, I didn't hightail it to the international departure lounge as soon as the

— Joe Saward's 2022 Green Notebook —

chequered flag had been shown but stayed on and joined the queues on Monday in the domestic lines and listened to Americans on their way home from the big race. This isn't difficult because Americans often talk very loudly and express their feelings for all to hear. Everyone had bought merchandise to reflect their support of one team or another, or the race itself, and it was fun to sit, plain-clothed, and watch all the interactions. The message was clear, they'd all loved it. It was cool, it was friendly and it had been fun. For many it was their first race – and they said they'd be back.

As there were not any VIPs on the flights I was taking, I didn't hear the complaints about the poor quality hospitality experience. F1 can blame the promoter for not using Do&Co, the experts who know what it takes, but in truth a share of the blame should go to the sport itself not insisting that the Austrian firm be used, in order to ensure the highest standards and justify the wildly expensive Paddock Club tickets.

The US Dollar is currently strong, or perhaps other currencies are weaker, but whatever the case, it has become an expensive place to visit. Three-day Paddock Club tickets were $12,000 a head, although they were changing hands on the back market at up to $35,000, a clear sign that the people buying were not there to go racing but rather for some other ego-related activity. Being there was what mattered. To give you an idea, a Monaco GP Paddock Club ticket will cost you $8,000, and the average European race will mean about $4,500 for the privilege. It felt like every VIP in Miami was there to be seen to have been there, perhaps with a selfie with a driver, or the ultimate prize, a selfie with Guenther F*cking Steiner.

The crowd capacity was only 82,500 but only around 50,000 were in grandstands. The rest were VIPs. And everyone was paying a lot. One had to be impressed by the scale of the event. It must have cost a fortune to create the whole concept, but it will pay back massively over the next 10 years, once the sort out the glitches. The track was terrific (but needs some work) and the hype was mad, but that is America for you. The Miami Grand Prix was a festival of self-absorbed people, getting ready to tell their friends that "You really should have been there".

The sporting event was the peg on which they hung their overpriced hats. From those of us from more reserved cultures it all felt a little much, but it was kind of magnificent in the same way. F1 often says it wants each F1 race to be like the Super Bowl, and this was definitely a step in that direction.

The paddock access, one can argue, went too far, which meant it was harder for those working. There was no possibility of quiet chats with team bosses because they were run off their feet by TV crews, selfie-seekers and VIPs who needed to be adored. Some of the team bosses, who don't need the adulation, took to hiding in their cramped hospitality units. And we all began to wonder what on earth it is going to be like when F1 goes to Las Vegas next year, where they have elevated such activities into an art form.

The great news in all of this is that Formula 1 is healthier than it has ever been, and its getting healthier all the time. OK, it isn't very chic, but in the end, who cares? This is the modern face of F1, brassy and filled with social influencers filming themselves and big watch-jangling types chest-bumping and talking about yachts.

In the future, with a little more work on transportation, the crowd in Miami can grow considerably and there really is no reason why racing fans cannot enjoy themselves alongside the party animals, mermaids and fake body parts. They may not start screaming when they see a driver (which seems to be a hallmark of the new F1 fan), but they can see the stars working their magic on the circuit.

The news that there will be another two series of "Drive to Survive" and that Formula 1 itself will spend $240 million to buy a piece of land in Las Vegas, to convert it into Party Central, is all good for F1. It's different, it's a little bit of an alien culture but you get bet your bottom dollar that it will pay dividends. So roll up, buy F1 shares, and enjoy the ride...

I guess that the number of VIPs is a measure of how good the event is, a bit like finding a good breakfast in the United States. You can go to a fast food joint but the best way to find a good place is to look for police cars. The more police cars there are the better the breakfast, unless it is a crime scene. There were five police cars at the place I chose on the first day in Miami and the breakfast was excellent Inside the F1 Paddock there was not much time for meaningful chatter, amidst all these other goings-on. There was the jewellery issue, which is obviously about safety and not about freedom of expression. The drivers banging on that drum need to spend more time in the real world. There was Sebastian Vettel showing off his crown jewels by parading in the paddock with his underpants over his overalls. If he wanted attention (or perhaps sponsorship from an underwear manufacturer) he succeeded, but it did not add much to the argument that F1 drivers be protected in case of fire.

And then there was Michael Andretti doing the rounds of the F1 big cheeses, hoping to be allowed a sniff of the action. It will not be an easy task to convince everyone and it is not being helped by the fact that it is all being done in the public domain, largely due to Michael's father Mario, who seems to be happy to talk publicly about the project. At one point Mario told Sky they were able to pay the $200 million to enter. "You get nothing for that... But we are ready," he said.

This is not strictly true. The $200 million is an anti-dilution fund which opens the way for a new team to immediately begin collecting prize money. This is valuable and means that new teams do not have to soak up pain for several seasons before being allowed to join the club. It also means that the teams will likely survive those early times, which was not the case before when most new teams went to the wall when the owners found themselves running on air, like Wile E. Coyote, and then plunged to become a distant cloud of dust at the bottom of the F1 canyon.

This money is (in theory) divided between the existing teams, to offset the loss of prize money that would occur if they agree to divide the funds 11 ways, rather than 10. This effectively means that they must each agree to take a 10 percent cut and gain another rival. So there is little motivation to make their own lives more difficult, particularly among the smaller teams. There are other less obvious problems that would result from an 11th or 12th team. Additional space is needed and additional freight must be shifted. Thus facilities and logistics operations have to be expanded.

There is a stupid argument that Andretti might take legal action and that the anti-dilution provisions are anti-competitive. It is possible they are but finding this out will take years of legal battles, will cost a fortune and will mean that if a team does eventually win, it will arrive in F1 one day with no friends, in a sport where alliances are important. So that is a non-starter because the important thing is to get an entry, which the $200 million does not buy. To get an entry one has to convince the FIA and the F1 Group that what you are bringing to the party is worthwhile and (most importantly) will add to the show. Andretti has therefore to convince everyone that he brings value, helping to build the sport in the US. The Andretti brand is widely-known in the world of motorsport and has enjoyed a fair amount of success, winning the Indy 500 five times in the last seven years, but has not won the IndyCar title since 2012, although the team collected four titles between 2004 and 2012. It has enjoyed more success in Indy Lights, where the opposition is less intense. The team runs various other operations in other championships. However, much of the brand value of the Andretti name derives from Mario's exploits as racer, albeit many years ago.

An illustration of the value of this came for me in Australia when I was asked to chat to a group of kids who are keen to get into F1. They had won the right to visit the F1 Paddock (a great prize). In the course of the chat, Sir Jackie Stewart appeared, in his trademark tartan trousers, in the company of Mark Webber. Jackie gave a few cheery words of encouragement and then continued on his way. The kids seemed none the wiser. So I asked: "Does anyone know who that was?" The response was 100 percent negative. "Has anyone heard of Ayrton Senna?" I asked. The response was the same. For traditional racing fans this might seem appalling, but this is the reality of the modern world. Success in other formulae and having loads of money does not guarantee success in Formula 1.

The first step in the process is to get the FIA and the Formula 1 group to agree to open up a tender process. The team must then win that process. No-one in F1 wants a team that is simply a passenger. The business model is key in this process and Andretti seems to be trying to create a team that operates from a European base, but using a US-built chassis. The Haas model relies on Dallara to manufacture the cars in Italy and the firm cannot supply two teams, so Andretti must either build its own capability (which will cost a fortune and take time) or find another partner to do that work. There are firms that could do it, but none of them has a proven track record in Formula 1, nor the level of infrastructure. And this is where the project runs into trouble because building all this – and sustaining it all for a number of years – would require so much money that it is still a better idea to buy an existing operation and get rid of all these problems. Andretti says that there are no teams available, although this is not strictly true as what he means is that there is no team available with a price he wants to pay. Audi is also in the market and obviously has more available cash.

If Michael was coming in with a US automobile brand behind him he would be very attractive, but it is not likely to happen.

– Joe Saward's 2022 Green Notebook –

If there is enough money, F1 is not a closed shop as Lawrence Stroll (Aston Martin), Dorilton Capital (Williams) and Finn Rausing (Alfa Romeo Racing) might all sell. McLaren says it won't, but it might if the numbers added up.

From an F1 point view, it is clear that the popularity of the sport is not dependent on a team, but rather on a successful driver, so what is really important for US growth is to find an American driver to get the country excited (as Max Verstappen has done in The Netherlands, Sergio Perez in Mexico etc etc). Michael's prize asset in this respect is Colton Herta, but he seems to be a path to join McLaren in F1, while he is also about to lose the last F1 American driver Alex Rossi, who is expected to join the McLaren IndyCar team in 2022.

On Sunday, Michael was accompanied on the grid by Mark Walter, the CEO of Guggenheim Partners and Daniel Towriss, the CEO of Guggenheim Life, the parent company of the Gainbridge insurance firm, but money is only everything if you spend it. The fact that money does not help much is also highlighted with a couple of other stories kicking about in the Miami paddock. One suggests that Williams is looking to change drivers for the second part of the year as Nicholas Latifi has not done a good enough job this year. Things are complicated by money that the Canadian brings and by contracts, but if that happens, expect Nyck de Vries to take the drive.

The other story along these lines is that of Audi, which is looking to buy a team. This has now been confirmed by VW group boss Herbert Diess. It is clear that Porsche will join forces with Red Bull and will effectively badge the Red Bull Powertrains engines, and there is speculation that there will be some kind of long-term option for Porsche to take over the whole team, if Red Bull decides that it has done enough in F1. Audi might come in sooner, because it has more to do, but it will be very difficult for the German firm to brand an existing team because of the current engine arrangements. If, for example, Audi was to buy Aston Martin, it could not run Audi-Mercedes cars, as the two firms are clearly in competition in the real world. Ferrari is unlikely to agree to Audi badging one of its engines, Renault says it is not even thinking about such matters, while Red Bull Powertrains has a deal with Honda which precludes any customer arrangements before the rule changes in 2026. Audi could build a current engine in addition to 2026 one, but that would be a little silly given the time scales involved and the best course of action would be to become a silent partner of a team and get things ready for 2026.

Audi appears to be focussed on acquiring either Aston Martin or Sauber. In both cases, the branding would change but Audi could not be used because of the engines.

Buying the Aston Martin team does not make a lot of sense, unless the current owners wants to offload it – which may be the case given that neither the team nor the car company are doing well at the moment. Aston Martin's Q1 results for 2022 make grim reading, particularly when compared with previous predictions of a resurrection led by the DBX, which was first unveiled in November 2019. Production began in July 2020 and Aston sold 1,516 DBXs that year. In 2021 the firm sold 3,000 DBXs, of which 746 were sold in the first quarter. This year that fell to 421, a drop of 44 percent, which suggests that demand is easing off. Other indicators are also not good. Overall sales in Q1 dropped 14 percent while net debt rose from £722 million a year ago to £957 million. The only real bright spot in the story was that sales of the expensive specials meant that overall revenues went up four percent. Although the company says hat things remain on target, it has dumped CEO Tobias Moers and has appointed the 76-year-old Italian Amedeo Felisa as his replacement.

The word is that Stroll and his investors are now actively looking for ways to sell the firm to Audi, which will give them a fig leaf of having saved the firm and handing it on to an industry major.

The racing team is also very disappointing. The team was in a mess in 2018 when Lawrence Stroll bought it (largely to provide his son Lance with an F1 drive) and the 2020 results were good because the team copied the Mercedes design, which resulted in Sergio Perez winning a race, but since the transformation into Aston Martin the team has failed to deliver, dropping from fourth in the Constructors' Championship in 2020 to seventh last year. This year it is currently ninth. Lance is quick from time to time, but is not the full package and has been overshadowed this year by Sebastian Vettel, despite the fact that the German missed two races with Covid-19. Vettel is seen in F1 as being well passed his best and prone to mistakes. Stroll is buying in talent and investing in a new facility which increases the potential value of the team.

The word is that Audi is now leaning more towards Sauber, which is for sale if the price and conditions are right. There is one key reason why this may be the best option. Sauber was owned by BMW between 2005 and 2009. It did well and was a

World Championship challenger in 2008 before BMW pulled the plug after the global financial crisis. The people who were at BMW at the time thus know that the team could be a contender with the right leadership and the right resources. Audi CEO Markus Duesmann was one of the BMW F1 engineers at the time and last year he appointed Australian Adam Baker, another ex-BMW man to formulate Audi's motorsport strategy. Another man who was involved in that era was Mike Krack, who is currently learning how to be a team principal with Aston Martin.

Many of the big names from Audi's glorious motorsport past have retired now and the new generation have yet to prove their worth and there are some in Germany who think Audi's reputation may now be a little overblown and the attitude a little bit too arrogant. Still, the people at the top understand the task in hand and seem to have the money to do the job... and they also know that Hinwil can produce competitive cars.

Other stories worthy of mention include the suggestions that the FIA has now agreed to the plan to have six F1 Sprint races in 2023, although it is not yet clear where these will be.

Calendars remain the source of much F1 discussion at a time before the Silly Season really begins and the sport has still to finalise a race to replace Russia in the autumn. This will be Singapore, if it happens at all. The plan is to have a two-day race meeting on the weekend before the main event, with the first race taking place in daylight, the second at night. It is a good opportunity for F1 to trial a two-day event.

Interestingly night and day is becoming an issue in Grand Prix racing for a rather left-field reason. There are some races that are stuck with certain dates and do not want to change: Miami, Monaco and Montreal being three of them. This means that F1 must fly backwards and forwards across the Atlantic, rather than adopting a more sensible strategy and creating a US "swing", with several races paired up to reduce costs and wear-and-tear. In a perfect world, Montreal and Miami would be linked but Montreal does not want to move forward from its summer-opening festival and Miami doesn't want to move earlier because of tennis. Australia might like to regain its season-opening date but the teams prefer to go to Bahrain so they can test and race in warm weather, without being too far from home, which means that when things go wrong, they can get stuff back to base more easily.

The night and day problem is because of the Muslim practice of Ramadan, the 30-day period during which they abstain from all the fun stuff and focus on religion and clean-living, at least during daylight hours. Going racing in Ramadan is obviously not a good combination. This year Ramadan was from April 1 until May 1, which meant that the Grands Prix in Bahrain and Saudi Arabia both took place before it began. The problem is that each year Ramadan moves and next year it will begin on March 22 and end on April 20, which means that the two races need to be on March 12 and 19, with the pre-season test on March 5. The teams want a break after Bahrain to avoid what is in effect a triple-header. That would mean that the season would need to start in February in order to get both races done before Ramadan. F1 argues that if the racing is at night, that would be OK, but that pragmatic approach might not square with all Muslim believers. And things are more complicated in 2024, 2025 and 2026 after which Ramadan will not be a problem again for F1 until the mid 2030s, when it will be happening in November.

This may explain why there is much interest in a race in Africa at the moment, because South Africa could, for example, take over pre-season testing and the first race at a time when the weather is best and there would be no jet-lag, and then F1 could return to the Middle East. F1 used to go to South Africa at the start of each year, although it has also started the season in South America in the past. One idea that is kicking around is a race in Colombia with a very solid project under development in the city of Barranquilla. The word is that this is funded with private money and will not need public funding, although perhaps the authorities will be asked to kick in some cash for infrastructure work. I heard in Miami that this would be called the Caribbean Grand Prix, which would create a race that could move around the region over time if other projects can come to fruition. This would operate along similar lines to the European GP title, which has been applied to different events in different countries. Colombia has a couple of young drivers beginning to climb through the ranks: Sebastián Montoya (son of) and Nicolás Baptiste, who is a protégé of Fernando Alonso.

This event might also help F1 with its problem of fitting in races in the US time zones as it could twin with one of the US events, or with Brazil, to streamline the calendar a little. The signs are that the new race in Las Vegas is going to take Austin's date in early November, rather than being held at Thanksgiving, which will mean that it will go back-to-back with the Mexican Grand Prix, which will keep its Day of the Dead holiday weekend.

This means that Austin will have to move to somewhere else on the calendar, which could mean a switch to the spring, to be twinned with Miami, because of the end-of-season is becoming more and more congested with races in Asia, Qatar, Abu Dhabi, Brazil and potentially Australia as well. Teams don't like triple-headers and so an Austin-Mexico-Las Vegas swing would not be popular.

The next new F1 race in America will be in Las Vegas at the end of next year and will be promoted by Liberty Media itself and so the profits generated will go straight into the F1 bottom line, without a promoter taking much of the loot and paying a fee. This is an important step as the Q1 figures for Formula 1 show that the hospitality is important. This year the sport raked in $360 million, compared to $180 million in the same period last year. There were two races this year, rather than one in 2021, but they were also held without any major crowd and hospitality restrictions, which was not the case last year. That is a big increase. F1's cash pile has grown from $2.074 billion last year to $2.265 billion but the sport is about to splash out $240 million buying a 39-acre plot of land in Las Vegas, where it will build a permanent pit lane and paddock complex. If that sounds profligate, it is clear that there is more to this than meets the eye and we can expect to see the land being used for other things as well.

The investment sends a strong message to Las Vegas that F1 is serious about the relationship, which is currently just for three years. It also adds the asset to the F1 balance sheet (which is important for the bean-counter types in Colorado). The whisper is that the land – which is located between East Harmon Avenue and East Rochelle Avenue, and between Koval Lane and Kishner Drive – will feature permanent facilities that will give F1 an all-year presence in Las Vegas, converting into garages and hospitality units for the race. This could be an F1 showcase which would highlight the history, heritage and power of the sport with permanent exhibitions, although there is also obvious potential for such things as convention space and even may hotel facilities, in addition to retail outlets.

If you think NASCAR Hall of Fame with garages, offices and so on, it is probably what will happen. The price for the land is high as the current owners 3D Investments, which is run by the Daneshgar Family, paid $130 million in 2019 for the land and another adjacent 21-acre parcel, on which the Harbor Island apartment complex sits. The project they had went west with the pandemic but they will make a killing on the F1 deal and will be able to develop the apartment complex into something nicer. As for the Las Vegas race itself, work is needed rapidly to get everything done and the word is that the F1-owned promotion firm will be headed by Renee Wilm, Liberty Media's chief legal officer, with the day-to-day management being done by F1's Emily Prazer, who has been Head of Commercial Development of Race Promotion up to now.

Finally, I hear that the project will include a facsimile F1 paddock area on land north of Caesars Palace casino on The Strip, where the public will be able to get a feel for the sport, up close and personnel, without disrupting the actual operations. This is good news for the battle-hardened F1 folk who fought through the Miami weekend.

From La Dynamite

26 May 2022

La Dynamite is such a great name for a village. I've always been a fan of eccentric place-names and La Dynamite is certainly up there with Little Snoring, Middle Wallop, Ecoute-s'il-pleut (Listen-if-it's-raining), Droop, La Roue-Qui-Tourne (The-Wheel-that-Turns), Bachelor's Bump or plain old boring La Machine.

La Dynamite is so-named because, in addition to being a good place to have a picnic and watch butterflies doing their thing, it is also the site of a very large explosives factory. This is why there are not many houses in proximity as the "blast wave overpressure" in the event of an accident would probably knock down reinforced concrete buildings and blow human being well into next week. From what I can gather, this has never happened at La Dynamite, although its sister works at the daftly-named Billy-Berclau, near Lille, suffered such an event in 2003, which led to its closure and the transfer of operations (by normal transportation methods, rather than by explosive wave) to an obscure part of Poland.

Anyway, La Dynamite is a good place to stop if you are driving the 400 miles from Barcelona to Monaco, as you do in F1 these days. It's about 250 miles into the trip. You could stop at the wonderful walled medieval city called Aigues-Mortes, which is slightly more off the route. This was once a port from which Crusaders departed to the Levant, but is now miles inland from the sea, because of the Rhône river deposits vast amounts of silt at its mouth, or rather its mouths, – as there are two of them.

Between the Petit Rhône to the west and the Grand Rhône in the east, is the Camargue, land that is as flat as a board with briney lagoons and reed-infested marshes. It is a weird and wonderful place with rice paddies and salt lakes, flamingos and cowboys. The latter, known as gardians, spend their lives corralling the famous black bulls and white horses of the Camargue.

La Dynamite is where it is because 120 years ago the area was empty of people but the PLM railway (Paris à Lyon et à la Méditerranée) passed through, hauling visitors to the Côte d'Azur. This could bring in the components of dynamite and carry away the finished product to the mines of the Cévennes. Railways used to be useful and they are becoming so again as everyone sees them as being more sustainable than a squillion road cars, all puffing out nasty smells and ruining the planet.

History is always useful (despite what some politicians will tell you) and back in the days before everyone had two cars, racing took place on the roads in many countries. Britain, being eccentric, insisted before 1903 that any rival to the horse-drawn carriage should require a person carrying a red flag to walk ahead of the vehicle. This handed leadership in road transport technology to the French, who allowed racing to take place on their public roads. In Britain things were liberalised after the Motor Car Act of 1903, but the 20mph speed limit on all public roads meant that racers had to go abroad, until someone with a lot of money decided to build Brooklands. The French raced everywhere and they often picked triangular circuits between towns with stations, which meant that the spectators could get close to the action.

Once more people had cars, circuits moved to places where only cars can go, which is exactly NOT what is required in the modern day and age. Huge traffic jams are no longer considered cool and even that most green of competitions – Le Tour de France – has a problem because while the riders produce little pollution, the 14 million car-borne spectators out-do all other sporting events in the world in terms of pollution.

The tragedy of this is that the racing circuits which we now consider to be classic venues are largely beyond the reach of railways and putting in new ones is vastly expensive. Le Mans twigged this years ago when the city built a tramway to take thousands of spectators from the city's railway station to the middle of the celebrated racing circuit.

Access is a problem for a number of famous F1 tracks, although Monaco and Monza are both served by railways, which makes life easier from them. But when it comes to places like Silverstone, Spa and Paul Ricard, it is a problem. The tragedy of Spa-Francorchamps is that it once had a railway station in the village and the path of the railway is still there, although the tracks were torn up in the 1970s and the path left was turned into a cycling track. A station would be invaluable today.

I mention all this because both the French and Belgian GPs are at the end of their current F1 contracts and the signs are that neither event will be renewed. Paul Ricard is struggling to meet the fee demands from the Formula 1 group, but Spa is in trouble because, despite support from the Walloon provincial government – which understands the value of the event for the region – the venue has serious problems with access. Spa has undergone a massive rebuild in recent months, in order to make it safer and to allow the track to run motorcycle races again, but the access problems will not go away. Last year's Belgian GP washout created horrendous snarl-ups after the usual car parks turned to mud – and fans parked wherever they could. And then didn't see a race... Obviously the weather does not help and although the hard core fans still love Spa – and so they should – it is not what Formula 1 is looking for these days. It is a long circuit but has a small crowd capacity of 75,000, which means that even when full (which it is thanks largely to the Orange Army that marches south each year from Verstappenland), it cannot produce the kind of numbers that F1 wants to see.

Adding more spectator areas might be possible, although ecologists would probably chain themselves to trees, but then access would become more of a problem because there are only so many ways in and out of the circuit... It does not help that the local police force has a reputation for imposing traffic management measures which seem to makes things more difficult, but some fellow with pips on his shoulder thinks he knows what he is doing and who are we to argue.

Spa's Commercial Director Stijn de Boever was in Barcelona for discussions with F1, but the word is that the series promoter isn't too keen on doing another deal, even if the provincial government ups the money, which it is willing to do. It may be considered a crime against humanity by hard core F1 fans not to have a race at Spa, but the sport wants to appeal to fans of all kinds – and Spa does not fit in this respect.

After the calendar disruptions caused by the pandemic, it is hoped that things will get back together more in 2023, but there remain question marks about China and how all the races will fit together next year. I bumped into Circuit of the Americas boss Bobby Epstein in Barcelona (he's often there) and he said it was news to him that his race might move to the spring. It sounds more like there might be an Austin-Mexico-Vegas swing, but F1 teams don't want more triple-headers if they can be avoided (as they were only supposed to happen during the pandemic).

The team bosses met with Stefano Domenicali in Barcelona and he explained that he would try to create a more regionalised calendar in order for things to be more efficient, more cost-effective and more sustainable (that word again). There are also the problems for the next few years with Ramadan, mentioned in the last Green Notebook, and so it could be that Australia will pop up at the start of the year again for a year or two to ensure that Bahrain and Saudi Arabia don't upset local sensitivities...

There could be a test in Bahrain and then a two-week gap to Australia and then the Middle Eastern races after that (before it gets too hot).

It would be nice to report that South Africa will be back in 2023 but it is going to be tough to achieve given the political instability in the country and the constant bickering that seems to exist within the ruling African National Congress party. These fights have become so bad that former President Kgalema Motlanthe recently said that the rule of the ANC, which has run the country since 1994, is coming to an end because it is steadily losing the support of the people. Against that background, it may be hard to get a race up and running any time soon.

The basic concept of regionalisation is to have a calendar that groups the races so that logistical problems are less complicated. Thus the season would begin in the Middle East in the early spring, with Australia and another Asia-Pacific race (normally China) following on. There would then be a swift double-header in the Americas before the European season in the summer. With some of the European races being weeded out, that opens the way for Eurasia as well. After the summer break (which no-one wants to lose) it would be a second Asian trip (logically Singapore and Japan). There is also the desire for a race in Korea, although there seems to be little interest in reviving either Malaysia or the GP that never was in Vietnam. The focus would then switch to the Americas again in the autumn months, with the likes of Mexico, Austin, Brazil, Vegas and perhaps something in the Caribbean, and then the season would finish off with a pair of evening races in the Middle East, to maximise global TV audiences for the finale. This would mean that Asia and the Americas would each get two hits of F1 per year, which will help build interest.

The problem with all this is that Montreal in June gets in the way. In a perfect world, Montreal would be twinned with Miami and held in May, when temperatures in Canada are a little lower. But that would move it off the traditional start-of-summer weekend, which makes it a big party for thousands of Canadians who don't actually attend the race. The event is coupled with graduation ceremonies and proms and it is a huge earning weekend for the city. Miami cannot go any later because of the heat in Florida in June. And Miami cannot have the Grand Prix in the autumn because of the NFL season that runs from September – January, which is the prime purpose of the Hard Rock Stadium. The Canadians have a contract that guarantees the current date and so to get them to change will be difficult, although the race promoter is now owned by Bell Media, which is also the F1 TV rights holder in Canada and so the date of the race may be negotiable given the other interests involved.

Monaco is still to be fixed as F1 wants more concessions and more money from the Principality and, if possible, a race track that allows for racing. Still, the race is no longer tied to the Ascension Day holiday and does not have an extra day, which makes it possible to be back-to-back with Spain, although it is a logistical struggle getting everything into and out of the pokey little paddock in Monaco, which is not VIP-friendly unless you have a yacht.

New races are adding to the prize money, but they also add to the costs and the human wear-and-tear. However, at the moment this is not the primary worry in the minds of F1 team bosses. On Saturday in Spain, just after qualifying, there was a very low-key meeting in the McLaren hospitality unit, involving FIA President Mohammed Ben Sulayem, the FIA's head of F1 Peter Bayer, Ferrari's Mattia Binotto, Red Bull's Christian Horner, Mercedes's Toto Wolff and McLaren's Zak Brown. Those involved entered and departed individually so it was not obvious – and the "smaller" teams were not part of the discussion. This was all about the impact of inflation on the F1 budget cap. Inflation was rising in many countries before the Russian invasion of Ukraine, because the global pandemic had created serious supply-demand imbalances. The war added new supply shocks to the global economy which we are now feeling with dramatic hikes in the price of many items and disruption in the supply chains. The big teams are arguing that $140 million is not enough (although, of course, they spend a lot more when all the exclusions are included). They have had to make serious reductions to adapt to the limits and now want to use the global situation to puff up the budget again.

The FIA seems to be smiling and nodding and letting them have their say, but there are no signs that the federation's cap will be doffed for anyone. This has led Christian Horner to suggest that the teams might not be able to afford the last few races and so will not appear, which is headline-grabbing but not realistic if Christian wants to keep his job. Still, given the amount of time he spends on Sky TV, he probably has a future in broadcasting if his days as a team principal ever come to an end (assuming, of course, that Sky is still around).

At the moment, the FIA seems to be more fixated at the question of jewellery, which seems to be a fight that is not really required, but must be viewed as arm-wrestling between the sport and the federation over who is the boss when it comes to the rules. Clearly, the boss of F1 is not Lewis Hamilton and so he may have to divest himself of his bling if he wants to race on in F1. This is sensible and logical – and safer – but Lewis seems to think it is against him, while others feel that it is a fight that F1 really does not need right now.

It is a time of change at the FIA and it is clear that we have not seen all the changes yet. More are expected in the weeks ahead as the new leadership cleans up the messes and structures left by the ancien regime. In the finest French traditions, some heads will roll.

As part of this process there is a new chief of staff at the FIA, with the appointment of 54-year-old British-born Anglo-Indian Shaila-Ann Rao. No-one seems to know what the difference is between a chief of staff and a CEO, but perhaps the President will explain that at some point once he has put out all the fires he has been fighting. Rao is a lawyer who spent years in TV rights negotiation with TF1 and Lagardère before joining the FIA as Legal Director in 2016. She moved on two years later to join Mercedes AMG Petronas... but is now going back to the federation, presumably because it has a new president.

The FIA was much in the news in Barcelona thanks to Aston Martin turning up with cars that looked like green Red Bulls. The team has "previous" with regard to copycatism and so the feds had to go through the process of finding out how this had been done without anyone nicking any designs or using photographs and scans (which are no longer allowed). This was a lengthy process which has been going on for a while under the radar and the FIA boffins say that there is no evidence of any wrongdoing. Red Bull says that some of its IP has been downloaded by staff who left the team but while that can be proved, it is hard to prove that it was used elsewhere. However, there is still the possibility of Red Bull taking action against individuals if they have breached their contracts, but showing that Aston Martin used the data is impossible. Cyber-security in F1 is well-advanced these days and there are almost certainly security markers hidden away in software to stop "cutting-and-pasting" of data. The fact that Red Bull knows about downloads says it all: there are elaborate systems that know exactly where all confidential information is, and who has accessed it. Everything is logged and there are multiple firewalls and multi-stage authentication techniques. Even if someone gets through all of this, the team will still know what data has been moved, which apparently it does... Espionage is thus a dangerous business.

Horner and his crew are good at technology and the word is that, in order to stay atop the rigging in F1, the team is now aiming to build a new windtunnel on its campus in Milton Keynes, because it fears that others may catch up. Windtunnels are huge, expensive, not sustainable and much work can be done these days with computational fluid dynamics (CFD), which simulates what windtunnels do. In a perfect world windtunnels would be gone but Red Bull still sees the value in them and has the money to spend on them... even if there are restrictions on how much they can be used. It would be better, perhaps, to ban them but then at least three teams would oppose this... because they are building new ones.

The budget cap has put value into the teams and the cost of buying a team has now risen dramatically, making life hard for those who want to break into the sport. At the same time, there is more demand as sports investors see the potential of F1 growth. Thus to get hold of a team today will cost about $700 million. This basically means that a buyer needs to have a billion or so to spare in order to buy and run a team. Obviously some of this would be offset with sponsorship (which is getting better) and prize money (which is also rising), but it does mean that Grand Prix racing is an expensive business. Every now and then one hears from financial circles that a team is looking for investors (or buyers) but most of these rumours seem to relate to "fishing trips" with the owners dipping their toes in the water to see if anyone bites at a big valuation. The most recent rumour is that Alpine has been sniffing around for a valuation, although it is unlikely that the team would be sold. However, bringing in partners to share the burden (as Mercedes, McLaren and others have done) is not impossible. Renault is still very keen on electric vehicles, although the bosses believe that ultimately the future lies in hydrogen, and it is worth noting that in recent weeks, the Nissan Formula E programme has been moved from the DAMS headquarters near Le Mans to the Renault motorsport engine facility in Viry-Chatillon. Elsewhere the Mercedes Formula E operation is being moved out of Brackley now that the team has been taken over by McLaren. This rather sums up the state of the car industry at the moment. Some folk running one way, others doing the opposite...

There is little chatter on the driver front yet although Williams sources say that the team is not going to kick out Nicholas Latifi and replace him with Nyck de Vries before the end of the year. There is no guarantee that the Dutchman will sign for 2023 because he's not a youngster willing to grab an F1 chance at any opportunity, but rather at 27 wants to make decent money from his career and can live without F1 if there is a high-paying job in sports car racing which would mean winning races, allied to a drive in Formula E. If one looks at Sébastien Buemi, one can see that there are lots of options. The Swiss used to be a Red Bull-sponsored F1 driver. Today he still works with Red Bull in the simulator, but also has a factory drive in WEC with Toyota and a Nissan works drive in Formula E. Quite how he has managed to represent two rival Japanese manufacturers at the same time is not clear, but he's probably pulling in a truckload of greenbacks as a result... and good for him.

From Solarium Beach, Monaco

31 May 2022

Monaco has always been a place that has lived off money from elsewhere, attracted by a scenic port surrounded by the high coastal mountain range, which shelters the town from cold northerlies. The fact that it faces south means that there is a warm microclimate so one can grow tropical plants and create exotic gardens.

The whole coastline – the Cote d'Azur – is like that and it became chic when wealthy members of the British aristocracy discovered that it was much nicer to spend their winters in the sunshine, rather than enduring British rain and fog – and that ghastly man Disraeli. They stumbled upon a small village called Nice, overlooking the Bay of Angels, and began to build villas. They soon added the Promenade des Anglais. Monaco at that time was remote and isolated. It was a fishing village with a castle on the hill above it. It was not rich and in 1856 Prince Florestan decided it needed more visitors and hit on the idea of building a bathing establishment and casino to pull in the deep-pocketed travellers.

His son Charles III thought the original building was insufficient and so built a much grander establishment on a small plateau to the east of the old port. Within a few years the Paris-Lyon-Mediterranée railway extended its railway line along the coast to Monaco and the area around the casino was renamed Monte Carlo (Carlo being Italian for Charles) and, hey presto, people began to arrive. Monte Carlo became the place to go to "break the bank" and it became tax-free to attract more wealthy individuals, including Americans and Russian émigrés. The Principality used sports to promote itself with the Monte Carlo Rally and then the Monaco Grand Prix. Then came the cinema. And when Prince Rainier married movie star Grace Kelly, the glittering image of Monte Carlo was complete. It has been riding that wave ever since.

But even surfers get old… so Monaco is forever building and tunnelling to make itself bigger and better. The elegant villas of old have largely disappeared now, as development has turned to tower blocks filled with tax-dodgers (or with empty apartments being used as residential addresses). Every time I visit I am reminded of Joni Mitchell's famous song "Big Yellow Taxi" and the lines: "They paved paradise and put up a parking lot".

But I still like Monaco, or at least I try to. At the moment they are building a whole new district in the east where there will be no cars, except in underground car parks. This will include a coastal promenade, 150 top-of-the-range apartments, villas and houses, a park, a port for parking yachts and lots of expensive new shops and restaurants.

Down in the old fishing village – now known as Port Hercule – they decided 20 years ago that they needed a way to attract more visitors and a new sea wall, known as the Nouvelle Digue, was built to allow cruise ships to stop by. Passengers swarm ashore and spend money. The Nouvelle Digue is actually floating (so they say) and was built in Spain (where labour is cheap) and it was then towed to Monaco and moored outside the famous harbour. On the outside of this concrete monstrosity, someone decided that it would be great to create a "concrete beach", giving access to the sea if one does not mind jumping in, and then climbing up a ladder to get back to floating "dry land". They have added trees recently to make it less concretey, but concrete it remains.

Having said that, if you are looking for peace and quiet in Monaco, it is a good place to go as few people get excited about concrete beaches (perhaps it is a little ahead of its time) and it is close to town. There is even parking nearby in the Parking des Pêcheurs (The Fishermens' Car Park) where F1 folk park their cars and where the Formula 2 Championship paddock is located. The top floor doubles as an indoor kart facility, where the Chuck Leclucks of the future can learn their trade.

The problem is that there is no space in Monaco and Formula 1 always feels cramped. The Paddock is a quayside. Everything is too narrow and so the Automobile Club de Monaco (ACM) employs countless folk who are there simply to move everyone on. It's a boring job, of course, and so these people tend to get blasé about how they treat others – and it not being a job that requires much in the way of education, they often have no clue who they are talking to. They all recognise the Prince and the ACM President, but they treat everyone else like dirt on their shoes. They are an anti-diplomatic corps. So, the Monaco Grand Prix is the event where the beautiful people cram into a small area which smells of fish, diesel and leaky portaloos. They trip over plastic cable covers that run everywhere, because no-once can be bothered to create mini trenches and the only people who are happy are those who get their kicks watching VIP after VIP trips over these things.

When you boil it all down, it's slightly less glamorous than a motorway service area, without the space. But, for most of the world, getting into the Paddock in Monaco is just the coolest thing...

The one area where there is a space has been eroded over time by a VIP hospitality area that was crept along the quayside (it makes money and so is interesting for F1) and it has now largely taken up with an area where TV crews are allowed to stumble over one another. Through this area sail the drivers, surrounded by their social media teams and PR folk, frantically filming and looking important, but actually being little more than human tugboats around sleek ocean liners.

These days, the written media is less and less visible in the paddock because no-one allows them into the motorhomes any longer (the teams made sure that something good came out of the pandemic) and so most stay inside the tatty exhibition hall on the first floor of the fading pink building that runs down the quayside behind the paddock.

The press do not bother going out, except to get food.

It is supposed to be a media sport, but no-one wants the media. The odd thing is that F1's new popularity comes from the Netflix series Drive to Survive, which takes people behind the scenes a little. But even this has major time constraints and so for those who really want to feel part of F1 the written media is the place to go, as it has untold acres of virtual space to tell the stories of life in F1 and to weave an interesting tapestry. F1 people and teams don't seem to realise this.

Many years ago, I realised that there was no point in trying to find people in Monaco and I use a couple of places where I hang out and let the world come to me. Sometimes one has to swat away security people to do this, but such is life. Terriers biting trouser legs can usually be kicked away. Watching the big boss of F1 Greg Maffei struggling through crowded alleyways surrounded by workers, caterers, people who want to be noticed, security people and endless VIP minders, made me wonder if perhaps he might not feel the need to buy a chunk of Monaco to create the right kind of F1 facility – as he has recently done in Las Vegas for a cool $240 million.

One gets the impression that the rather tatty block behind the Paddock might be demolished and things reorganised, to spruce up the poor end of the Quai Albert Ier, giving Monaco a nicer space for events and F1 a better paddock. I am sure that such a scheme could make money because one can always sell or rent new apartments in Monaco to the rich – and some new apartments could easily be built into any development.

I see from the US that Roger Penske, the owner of Indianapolis Motor Speedway, has also gone down the same path by buying the Speedway Monogramming property, that has existed among the Speedway's parking lots, opposite the South Chute Tunnel, for the last 30-odd years. This means that one day soon, this will be demolished and the Brickyard can get the kind of "front door" that such a facility requires.

Anyway for now we are stuck with a dingy Monaco Paddock, with a race track where overtaking in impossible. It was ironic that this year's Monaco GP slogan was "Let's Race", which, of course, is the last thing that happens on the current track... Add to this the fact that the TV coverage is awful and advertising and hospitality are both sub F1 standard. And the race pays a much lower fee than all the others.

While we all love the concept of Monaco, it is one of the worst races – by a long way, although the ACM seems unable to grasp the concept that it is not the best race in the world. One good indicator of the arrogance in Monaco is that one never sees ACM people at other races looking at what rival promoters do... to learn. The ACM thinks there is nothing to learn.

Ah well, ignorance is bliss. F1 is telling Monaco it might not agree a new contract, but the ACM thinks it is impossible that F1 would drop the Grand Prix. It is not impossible...

The Paddock did not buzz with news as a result of all the restrictions on movement, but the press conferences did see a performance worthy for an Honorary Palme d'Or at the Cannes Film Festival. This was Christian Horner explaining how tough life is for Red Bull with the F1 budget cap. It is almost tragic to have to report that this was lapped up by open mouthed media (yes, there are a few mouth-breathers in the media) who do not realise when someone is feeding them information for reasons other than admiration for what they write. Grown men had tears rolling down their cheeks as Christian soldiered onward with stories of Red Bull staff being laid off and how they would have to busk at the roundabouts in Milton Keynes. He stopped short of launching a TV appeal for little old ladies to send in their savings to help these lovely cuddly people, who would be cruelly wronged by the evil budget cap.

The truth is that while inflation is a problem, Christian & Co have forgotten to mention that F1's business is largely conducted in US dollars, including the all-important prize money payments, much of the sponsorship and, the budget cap itself. He also forgot to mention that in the last 12 months currency traders have seen the dollar as the safe haven and so it has appreciated significantly against its European counterparts. Teams earn in dollars and spend in local currencies (be that the pound, the euro or the Swiss franc). If one looks at the numbers, inflation in Europe is about seven percent and might rise to 10 by the end of the year. The dollar has appreciated against the euro by 15 percent, 13 percent against the pound and eight percent against the Swiss franc. Anyone who has travelled to the US recently will attest that it has become a very expensive place to be.

This means that teams have up to 15 percent more money to play with, in their local currency, than they used to have. Inflation has reduced the value of this extra money, but they still have more than they used to have. It is true that many costs have increased impressively, particularly the costs of electricity, fuel, air freight and air tickets, but these are not the major items in team expenditures. This all means that claims for a higher budget cap are really only big teams trying to get more money to help them beat less well-funded teams...

Incidentally, Red Bull is now discussing building a new wind tunnel in Milton Keynes in order to stay competitive, at a time when wind tunnels should be a thing of the past. They are doing this, so Christian told me, because Lawrence Stroll needs one for his son. Someone really needs to whisper to the Canadian billionaire that you cannot buy the World Championship for one's offspring. It has been clear for some time that Lance is good, but not quite good enough. It is a similar story with Mick Schumacher who keeps having big crashes while trying to out-do Kevin Magnussen. This is wearing thin for Haas and there is talk that it would probably like a different driver next year, although Ferrari does have a say in the matter. The problem is that Ferrari has a gap in its young driver conveyor belt at the moment because the only Ferrari youngster who looks even vaguely ready for F1 is Robert Shwartzmann, a Russian. Antonio Giovinazzi is still there but he has been around the block a few times already. British driver Callum Ilott is still a member of the Ferrari programme, but seems to be settled in IndyCar (where he damaged his wrist last weekend when he crashed during the Indy 500) while the next Ferrari youngsters are Formula 3 drivers: including Arthur Leclerc (The Sequel) and Oliver Bearman.

The rumour in Monaco is that Mick's people are now looking at other options for the future and that Aston Martin might be a good choice for him because he's German, younger and less hairy than Sebastian Vettel, and he is not too fast for Lance.

The thing is that billionaires always seem to think that because they are billionaires they can be successful in everything. No-one dares to tell them that may not be the case. Similarly, it seems to me that billionaires should buy smaller trousers because having really deep pockets and high belts is never a great look. But, hey, who decides what is fashionable? Money is always in fashion.

The recent fiasco with Formula 1 VIP hospitality in Miami seems to have led to a rethink about the way the system should work in the future. The deal in Miami allowed for the local promoter to select its own catering, and it chose a local firm because it was less expensive that F1's usual supplier, the Austrian caterer Do&Co. The result of this decision was a lot of very unhappy VIPs, teams and sponsors, who all felt – quite rightly – that if one is paying $12,000 for a ticket to an event, one should expect top level hospitality. The problem for Formula 1 is that the guests do not know, nor care, about the sub-contracting arrangements. For them the Grand Prix was a failure of F1 itself and the danger of this is that the sport will get a reputation as being a rip-off – and that is clearly not what is wanted. The best way to maintain quality control is to dictate what happens.

In the future, F1 will be doing that…

There was not much else. Former Formula 1 driver Kimi Raikkonen is going to race in the NASCAR Cup Series later this year. Now 42, the monosyllabic Finn will race for the Trackhouse team at Watkins Glen on August 21. The deal is part of a new initiative launched by Trackhouse called Project91, which will field a Chevrolet with #91 for a series of international racing drivers, in an effort to increase worldwide interest in the stock car series.

Not everyone goes to Monaco because they want to be noticed. Some go to see the event because they have plans of their own to host races and DON'T want to be seen. This is a daft idea, of course, because in Monaco, everyone is looking at everyone else to see who they are, and anyone who believes that they can hide in plain sight is taking a big risk. If one sneaks on to a boat one can get away with it, if they crew don't blab, but if you are in the paddock you can be spotted not only by the way you act, but also by how those around you behave.

Years ago I developed a strategy for spotting these people. If I saw someone accompanied by leggy blondes with diamond earrings, this suggested that the gentleman in question was wealthy and I would rush up and say "Hello, I'm Joe," and they would say: "Hello, I'm Such-and-Such" and we'd get chatting and I'd find out who they were. This worked very well with a man who replied: "I'm Steve. Steve Wynn." He was in Monaco because he wanted to have a Grand Prix in Las Vegas and told me all about it.

I might have done the same thing this year with a chap in a Williams hat, as all the big cheeses in the team were fawning over him in the Paddock alleyway. I even heard one of them say: "This way, Peter" and that got me thinking. Back in the summer of 2020, when the Williams team was sold to Dorilton Capital, there was much interest and speculation about who was behind the mysterious investment firm. It was based in New York, but was clearly not an American firm. It was identified only as being a private investment office for an unidentified high worth family.

I got a tip that the buyer was a Jersey-based entrepreneur called Peter de Putron, but no-one in the team would talk about whether these stories were true. De Putron is so reclusive that there does not seem to be a single photograph of him on the Internet, which makes it quite hard to identify him. Did Peter's pass say de Putron? I wondered. There is a picture on the Internet of his brother and the two people seemed to have some striking similarities.

I suppose I could have employed some ACM security person to be annoying and look for me, but in the end I concluded that with modern telephones one can take pictures that blow up very large. Anyway, to cut a long story short I am certain that de Putron is the man behind Dorilton – and I'll not post any pictures of him because he does not want to be famous. And now he owes me a favour… which is never a bad thing.

Among those in Monaco who were not hiding was William Hornbuckle, the CEO and President of MGM Resorts International, one of the biggest casino operators in Las Vegas, over to take a look at how things are done. There was also a delegation of Africans (which is quite unusual in F1) and I was told that they were from South Africa, present to discuss the possibility of a new F1 event at Kyalami.

In my years in F1, I have always found that there is no better way to upsetting celebrities than asking them how they became famous. I don't do it any more and am blithely unaware when I stroll past some pouting social influencer with a squillion followers, a cage fighter or a jingly-jangly bling-covered football player with tattooed nostrils. As usual, Hollywood's finest (apart from Horner) didn't turn up for the photo op in Monaco.

Flavio Briatore could not stay away, of course, dying as is he is for publicity and surrounded as always by fashion models of yesteryear, reminding us all about how much F1 has moved on since his inauspicious exit from the sport more than a decade ago. A Formula 1 version of The Ghost of Christmas Yet to Come...

Bernie Ecclestone was not there (he's always been smarter than Flav) but he did manage to get into the news in F1 by being arrested while trying to get on a plane in Brazil with a small revolver in his luggage.

"I haven't had any publicity lately and I thought I ought to do something to get some," The Bernard told Reuters. Some in the cynical world of F1 think that this is possibly the real story.

Anyway, the race was interesting enough, but when we left on Sunday night I didn't say: "See you next year" to the ACM folk, because I am not sure we will be back in 2023. I hope so, but if we are back I hope that there will be some changed attitudes. F1 is deadly serious about getting what it wants from Monaco – even if that hurts for a year.

The ACM should perhaps take note of advice from Joni Mitchell. "Don't it always seem to go that you don't know what you've got 'til it's gone..."

From a quiet valley in Normandy

14 June 2022

Down the road from the ruined abbey and the picturesque duck pond, not far from an old farm where I sometimes go to buy exquisite charcuterie, there is a house that flies the Red Bull Racing flag at all times.

One day I must stop off and say "Bonjour", and find out why there is such passion for the team in such a un-Red Bull kind of place. Perhaps they are Max Verstappen fans, or maybe it is Dr Marko or Christian Horner who stirs the passion. I doubt (very much) that there are Mexicans in the neighbourhood.

I smile every time I pass by, which is quite often these days, as it is on the route I like to take to get to the airport. The road (eventually) links up to the old Roman road (known as the Chaussée Jules César), that runs as straight a die towards Paris, and Charles de Gaulle airport. I am taking this route three times in eight days: once returning from Baku, once going to Montreal and once on the way home from Canada.

Baku was (how can I put this politely?) dull. It's a nice enough place, if you don't look too closely, but it was incredibly quiet for the F1 weekend, perhaps because it came after three busy races in Miami, Barcelona and Monaco.

Admittedly, most of the locals cannot afford tickets, and in F1 only those who are really keen on the sport make the trip. It is not the kind of place where there is much in the way of B2B action, although the canapés in the Paddock Club probably make Monaco catering look good.

If they wanted to offer $10,000 as a reward for spotting a VIP, they would probably have got away without having to pay, although Flavio Briatore (who passes for an ageing celebrity) was probably there somewhere, picking up his commission cheque (or cash) for having put the deal together originally.

I didn't see him on the grid, which is where such people like to be seen. In truth, the grid was like high noon in Hadleyville, New Mexico, except that Gary Cooper had (unsurprisingly) decided NOT to forsake his darling Grace Kelly on their wedding day. So it really was rather quiet. Stefano Domenicali was walking around with FIA President Mohammed Ben Sulayem, without any celebs to shepherd around. It made me wonder what F1 is doing in Baku these days. In an era when F1 wants to put bums on seats and have big parties, is Baku the place to be?

It is actually a really interesting place. It was the scene of the world's first oil boom and although hydrocarbons are out of fashion these days, there is still plenty of the stuff to see in Baku. They have the pre-requisite silvery constructions that oil-rich places love, but there is old stuff too.

I concluded that Baku will need money to keep F1 interested, particularly at a time when the sport is

— Joe Saward's 2022 Green Notebook —

heavily into "regionalisation". Azerbaijan would fit into a notional calendar in April, perhaps on the way back from early season Asia-Pacific races, but it does not make a lot of sense in June.

Having Miami and Montreal in early May before the European season gets underway with Spain and Monaco (if a deal can be found for the latter) is much more logical. As Baku's deal runs out after the next race, it is fair to say that the boot in this negotiation is firmly on the F1 foot. If Baku doesn't want to play ball, it will lose the race. There is no negotiating position beyond cold hard cash.

Still, Liberty Media seems to be interested from time to time in places with horse-choking wedges of greenbacks, even if they do not quite fit into the pristine world inhabited by the Securities and Exchange Commission (SEC).

Although it doesn't always seem that way, Formula 1 is listed on the NASDAQ in New York and so there always a risk that the regulators might deem it unfortunate to go to places that rate 128th on the Corruption Perceptions Index (CPI). Now that Russia is gone from the F1 calendar, Azerbaijan is Bottom of the Pops on the CPI.

F1 has done much of what Baku wanted (putting the place on the international map), but tourism numbers have been slow to recover since the pandemic and have not been helped by the war in Ukraine, which has effectively wiped out all visitors from Russia and Ukraine. Russia was previously the major source of visitors to Azerbaijan. Without the Russians, the grandstands in Baku were, um, well, pretty unfilled.

Baku was pondering an Olympic bid a few years ago but, with the International Olympic Committee already having deals in place for Paris in 2024, Los Angeles in 2028 and Brisbane in 2032, there no possibility of the Games going to Azerbaijan until at least 2036, which is a long time in the future. And there are small signs that Azerbaijan is less interested than once it was. The infrastructure for F1 was left up for the whole of last year and is now suffering from wear and tear – and the current contract ends next year. So some fancy footwork may be required to get a new deal. F1 is in two minds about the future. Money is good, but…

Anyway, the FIA World Motor Sport Council will meet in the week after Montreal and we should not expect a 2023 calendar by then because there is too much under discussion. Stefano Domenicali flew off to South Africa after the race in Baku to talk about F1 going back to Africa, a deal that would probably help the F1 share price.

Baku hasn't changed much since we first started visiting in 2016. It is a little more welcoming perhaps. I seem to recall that the first visit involved an immigration officer with all the charisma and humour of Vladimir Putin's country cousin. This year the immigration officer was efficient and charming… and very beautiful. She was, in fact, the perfect antidote to the gormless rubber-stampers of old. But, there are still lessons to be learned. The people in Baku are generally very friendly. The hotelier sent me a message warning that "the price of a taxi from the airport to the hotel is 10-15 AZN". Sadly, I did not receive this (because it was too costly to turn on the roaming on my phone) and so I trusted the Taxi Desk in the Arrivals Hall where a dubious-looking individual assured me that 55 AZN was the going rate. Everyone got kinked. You can tell a lot about a country from its cab drivers…

Anyway, if Baku really wants to promote itself as an international tourist destination, it really does need to do something about the thieves who drive taxis. The hotel, of course, didn't take credit cards and naturally the card was blocked after two identical transactions to get cash, because credit card companies assume that there is criminal activity if you try the same transaction too many times from a place like Baku. There is, you see, still a reputational problem…

Anyway, I could walk into the paddock from the hotel, so life was not too bad. The only problem was that nothing was happening.

The signing of Sergio Perez by Red Bull (announced after Monaco) meant that the focus in the F1 driver market has moved to the next most competitive teams. Barring upheavals, Mercedes, Ferrari and Red Bull are now settled for 2023. This means that the focus has shifted to McLaren, Alpine and Alfa Romeo. McLaren has Lando Norris under contract and Daniel Ricciardo should still be there, although his results have been very disappointing, for the second year running. Thus there is a possibility of change and the theory is that McLaren can have Colton Herta, an American, if he does well in F1 testing (which will soon begin). Is that realistic? Perhaps not. I can see Herta replacing Ricciardo in 2024 as the American still has so much to learn.

Over at Alpine, the signs are that the current two drivers will stay. Esteban Ocon has a contract and the team is keen to keep Fernando Alonso. This means that Alpine must find Oscar Piastri a drive or risk losing him – which would not be very smart. I heard stories that Williams has done a deal with Piastri but, leaning against a wall in the paddock, I saw Mark Webber (Piastri's manager) talking in animated fashion to various people, which suggested that no deal is done. If it was done, Webber would have been somewhere else… Williams is the obvious spot on for Oscar, but a deal must be done. It was interesting to note that Williams had very much a skeleton staff in Baku, with no sign of team principal Jost Capito, let alone the owners.

Haas might be interested in Oscar but the truth is that Ferrari has a say in the second Haas driver and as Mick Schumacher is not delivering the good, the word is that Haas will probably end up with Ferrari's reserve driver Antonio Giovinazzi in 2023.

As for Alfa Romeo, no-one will want to drive there unless they can stop the cars breaking down. It is a really quick car but the results are less than impressive. In terms of speed, the team might be third in the championship if the car worked properly.

So, the big story in Baku was that there was no story, although the hyperbolic individuals in the F1 media decided to get excited about a possible salary cap. No-one seemed to know from where the story had come, which means that it was planted, but in truth it does make a lot of sense. Now that we have a budget cap (even if the top teams are whining about what they agreed), the exclusions make less and less sense. If you are slashing salaries inside a team, how can one justify going on paying vast sums to drivers and top people (these being excluded from the current cap)?

The fact that there is inflation and it is painful for the top teams is not that interesting, although one might ask the question about why no-one properly considered what impact inflation might have, presumably because there are not so many folk old enough to remember bad inflation in the world.

Anyway, there is an easy fix. Teams that are short of cash can simply turn off their wind tunnels for a few weeks… The purpose of the budget cap is to balance up spending and this is exactly what it is doing and the FIA and the smaller teams see no reason to change that because the big teams are having to pay more for their electricity.

No team is going to miss races.

Bringing everything under the budget cap is a good idea C and is already being used in any number of sports. What people in F1 miss is that there are many different ways to have a salary cap. And it does not mean that drivers will get less money. It is not an assault on their value, nor a restriction of free enterprise nor trade, it is simply a way for teams to better use their resources in a controlled fashion – which means that they will make more profits, and become more valuable.

What is needed is a step back from the F1 coal face.

There are salary caps in the NFL, the NBA, the NHL, the MLS and many other smaller leagues in the US and in many other sports across the world. A salary cap merely restricts what a team can pay a player/driver. It does not restrict what a sponsor can pay. The only thing required to make it work is for the teams to give up the current practice of taking all the drivers' marketing rights and all their time.

If they do that, which they must if there is to be a salary cap, then nothing is impossible and such an agreement would promote parity between the teams – and help control costs (and thus generate profit) even more. With a salary cap, each team has the same economic power to attract stars. Salary caps can be on a per-player basis, or as total figure for all the players. It can be a combination of the two and it can also have different styles of cap, with hard caps resulting in punishment or fines and softer caps allowing teams to overspend on occasion, as long as they pay a "competitive balance tax" which means that they must contribute money to an industry growth fund if they overspend substantially.

This discourages them to do so… while also providing funding that allows the sport to develop. Such restrictions are not necessarily only for drivers and might also include the highest-paid employees, so that a team might wish to invest more in engineers than in expensive drivers, as long as everything came in under the salary cap.

The F1 drivers argued in Baku that people will not invest in youngsters if there is no return on the investment. This was clever but was ultimately poppycock. Teams will be looking even harder for the best youngsters because they will ultimately cost them less than paying for the stars. Thus one can argue that there will be MORE incentive to promote youngsters than is the case today.

The key is that the stars can make money from endorsements and so investors who put money into

– Joe Saward's 2022 Green Notebook –

youngsters will still get their share of the overall returns. They will not go hungry. These days, drivers may not be keen to run their own commercial operations but they can afford to pay people to do so, rather than relying on the teams. Drivers can thus earn a lot and, if they want more than the salary cap allows them, they can work a little harder to get it. It is actually more of a free market than is currently the case... So what it really means is that there would be a realignment of the money flows, rather than a loss of revenue. It will add more value to the teams because they will have to pay out less, but it will not impact on sponsorship revenues, as long as the sport remains popular...

It may seem an odd thing to say but I think that F1 "franchises" are still under-valued. Yes, it might cost $700 million to buy an F1 team when two years ago one could pick up a team for $200 million, but things have changed. The budget cap and increasing revenues in the sport have made it more attractive and now the big guns of sports business are turning towards F1 because thanks to Liberty Media, they now understand the business model. In the days of Bernie Ecclestone, F1 teams were money pits into which owners threw their money, in order to become famous.

Today, they can still get to be famous but can make money too. So the sport ticks a lot more boxes than it used to. If you look around global sport there are some impressive deals being done. But it is a game only for the super-rich. The other day, Rob Walton agreed to pay $4.65 billion to acquire the Denver Broncos, an NFL team. It is most expensive purchase ever of a sporting franchise. The fact that Walton and his family are worth $200 billion or more (thanks to Walmart) is not a big issue, but it is worth noting that he has a car collection worth $200 million and as even been known to race his own cars.

Walton's deal beat the recent sale of Chelsea for a similar kind of number. The buyers were Todd Boehly, who owns three sports teams in Los Angeles: the LA Dodgers, the LA Lakers and the LA Sparks. What is less known is that Boehly is a partner in a number of businesses (including Chelsea) with another investor called Mark Walter, co-founder and CEO of Guggenheim Capital, and that Walter is the man behind Michael Andretti's bid to buy an F1 team.

No-one wants to sell their teams for the kind of money that Walter & Co want to pay (this is because they were not as quick on their feet as Dorilton Capital and Lawrence Stroll who picked up teams cheaply before other realised that the sport was going in the right direction). So today, investors either have to bite the bullet and pay to acquire a team, or they have to somehow convince the sport that it needs new teams (which it really does not). Still, the Haas model – of buying in as much as possible – is a good one to get a new team going. The problem is that there are not many Dallaras out there. Finding a partner to manufacture cars is key to success because trying to build up composite departments is REALLY expensive. Thus I was interested to see a deal between Lamborghini and Ligier in relation to LMDh chassis.

You might say: 'What has this got to do with F1?' apart from the fact that there was once a Ligier-Lamborghini F1 car, but if you start digging you soon find that Ligier these days is a very impressive business. It is one of the four firms that were selected to build chassis for LMDh sports cars.

What is interesting is that Ligier's parent company is called Everspeed, which is owned by French businessman Jacques Nicolet. The group also owns HP Composites, an Italian firm, which has more than 20 years of experience building composite chassis for motorsports and for road cars. It has done work for Audi, Ferrari, Bugatti, Porsche, Lamborghini, Minardi and some of the Italian motorcycle firms as well. To put it into perspective, when Dallara decided to build its own road cars, HP Composites did a deal to manufacture the chassis... So watch out for Ligier if F1 agrees to allow new teams. It may not be a team like before, but it could be a sub-contractor like Dallara is for Haas.

Anyway, even if F1 was not big in Baku this year, the sport continues to gain traction in the world and Lewis Hamilton's involvement in a movie project with Brad Pitt and Apple Original Films sounds interesting. Th only thing that alarms slightly is that Pitt is now 58 years old and although he obviously treats his body like a temple, age is age. The script, it seems, is also about a driver who comes out of retirement to compete alongside a rookie driver. This means that Brad is a good 20 years older than the average F1 comeback merchant... One should perhaps remember at this point that Sylvester Stallone once made a movie along similar lines. He was 54 at the time. The movie, which ended up being about IndyCars because F1 realised it was not a good idea, was called Driven, although in the racing world it is now known as Drivel, and lives up to its name in spectacular fashion.

The problem with making fiction-based movie about racing is that reality is always stranger than fiction and so fiction is never convincing. Unless it is completely bonkers. It is also worth noting that the biggest movie about racing in recent years has been a cartoon called Turbo, which is about a snail who wins the Indy 500. If you have kids or grandkids, you will probably already know it. If you don't, check it out. It's brilliant. Rubbish, but brilliant…

Right, I must stop now, as I need to work on a film script called "Escargot" – a snail that wants to win Monaco. I should be able to bang something out before I head off to Canada.

And, in the worst case scenario, here in France, one can always add a little garlic and some parsley and eat the star…

From Pierre Elliott Trudeau Int'l Airport

22 June 2022

The ultimate accolade for any politician is to have an airport named in your honour, although to be quite honest if an airport was named after one or two of the modern politicians I would prefer to fly elsewhere, as the naming of the airport indicates the political feelings of the city.

These, of course, change over time. If you follow such matters you will know that Jan Smuts International in Johannesburg is now called Oliver Tambo Int'l.

In a world where little history is studied, kids probably don't know much about John F Kennedy, but they will travel through JFK, they might also know CDG, without knowing the first thing about Charles de Gaulle. It's the same with Napoleon Bonaparte Airport in Ajaccio, Ben Gurion in Tel Aviv and so on.

Montreal's principal airport, once known as Dorval, is now known as Pierre Elliott Trudeau International, a former Prime Minister of Canada, and father of the current Prime Minister Justin Trudeau.

It needs work...

I used to love the place because it was the entry point to a city that I have always enjoyed, although I have never been in the winter – and do not wish to do so. Why? Because in the winter Montreal is cold. It is so cold, in fact, that the mighty St Lawrence River freezes over, which is hard to imagine in the summer months. The extreme cold is why Montreal boasts "La Ville Souterraine", the world's largest underground city. This consists of 20 miles of tunnel in a five square mile area. From this network one can access bus, train and metro stations, apartment blocks, hotels, offices, universities, shopping malls, concert halls, cinemas, the Bell Centre arena and, of course, cavernous parking lots. The underground city provides access to 80 percent of the city's office space and every day in the winter around half a million troglodyte souls traverse these passageways.

If it is pouring with rain in the summer, it is very useful because you can get across town without getting wet, although you need good navigational skills not to get lost in the maze. The good news is that unlike the multi-level railway stations in Tokyo, where even Marco Polo would get lost, there are people in Montreal who speak English and French, although their accents can make them utterly incomprehensible.

Generally-speaking, I have a rule not to write too much about the stresses or strains of international travel, because people don't really want to know, but sometimes these stories are worth telling, in order to get the airline or airport involved to get its act together, by hearing things said publicly they do not wish to hear. The litany of incompetence during this year's trip to Montreal was the worst I have seen anywhere in the world in 39 years of non-stop travelling. And the same kind of disaster befell many other people. All three partners in our e-magazine GP+, travelling on entirely different itineraries, suffered serious multiple delays (more than eight hours) getting into Montreal – and all three lost our luggage (including cameras). The lost luggage service was there in name alone and after waiting the whole weekend for my bags, which had been promised within 24 hours, we went to the airport on Monday, hoping to see if any progress had been made because it was impossible to get any other information. On the off-chance it seemed sensible to take a look in the baggage hall rather than believing the people there and, sure enough, there it was, standing out from the crowd of black bags as it always has done. Clearly no-one had even tried to look for it.

Suffice to say, by the end of the weekend we had all sworn never to do business again with Air Canada

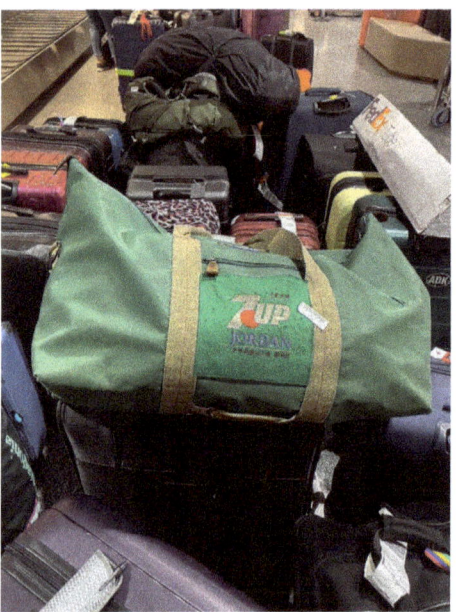

and while we may not be able to avoid the airports (although it had been at least 15 years since my last visit to Toronto, when similar incompetence led to the decision to avoid the place at all costs), this took the pleasant edge off what is usually a joyful weekend.

If you asked a cross-section of the F1 Paddock to list their favourite races, the vast majority would include Montreal. It is a quirky and cosmopolitan city and it has always felt like a big party, with everyone staying in the downtown area and enjoying life a little bit more than usual. It helps, of course, that the Grand Prix coincides with the annual graduation ceremonies and proms. It is a joyful time. It is also Canada's biggest annual party with as many as 450,000 people coming to town, although only a third of them attend the race. The rest are there to party, drink, dance and canoodle. It is the most important weekend of the year for the city's entrepreneurs. Hotels are fully booked and prices are up to 10 times normal rates. The problem with this is that there comes a point at which even F1 people decide that there must be better choices, which means that the circus disperses more widely, rents cars which that means that everyone is more constrained in what they can do, and the sense of community that was once prevalent disappears.

And of course the weather does not help because, if it rains at the circuit, team people stay inside their hospitality units. So gossip was thin on the ground. The race attracted a three-day cumulative crowd of 338,000, which was a decent score, and the US TV audience averaged 1.7 million viewers, up 50.6 percent compared to 2019, the last time the race was held. Most exciting was the fact that F1 blitzed all other forms of motorsport in the 18-49 age group in the US and that it was the most-watched Canadian GP in American TV history. This is important as negotiations continue for the Formula 1 TV rights for the United States market. The word in Montreal was that a decision is now close and that there are three serious bidders: Disney (which owns ESPN and ABC), Comcast's NBC, and the TV streaming service Amazon Prime Video. The deal will go to one company, rather than being split up as NASCAR does, although there is a possibility that a small part of the rights may be carved out of the main deal, to provide non-live highlights to other audiences and thus push up the numbers still further.

F1 growth is very exciting at the moment but for those who are hoping to see a 2023 calendar, there is going to be a bit of a wait, with an announcement not expected until the end of July. There will be some changes compared to this season and it seems that at the moment there are two different drafts of the 2023 calendar: one with 23 races, the other with 24. At the moment both drafts include the Monaco Grand Prix, although it is by no means certain that this will still be there. The difference in calendars appears to be the Chinese Grand Prix in Shanghai, as it is hard to know what the Chinese are going to do because of their attitude towards the Covid pandemic. The other calendar does not, but this obviously impacts on other dates.

Both drafts apparently include a South African GP, underlining F1's desire to have its first race on the Africa continent since 1993. This will be at Kyalami, near Johannesburg, but there are still questions that need to be answered about the race because of ongoing political problems in the country.

The other new race will be Las Vegas. Obviously if you have a 22-race calendar in 2022 and you add three races (South Africa, China and Las Vegas), you reach a total of 25, and so some of the current events must disappear. Fortunately, Russia has taken care of itself.

At the moment, so they say, France and Belgium are not on the 2023 schedule so I'm not quite sure how we would get to 24 races, but I guess this might relate to a notional new event in France. The suggestion made by Stefano Domenicali last week in an interview with the French sports daily L'Equipe is that there might be a French GP in Nice. Domenicali gave no details, but the rumour mill suggested that the idea is to lay out a street track around the Allianz Riviera stadium, in the Saint-Isidore district, in the Var valley to the west of the city, adjacent to the ring road that loops around Nice, en route to Monaco and the Italian border.

It is a relatively new neighbourhood, carved out of what used to be farmland, with the stadium opening in 2013. It is the home of the local soccer team OGC Nice and is used also by the Toulon rugby club. The only link to motorsport is that there is a street named after the late F1 driver Jules Bianchi, who died in 2015, after a crash in Japan in 2014. This would be incorporated into the circuit.

The history of racing in Nice is quite impressive and pre-dates Monaco, as the first Nice Speed Week was held in 1897, and the celebrated Nice-La Turbie hillclimb, one of the biggest early events, ran from 1901 onwards. There were land speed records set on the Promenade des Anglais and there was a Nice Grand Prix in the 1930s and then again post-war. The 1946 race is often said to have been the first event run to Formula 1 rules.

This all sounds rather a good idea, as F1 has decided against continuing with Paul Ricard and it suits the Grand Prix promotion company, which is headed by Christian Estrosi, the Mayor of Nice. It is also convenient for F1 that the idea has come up as it is in deep negotiation with Monaco. The celebrated street track is just 12 miles to the east of Nice and while the latter cannot put an F1 track through its port and streets, it could (and should) be conceived as a threat to Monaco, if F1 cannot get the deal it wants with the Automobile Club de Monaco.

The shape of the 2023 calendar may be a little different than today, but the signs are that it will begin with a big test/F1 launch in Bahrain, followed a week later by the first race. There will then be a weekend off before a race in Saudi Arabia, followed immediately by Australia. It is not clear what will happen after that because this is the time when China would be fitted in, perhaps back-to-back with Baku, or with South Africa slotting in there. It is clear when one tries to piece together the calendar that there are too many question marks to have any definitive answers. What is clear is that it looks like F1 is stuck with having to do two Transatlantic trips each spring as Miami is stuck in May and Montreal will not move from its June date. This is inefficient in every respect, but F1 is stuck with the contracts it agreed or has to renegotiate… The desire remains to try to regionalise the calendar more than is the case today.

The desire to grow F1 in the Americas is stronger than ever and team owners are unwilling to sell because they feel that the value of the teams will increase dramatically as the sport grows and big sports investors come wading to try to make a profit. If you don't have at least $1 billion, however, there is not a lot of point in even trying to buy a team at the moment. Having said that, building a new team costs about the same when you take into account all the money needed and, in any case, a new team is unlikely to be as competitive as a well-established one. This is the frustration that currently exists for a number of people keen to become team owners, not least Audi and Michael Andretti, not to mention Hitech Grand Prix and some others still in the shadows.

There is no desire within the sport at the moment to add new teams because no team wants to reduce its share of the revenues (even if they are increasing) and have more rivals. Michael Andretti's only real hope of being granted a new entry would be if he could bring Ford or General Motors into the sport, then the doors would open very quickly and an 11th team could be put together and everyone would see value in adding another manufacturer to F1. If one cannot buy an existing team and it makes no sense to build a new one, the only way for those with ambition is to invade the sport from within. At any given time, a number of F1 teams are not being run very well, and so there is always potential for outsiders to be offered jobs if the F1 team owners think they could find better management, if indeed the owners recognise that there is a problem – which is not always the case. If you look back, you can see this happening in the last 15 years with the likes of Christian Horner, Eric Boullier and Frédéric Vasseur, moving up from the junior formulae, with others such as Franz Tost, Jost Capito, Mike Krack, Andreas Seidl and Otmar Szafnauer coming in from manufacturer roles, and Guenther Steiner from running a successful composite business in the US.

There are not many team principals who have come through the ranks, with the obvious exception of Mattia Binotto and Sauber's previous team principal Monisha Kaltenborn and one can, I suppose, add family members to this, notably Claire Williams, although in the distant past there were also folk like Bob Tyrrell, Ken Tyrrell's son. Toto Wolff is unusual in that he is an investor who has moved into management roles.

This is where, perhaps, there is potential for takeovers, with people offering both money and management skills and then gradually gaining ownership of a team from within. That was a route that allowed Ron Dennis to take control of McLaren way back in the early 1980s and how Wolff got into an executive role at Williams. One suspects that Zak Brown may be doing something similar at McLaren but shareholdings do not need to be declared until they reach a certain level, so for the moment there are only whispers that he is a shareholder. Those who bring in big sponsorships can sometimes take shares rather than a big commission…

The other way would be new to F1, but not unusual in the business world where weak companies are targeted by bigger players, who win control by buying up shares and gaining enough influence to oust the original owners. This is, to some extent, what happened when the late Fiat boss Sergio Marchionne won control of Chrysler back in 2014.

It was not uncommon in the car industry for investors to kick out the founders of businesses. Henry Ford's first company, the Detroit Automobile Company, was shut down by investors. His second, known as the Henry Ford Company, saw him ousted and the firm renamed Cadillac, and it was not until his third attempt that the Ford Motor Company emerged.

The same was true of Audi which emerged only because its founder August Horch was ousted from his own company in 1909 and so started a rival business called Audi. Horch in German means listen which translates into Latin as Audi.

Of the current F1 teams Mercedes, Ferrari, Aston Martin and Alpine all belong to listed companies, while there is now talk of McLaren being listed on the stock exchange at some point in the future.

It might not be easy but one can imagine someone seeing an opportunity to buy control of Aston Martin in this way in order to get control of the brand. Mercedes owns 20 percent of Aston Martin shares and, if it wished to offload these, a buyer could acquire them and then hoover up smaller shareholders (which make up more than 50 percent) by buying shares at a premium. Under current rules, a purchaser would not have to declare a significant interest until they have 25 percent of the business, but there are all kinds of ways to gain control with, for example, debt-equity exchanges, in which debts are acquired and turned into shares, thus diluting the share value but making the company more solid. The devil is in the details, but weak companies are exposed and disgruntled shareholders are prime targets.

There seemed to be little new on the driver front, although some of the known deals did get confirmed with AlphaTauri's Franz Tost saying that Pierre Gasly will stay on in 2023.

The other key point was that Otmar Szafnauer, Alpine's team principal, said that Oscar Piastri will be racing in F1 in 2023. This is no surprise as Alpine will lose control of the Australian if he does not have a race drive next year. There is presumably a date by which a deal must done by Alpine or Piastri can go to market as a free agent. Thus there is some pressure on Alpine to find him a seat. The only obvious choice for him at the moment is Williams, where Nicholas Latifi will lose his drive at the end of the year, if things do not pick up. This has led to suggestions that Williams might change engines, but that makes little sense because it is too late for 2023 and that would mean only two years to get up to speed with the current engines in 2024 and 2025. It is probably better from Alpine and Williams to talk engine deals from 2026 and beyond. This is not a bad move for Williams as the team would become the second Renault team, rather than the fourth Mercedes operation. It would also give Williams an impressive driver line-up and provide the team with time to develop its own young driver Logan Sargeant, who needs more time in Formula 2.

That aside, there was little gossip in Montreal, although there were some interesting faces on the grid, including some people from Melbourne who had dropped in to look at the pit facility at the

Circuit Gilles Villeneuve, as they need to start work on upgrading the facilities in Albert Park, which are now 25 years old and outdated. In much the same way, Steve Hill, the CEO and President of Las Vegas Convention and Visitors Authority (LVCVA) was in Montreal to see how the Canadians run a Grand Prix. Las Vegas is making rapid progress in preparation for its first race in 2023 with the aim being to build a permanent three-storey pit facility similar to the one in Miami, with garages on the ground floor, hospitality on the second and on the roof, with Race Control and other necessary facilities integrated into it. This would be turned over to other uses for the rest of the year when F1 is not in town.

By Sunday night, everyone was keen to get home, although there were the delights of the airport and the flights home still to come. You know that tiresome moment at an airport when you (and your hand luggage) have to go through a security check. Working security is not an easy job – because people are in a hurry and do not like queuing. Things are bad at the moment and Montreal has adopted Disney-like policies of hiding queues. While one does not expect the security folk to be Rhodes Scholars, it is a job that can be done with grace or humour. It's dull work, explaining why one cannot carry a whole tube of toothpaste, and confiscating nail scissors because they are lethal weapons…

With all the paraphernalia required by itinerant F1 journalists, it is not unusual to be stopped, but normally the security people quickly see that nothing is amiss and off you go to find the gate. Alas, with a shortage of staff since the pandemic (the primary problem for all the troubles at the moment), there are new folk employed who do not have much experience. The security girl I encountered insisted that I had "a multi-tool" somewhere in my multi-pocketed bag.

"There isn't," I said, with as much patience as I could muster. No professional traveller carries a multi-tool. It is plain stupid. I'm not saying that she should instantly believe everything, but after 25 minutes going through my bag (no exaggeration), it all felt a bit too much, particularly as others were queued up behind waiting to have their bags inspected.

"You've already looked there," I said, politely, on several occasions. She got excited when she found some pen refills, but could not figure out how these might be deemed to be murderous devices, although I was on the verge of showing her by that point. To be honest, I've known dogs that were smarter than this person, but finally there came a moment when she had to admit defeat. I was not a professional assassin, nor an international terrorist. She would not get promoted for finding my hidden weaponry. She shoved the plastic tray at me gracelessly, leaving the bag unpacked, as she did not have the mental capacity required to put it all back together again so it all fitted.

There was no "Sorry, I was wrong", nor a "Sorry, I have wasted your time because I am incompetent". With Air Canada at the moment there was no need for "Sorry, I've caused you to miss the flight", because I doubt the airline managed to get a single flight out of Montreal on time last week.

As I walked away from this experience, I chuckled. There was one pocket that she never did find – even if it didn't have a multi-tool in it…

Still, with every cloud there is a silver lining. The barman at least was good at his job…

From Mauquenchy

7 July 2022

Getting home from the British Grand Prix normally involves driving south from Silverstone, around the miserable M25 and then towards Newhaven (which has not been new since the 16th century). This is a small port on the coast on England, to the east of Brighton, between chalk cliffs. From there, one takes a ferry across The Channel to Dieppe, a similar port between two chalk cliffs. The journey takes around five hours and one can get a cabin and sleep half a night before setting off across France.

The Newhaven-Dieppe ferry is not very glamorous, although those with a taste for the bizarre might like to know that Vietnamese revolutionary Ho Chi Minh spent time as a crew member on the ferry route, going backwards and forwards between France and England. It is doubtful that he gained much inspiration from this, although white cliffs have been known to inspire.

When you leave the ferry port in Dieppe, the road climbs quickly to the top of the chalk plateau (the reason for the white cliffs) and soon you arrive at a roundabout. Dull stuff, unless you know the history.

If you turn to the east, you are on the main straight of the Circuit de la Seine-Inférieure, home of the second the Grand Prix de l'Automobile Club de France in 1907. There is nothing there now, but once there were pits, a vast ornate wooden grandstand and a giant scoreboard, which was never up to date. Today most travellers turn west and the road they take descends into the flat valley of the River Arques, close to Dieppe's hippodrome and to the Alpine car factory (Dieppe is Alpine's home town). You arrive in the strangely-named suburb of Rouxmesnil-Bouteilles, now a drab industrial area with its only saving grace being a kart track, hidden away behind a Nestlé factory, where they manufacture Nescafé. You are soon out in the country and it is a delight to be rushing through the lanes at an hour when these still belong to crows and rabbits, with occasional cats on the prowl for small animals to torture. It is a bewitching time of day, particularly in the summer, when the warmth from the earth rises into the cool sky and mists form before your eyes. If lit by the sun, these turn the world into an unworldly and beautiful place.

And thus it was that I found myself in a misty Mauquenchy, the perfect antidote after the Silverstone weekend, filled as it was with people and traffic jams.

There was a time, 35 years ago, when the village of Mauquenchy nearly became famous in Formula 1. The Automobile Club Normand (ACN), which ran the Rouen Les Essarts racing circuit, realised that its track was too dangerous for international races and was looking for somewhere to build a new F1-spec race track. Mauquenchy has a quiet and secluded valley, surrounded by hills on all sides, and the ACN thought this would be a great venue for a circuit. The mayor of Forges-Les-Eaux, a picturesque spa town nearby, was excited by the project, as was Jean-Luc Thérier, a local who was one of France's biggest rallying stars at the time. The Larousse-Calmels F1 team also liked the idea as it would provide them with a new home, which would develop into a motorsport hub and thus help the local economy. It was all sound logic.

The bad news was that France's President at the time, François Mitterrand, was a man who knew how to keep his friends happy and had a plan to redevelop the Magny-Cours circuit. This would become the home of the Ligier F1 team (and a motorsport hub... etc etc). With the help of Pierre Bérégovoy, who was the mayor of nearby Nevers (and Mitterand's Minister of the Economy), the project in Magny-Cours trumped Mauquenchy. And so the Norman plan was recycled and they built a hippodrome instead. This pulls in a few people, no doubt, but for Forges-Les-Eaux many of its visitors today come on two wheels, on a cycle path that links London to Paris, known as the "Avenue Verte" (the green avenue), which uses disused railways converted into cycle paths. It always make me smile when cyclists try to exercise their moral superiority about the environment, because it brings out the devil in me and I ask: "What's the most polluting sporting event in the world?" The answer, of course, is the Tour de France because while the 176 riders involved don't leave much of an environmental footprint, the 14 million fans who drive to watch pump out a lot of exhaust gases.

Protesters do not generally target the Tour de France because everyone thinks that riding bicycles transform a person into an angel with toe-clips. F1 on the other hand, ends with up a bunch of people thinking it is smart to walk on to a racing circuit to draw attention to the use of oil.

Well, David Baldwin, Emily Brocklebank, Alasdair Gibson, Louis McKechnie, Bethany Mogie and Joshua Smith (collectively known as the Silverstone protesters), if you knew what you were talking about, you would have targeted the Tour de France.

I bumped into David Richards of Motorsport UK at one point during the weekend and he said that he was busy trying to get a meeting with the protesters, in order to explain to them why they would be wrong to target the Grand Prix, because they obviously did not know about F1's amazingly efficient engines and how this is filtering down through the industry...

Silverstone saw the launches of various worthy projects, designed to create a perfect world. I do worry about the F1 campaign to be carbon neutral by 2030, not because I am opposed to the concept, which clearly I am not, but I do think that if the sport is going to make such claims, it must also include the emissions created by spectators in the calculations.

What the sport has to do is to tell the story of what it is doing for emissions technology (which is amazing) and to argue that it should be viewed as part of the solution, rather than the problem. In this respect the sport has only itself to blame.

The Formula 1 group is looking more and more at urban circuits with mass transit in order to address this problem, but the down side of this is that in time we will lose some famous places if the strategy continues. Races in the middle of nowhere are no longer popular. Circuits out in the wilds are struggling to get F1's attention. The Nürburgring is gone already. Paul Ricard and Spa are on the verge of disappearing. Everyone loves Spa, despite its drawbacks, but it is hard to argue that because it is a famous place in racing, it should be allowed to produce lots of emissions. The ultimate irony is that Spa was originally laid out where it is because it had railway stations in Francorchamps, Stavelot and Malmedy. The latter two were lost when the circuit was shortened and passenger trains to Francorchamps stopped in 1959, with the rails being torn up in the early 1970s. You can still see where the tracks used to run and ponder that if they were still there today, the track might have a very different future. Putting back railways costs a fortune but at Spa the path of the old railway was transformed into a cycle track, known as Pré-Ravel Ligne 44a and so those of an energetic nature can still cycle to the races. But will they?

A sport is only as good as its fans. It's no good fixing all the F1 emissions if the fans arrive in gas-guzzling urban tractors and sit in jams for hours on end, pumping out exhaust fumes. We had a race last year at Zandvoort where most cars were banned and fans came either by train or by bicycle and it worked out very well. The truth is that if these old rural circuits want to survive, they need to adapt and transportation infrastructure is important.

All this brings me, by a roundabout route, to the big rumour of the Silverstone weekend which is that Audi AG has reached an agreement to acquire the Sauber team. We already know that Porsche is leaping enthusiastically into bed with Red Bull and now its sister brand Audi wants to go racing as well. Why? Because the new F1 rules in 2026 are exactly what the industry wants as it heads towards sustainability, with hyper-efficient engines and synthetic fuels. There may be others that want to jump on the bandwagon as well...

The whisper is that the deal is worth around $450 million and will see Audi acquiring 75 percent of the shares in the team, valuing it at $600 million. The sale is conditional on the technical rules of F1 for 2026 being confirmed by the FIA but will be a phased deal over three years with Audi taking control of a first 25 percent of the shares in 2023, another 25 percent in 2024 and a third 25 percent in 2025. The remaining 25 percent will be retained by Finn Rausing – who is one of the owners of Tetra Pak Laval, a firm which has annual revenues of $16.3 billion.

The team will go on using Ferrari engines and being called Alfa Romeo until the end of the current formula at the end of 2025. After that it will transform into an Audi operation, with engines being built by Audi Sport GmbH in Germany. It cannot happen any quicker than that because you cannot have an Audi chassis powered by a Ferrari engine.

There was another interesting rumour kicking around in Silverstone about Alpine selling some of its shares to the Chinese car company Geely. This makes perfect sense given that Geely owns Lotus and the Norfolk firm is involved in joint venture with Alpine to build electric cars, while Alpine's parent Renault and Geely are reportedly planning a joint venture to sell hybrid cars in the Chinese market. Renault is also helping Geely get into the US market using the Renault Samsung plant in South Korea. There is a trade deal between South Korea and the US which allows Korean automakers to import vehicles into the US tariff-free. There is no doubt that the best way to promote Lotus would be to use Grand Prix racing, where the firm has huge heritage, so perhaps we might one day see Alpine (which was called Lotus F1 a few years ago) either reverting to that name or with an engine supply to a Lotus-branded team. Who knows?

While on this subject, it is also said that part of the Aramco sponsorship deal with Aston Martin was a commitment from the team to build its own F1 engines in 2026. That will cost a lot... Aston Martin's financial situation is creating headlines in financial newspapers as the firm's share price is light and its debt load heavy. The company continues to make positive noises but the number-crunchers are sceptical. There are rumours that the Saudis might buy into the business.

Billionaires have different rules to the rest of us, although the presence of Vijay Mallya was a reminder that things don't always end up well. Still, the bigger the billionaire the more fluffy the cushions that they have to break their fall. When it comes to billionaires, F1 has a lot of them – some with more cash than others. One thinks of Mateschitz, Latifi, Rausing and the Strolls. Not to mention the Al-Khalifas of Bahrain, the Agnellis and others who like to play at the F1 tables.

I've always found that the richest folk always make the least noise and that was definitely true at Silverstone where there was a man who is worth more than Mateschitz, Rausing and the Latifis combined, walking around the paddock. Rob Walton mentioned in conversation that he was a small investor in McLaren, as a member of the consortium that owns about 33 percent of the team. He does like cars (he has a car collection worth several hundred millions) and it is said that he has about $60 billion to play with thanks to the family's involvement in Walmart... and so F1 does not really faze him. He seemed to be enjoying his weekend.

When one considers the big players in this world, the scrambling over a few millions seems somehow rather tawdry, but that is part of the F1 game from week to week.

The driver market is beginning to burble and it may be that we are going to have some earthquakes soon. There are lots of assumptions being made about who will go where in 2023 and I sense that some of them are false assumptions.

There have been rumours for some time regarding the future of Sebastian Vettel at Aston Martin F1, with the suggestion being that the four-time World Champion will retire at the end of the year, at the age of 35, and will be replaced by 23-year-old Mick Schumacher. There is much interest as well in Alpine. The team is saying that there are no decisions yet about the team's driver line-up for 2023, but things seem to be on the move. Esteban Ocon is under contract until the end of 2024, while Fernando Alonso's contract with Alpine finishes this year. The team's third driver Oscar Piastri has a contract, but Alpine must provide the Australian with an F1 drive in 2023 or else he is free to leave.

As with all F1 contracts, there is an option date by which point a deal must be agreed. This is often the end of July, which means that a driver who does not have a deal for the following year still has the time to find an alternative. The thinking in recent weeks has been that the team would agree to another two-year contract with Fernando Alonso for 2023 and 2024. Alonso is 41 at the end of July and so would be 43 by the end of the contract. Having said that, Fernando is obviously still quick, having started on the front row of the grid in Canada recently. Dropping Alonso in favour of Piastri would be a controversial thing to do, even if the logic is to prepare Piastri and not risk losing him. On the face of it, Piastri's only real option was to join Williams, replacing Nicholas Latifi, but Piastri's manager Mark Webber is a cunning fellow and also a mate of his former Porsche colleague Andreas Seidl, now team principal of McLaren. Seidl, it seems, is interested in Piastri.

Daniel has a McLaren contract for next year but it is fair to say that he has been a disappointment, despite winning last year in Italy. One might conjecture that McLaren might offer Daniel an elegant exit by putting him into IndyCars as it has not yet confirmed whether Felix Rosenqvist will race IndyCar or Formula E next year. But spies in the US are suggesting that this is not a real option as McLaren will be running Pato O'Ward, Alexander Rossi and Alex Palou, the present IndyCar champion currently racing for Chip Ganassi.

If McLaren makes Piastri an offer, it would probably be a better choice than a Williams' seat and so one can see that Oscar would prefer that. It is also a splendid lever to get Alpine to ditch Alonso because Piastri is seen as the real deal, rather than being Alonso the real deal from 20 years ago, who never quite delivered on his potential.

Alpine has already lost Guanyu Zhou to Alfa Romeo and the Chinese driver is now beginning to show his paces and his value for the Chinese market...
The thing that might mess up this scenario is that McLaren remains intent on becoming an American-style F1 team with Zak Brown, some US investors, who have the clout to buy out the Bahrainis, if they wish to depart and the possibility of Colton Herta being good enough for F1. He should begin testing soon and so we can find out, but he has an IndyCar deal with Andretti for 2023 so his arrival would not be before 2024.

The only other story of major interest in the Green Notebook in Silverstone is the suggestion that South Africa will definitely have a place on the 2023 calendar. The word is that a deal has been agreed with a South African promoter to hold a race, but that the event will no have any overt funding from the government. This does not mean the authorities will not help with tax breaks and such things, but it will not provide actual funding, because President Cyril Ramaphosa does not want to put himself into a situation where he could be accused of spending government money on a sport he enjoys, when the country (and he himself) have other problems. The government can always get involved later if things improve. Formula 1 wants to visit Africa in order to strengthen its inclusion programmes, which aim to treat everywhere the same – and make money from everyone.

As I finish writing up these notes, I find myself in Nuremberg, bound for Austria where we will have another race… and another Green Notebook…

From Walhalla

13 July 2022

When your average Viking was slain (messily) in battle, a complicated business followed. A Valkyrie would arrive (presumably with a clipboard), alerted by mystical forces. Valkyries are female. Their role is to guide dead warriors to one of two places, depending on their mood. The cool place for a dead Viking to go with his Valkyrie is Valhalla, a sort of hall of fame for newly-departed Norsemen.

The mythology has all been confused by Aston Martin, which likes to have cars with names beginning with V. The Vegetarian, Vanilla, Vacuum, Va-va-voom, Vesper and Verruca may be still to come, but the recent models have been the Valkyrie, followed by the Valhalla.

I guess this is because Valkyries have been cool since the days Francis Ford Coppola used Richard Wagner's Ride of the Valkyrie, from his Der Ring des Nibelungen series of operas, as background music in his drug-influenced but impressive Apocalypse Now movie.

Anyway, before there was a united Germany, there were lots of Germanic folk in search of a nation to belong to, and some felt that they should unite and become one nation, rather than slaughtering one another. It was a good idea.

While this process was going on, Crown Prince Ludwig of Bavaria (later King Ludwig I) came up with the idea of creating a hall of fame for eminent German sovereigns, politicians, scientists and artists and decided it should be called Walhalla (Germans pronounce W as V). Ludwig believed that a hall of fame needed a hall (which is not the case today) and so funded the construction of a neo-classical box, atop a hillside overlooking the Danube, to the east of Regensburg, where he put busts of famous Germanics. It isn't exactly Disneyland... but it happens to be just off my usual route to the Austrian Grand Prix and so this year I stopped off to check it out.

The purpose of this visit was really to get away from the vast numbers of Dutch cars that were pottering down the autobahn towards Passau. It was reckoned that there were 55,000 Dutch folk in Austria, following the cult of Verstappen, creating other problems in Styria, not designed to have so many Dutch(wo)men all visiting on the same weekend. The result of this was that while many of the orange-folk stayed in camper vans, tents, transit vans, or simply lay where they fell, others booked every available room for many miles around, and there are not that many... This year the first available hotel I found when I first looked was 75 miles from the track, admittedly on the motorway. But this was ridiculous and so I kept looking and found something about 25 miles away. It looked fine, but I didn't really check. I was happy to have it, whatever it was. We learn lessons in life and I discovered that the route between Zeltweg and the oddly-named Maria Lankowitz is about 25 miles, but it has to climb up the Lavanttal Alps, through the Gaberl Pass. The road made the old Nurburgring look dull. I did it eight times in total and to pass the time I counted 215 corners (all quite quick). By the end of the weekend, I had concluded that it was roads like this which nurtured talents such as Jochen Rindt, Niki Lauda, Gerhard Berger and Helmut Marko. What I also discovered was that of the 16 Austrian F1 drivers, four went to the same school: Rindt, Marko, Lauda and Harald Ertl. It was a place in the town of Bad Aussee, designed to get troublesome children back on the straight and narrow. This was run by a man who could have been a character from a John Le Carré novel. His name was Wilhelm Höttl, who in addition to being an author, had served with the Sicherheitsdienst (SD), the rather nasty security service of the SS, in Hungary during the war. Höttl was clever and recognising that he did not have much of a future, offered his services to the Americans and became a key witness against SS members in the Nuremberg Trials. The Americans used him to organise a couple of anti-communist spy networks in Austria and then let him run his school. Instilling some discipline in wild youngsters was probably not such a big deal for a man with such a background, but whatever he did, the school produced young men who knew how to get what they wanted...

Marko runs the Red Bull operations with an iron fist and if you do not do the job he wants, you get axed without emotion, even if it means that your career is over. He has made a lot of stars and destroyed a few others, who did not fit his view of what makes a great racing driver. The man behind Marko's empire is Dietrich Mateschitz, who has created all things Red Bull. The next big deal was going to be announced last weekend but faffing about at the FIA (and some can-kicking by rival manufacturers) has meant that the 2026 engine regulations are still not yet finished and no-one is announcing anything until these are set in concrete. And so Porsche's F1 plans will have to wait – and Audi's as well. Some rapid action would now be a good idea as there are others who are thinking along similar lines.

This has combined with a subtle industry-wide acceptance that electric cars are not perhaps the immediate future – and the Tesla share price has been trending downwards for some months. The problem is that, in this world of judgemental idealists with social media tools, no-one wants to admit that the only really sensible stop today is efficient hybrids with synthetic fuels, which will buy the industry more time to get electric cars to a point where people want to buy them. F1 completely failed to tell the world about its amazing engines back in 2014, but the car manufacturers have now begun to realise (and accept) that F1 got it right.

The true genius in F1 came when Chase Carey talked the teams into accepting a budget cap, thus ending the unlimited spending that had driven the car manufacturers away. Now, they are looking at F1 and seeing a business that will not only put value in to their firms, but will promote their activities as well. It really is a win-win despite the best efforts of those who want to go on spending crazy amounts to stay ahead. One might add that, when you boil it all down, some of the teams these days are frightened of Porsche. Anyway, the new engines will be simpler, cheaper and more relevant for series production and when one adds this to the sport's advertising power and its growth in new markets – team ownership is not a bad idea, which is why the value of teams has sky-rocketed.

The problem is that those who did not see the opportunity have now missed the boat and if they want to get involved they will have to pay more. But for big manufacturers the billion they need to get into the game is no big deal, while for some of those currently involved, landing that kind of money for selling the team makes a heap of sense.

This is not just conjecture because in Austria, the entire top management of Honda popped up in the paddock, led by President Toshihiro Mibe, chairman Seiji Kuraishi, Honda Racing Corporation president Koji Watanabe and the man in charge of Honda's F1 efforts Yasuaki Asaki. I don't think it is unfair to say that Honda screwed up in 2020 when the firm decided that it should focus on electric cars and quit F1, agreeing to sell its IP to Red Bull. That was a decision taken by Takahiro Hachigo, the then president. And guess what, in the finest tradition of Honda in F1, the next year saw success... Hachigo was politely shown a different future by Honda in April last year and the signs are that Mibe may reverse the decision, but now he must find a team to take over. Several are for sale if the sum of money offered is sufficiently high.

Another rumour that has popped up in recent days, as the result of a possible road car deal between McLaren and BMW, has been the suggestion that the Munich firm might come back to F1, in order to compete head-on with rivals Mercedes, Porsche and Audi.

McLaren and BMW have long history back to the F1 supercar programme in the 1990s. McLaren does not have the money to do its own F1 engine programme, so perhaps falling into bed with BMW might be a good idea.

For the moment, Formula 1 is still allowing manufacturers to get a free ride in F1 with Aston Martin, Alfa Romeo and McLaren all using engines which are coming from elsewhere. How many fans really know that the Alfa Romeo team is really Sauber-Ferrari, that Aston Martin is Aston Martin-Mercedes and that McLaren is also running Mercedes engines? I see a marketing problem with this but not really an issue if manufacturers can get away with it. Th word is that Aston Martin will be building its own F1 engines (with help from Aramco), while the Sauber-Ferrari operation will be taken over by Audi. Alfa Romeo will be looking for alternatives – it is interesting to see that Alfa Romeo CEO Jean-Philippe Imparato was in Austria – and while continuing to use Ferrari engines is a possibility, it might also be sensible for Alfa Romeo's parent company Stellantis to invest. Why? Because it has 14 different brands that it wants – and needs – to promote. A Stellantis-engine could be branded by several of them... and why not have a Dodge F1 engine alongside an Alfa Romeo or even a Peugeot? If the brands share the cost, it is really not a big deal and Dodge could be portrayed as an American team, which might stop Michael Andretti saying silly things about F1 in interviews because at the moment he cannot find a cheap way into the game. If he turned up and promised to deliver an Andretti-Dodge F1 car, F1 might be more interested in having him aboard. Last summer, Stellantis confirmed plans for the launch of a Dodge plug-in hybrid, to be known as the Dodge Hornet, a revamped version of the Alfa Romeo Tonale, and it makes sense to share F1 technology around as well.

But really gets sales going is not the involvement of a certain manufacturer, but rather the success of a driver. Everyone wants an American now that F1 is getting bigger in the US and Zak Brawn at McLaren seems to be trying to get his team to look very American. In recent days the Colton Herta testing programme has begun with a 2021 McLaren MCL35M being run in Portugal for Herta. Brown says that Daniel Ricciardo is still going to be at McLaren next year but Herta is obviously someone who might replace the Australian in 2024. It would be lovely to report that Daniel is getting to grips with the car but after a year and a half with the team, he is still having weekends like Silverstone. It is also interesting to note that the only other driver who is close to Formula 1 – Formula 2 racer Logan Sargeant, a Williams young driver, has recently started looking very good, winning two Feature races (the ones that count), and is now second in the championship, admittedly a ways behind the leader Felipe Drugovich, although he is in his third year of Formula 2.

Of course, everyone would love to have a Chinese driver as well, if we can get a Chinese GP back on the calendar again.

China is a monster market where F1 could make a big impact if Guanyu Zhou does well. Thus far he's doing a very good job, scoring twice so far but suffering three mechanical failures and the crash in Britain, which was not his fault. In other races, he has been hobbled by pit stops that have gone wrong and in which strategy calls did not work out, so while it looks Valtteri Bottas has dominated him, it is worth pointing out that this may not continue. He has out-qualified Bottas on three occasions which is good given their relative F1 experience.

The word is that Zhou will stay where he is next year and Sauber protégé Théo Pourchaire, has been pretty disappointing. Pourchaire has pace, but expectations were perhaps too high after last year.

F1 does need to sort out China, but it is hard at the moment because of politics. The biggest thing is the 20th National Congress of the Chinese Communist Party, which will take place in Beijing in November. No-one really doubts that Xi Jinping, who has ruled the country since 2013, will stay in power, but the big question is who will be around him and whether the same bosses will survive in Shanghai. If not, there have long been rumours of a desire to move the Chinese GP to a street venue in Beijing. But then there is also the question of Covid... If there is a Chinese GP in 2023, it will be in the autumn, which will give the Chinese time to sort out more stuff.

The calendar is still only chugging along but things may become a little clearer after a meeting between F1 and the Automobile Club de Monaco, which is scheduled for the French GP weekend...

Elsewhere, Sebastian Vettel is beginning to behave more and more like a driver who will be off at the end of the year. His decision to walk out of the Drivers' Briefing in Austria meant that he has been fined €25,000, although this is suspended for the rest of the season. Vettel fixed things up with Race Director Niels Wittich afterwards, but this is not the act of someone who is trying to build good relations with officials who will probably be around for a while...

Never mind, perhaps he will get a place in Walhalla (the earthly version) instead, although it is not easy and it takes time. Richard Strauss died in 1949 and only got into Walhalla in 1973. Albert Einstein died in 1955 and only snuck into the hall of fame in 1990. Konrad Adenauer, who oversaw the rebuilding of the country after World War II, made it in 1999, 32 years after his death while Johannes Brahms was in transit with his Valkyrie for 103 years before being allowed into Walhalla in 2000.

From the Pyramids

25 July 2022

If you happen to be in Monza and go north on the Arcore road towards Lecco, you will soon find yourself in a town called Cernusco Lombardone.

While the name sounds like a Soprano, it rolls off the tongue like a lazy river meandering through linguistic meadows. Turn to the left there and you will pass through Quattro Strade, a place name that tells you (with admirable brevity) that the town has four streets. You will then see signs to Montevecchia, the old mountain, which explains nothing of an extraordinary place where a few years ago geologists, archaeologists and astrophysicists worked arm in arm to discover three pyramids built by an ancient civilisation. Really.

Just like the Egyptian pyramids, but taller. And without burial chambers within. They were built by shaping limestone hills into matching monuments, which were used for reasons unclear, but were probably related to astronomical or religious beliefs. I guess you might call it an Italian Stonehenge, but built without moving mountains.

Why am I going on about pyramids in Italy when the last Grand Prix was in France? Well, the world is filled with surprises that we often rush past without even seeing. I was pottering through, bound for Budapest and the pyramids attracted my attention… Paul Ricard is a monument of sorts, recalling a very smart man who created not only an eponymous drink, a kind of hooch called pastis, which is flavoured with Provençal things and is 45 proof. Having done this in 1932, he got very rich and then used a bulldozer to turn his name into a global advertisement for an alcoholic drink which today cannot legally be advertised. Yes, the Circuit Paul Ricard is a monument to Ricard, but it is also an advertisement for his drink…

Anyway, it will still be there for many years to come, but the French Grand Prix is unlikely to be. There is a break clause in the contract and Formula 1 wants one. It has other venues in better places, willing to pay more, or without all the hassles that come with a drinks magnate building a circuit in the middle of nowhere – with no possibility to improve the access roads… We'll not talk too much about French policemen, of course, but let us just say that perhaps they lack imagination and do what they are told to do without ever applying logic to the situation. Thus even team bosses and other stars of Drive to Survive were turned away from the logical route to the track because a special lane had been invented for F1 people, even if that meant you had to drive 30 miles to get to the so-called "F1 Lane". To be honest I had no problems getting into the track, but I was getting there every day at seven o'clock in the morning because I hate wasting time in traffic jams. The evenings were less successful. The access problems are certainly not unique in F1 and France does not appear to have a problem with money, but the decision not to race in France is rather a case of the Formula 1 group not being happy with the

— Joe Saward's 2022 Green Notebook —

venue. It is 37 miles, much of it on wiggly roads, from Marseilles and there are some who dare to suggest that the city is not really a destination city (at least not in the terms F1 applies) and there is no getting away from the fact that while there have been attempts to regenerate parts of the city, it still has a bad image and people are nervous about visiting. This is based on the poverty that exists there and in consequence a high level of crime, often very violent. It is one of the biggest ports in Europe and rather a lot of dodgy stuff comes in and causes problems amongst the crime gangs.

The nearest "destination city" is probably Nice, as Toulon is traditionally a naval town, filled with rowdy sailors.

This is not to say that the region is not delightful. The coastal towns between Marseilles and Toulon are wonderful but there are still insufficient hotels for F1 and while the circuit could increase its crowd capacity quite easily and its VIP count, the problem remains: where are these people going to stay when they emerge from the traffic?

This is not to say that I am favour of dropping the French Grand Prix from the calendar. It does not seem right to do that. History may not matter much in the F1 world, but it should always be remembered that once there was only one Grand Prix a year – and it was French. Originally known as the Grand Prix de l'Automobile Club de France, the race was hugely significant not just in terms of racing, but also in the car industry. France was so dominant in the early years of the sport that the FIA was headquartered there, squatting in a building next door to the Automobile Club de France. Does that mean that it should always be on the calendar? No, perhaps not, but running Grands Prix without France is a bit like running the IndyCar Championship without the Indy 500 – or at least one can argue that case.

Actually, when it comes to races that argue such things, Monaco seems to have the belief that F1 cannot exist without it. However, I believe there was a meeting recently at which some of the points of contention between F1 and Monaco were fixed, although there still remain significant problems between them. There will come a point at which a calendar will need to appear and we will see how serious F1 is about getting the deals it wants. What is very interesting is that the company that organises the French Grand Prix is called "GIP Grand Prix de France". This can organise a race wherever it wants to host one, as long as the local ASN, the Fédération Française du Sport Automobile (FFSA), agrees. At the moment the firm rents the Circuit Paul Ricard, but it could do whatever it wants. The man behind this firm is the mayor of Nice, Christian Estrosi, a former racer, who is a political fixer, and a former government minister, close to President Emmanuel Macron. The President recently said that France must protect its Grand Prix and that "the state is ready to participate". The other point worth noting about the French GP weekend was that there was a dinner on Saturday night that featured around 15 of the CEOs of France's biggest companies, which are included in the CAC 40 stock market index. These included L'Oréal, Sanofi, Bolloré, Accor, Air France and Pernod Ricard. So there is some serious clout beyond the idea of a French GP, if the country can find a venue. At the moment, they are trying out the idea of a race around the Allianz stadium in Nice. Oddly enough, on Monday morning, as I was heading towards the pyramids near Milan, it struck me that perhaps I should stop and visit the stadium as it would be a logical time for F1 types to visit and I might bump into them as they inspected the idea. In the end, I didn't bother because I don't like the idea and I don't think it will work.

The irony, of course, is that France has three tracks that could host F1 races without too much trouble: Ricard, Magny-Cours and the Le Mans Bugatti circuit. The problem is that Ricard and Magny-Cours are both deemed wrong for F1 because of their infrastructure and access (and image) problems and Le Mans does not want a Grand Prix because the Automobile Club de l'Ouest is worried it might undermine the status of the Le Mans 24 Hours….

So, if France wants a Grand Prix any time soon, it is going to have to create a new idea. There have been some good ideas over time but nothing happened mainly because of money but also because of environmental questions. This is daft in an age when F1 is really setting the trend for environmentally-friendly engines that people want to buy. Formula E has been brilliant at promoting itself as being the best of all possible worlds, but in truth electric car sales are still pretty hopeless when you look at the big picture, because people just don't want to buy them. Smoke and mirrors from Formula E boss Alejandro Agag has kept the plates spinning up to now, but it's a high wire act. Formula 1's approach is a great deal more practical and the industry seems to like it.

Anyway, I have long had the belief that the best idea for the French GP would be to hold the race in the Bois de Boulogne, the huge public park that sits next to the city's famous Boulevard Périphérique, the city's inner ring road. For those who don't know Paris well, if you go under the Arc de Triomphe and go straight on, down the road directly opposite the Champs Elysées, you arrive at the Porte Maillot. This is where the Bois de Boulogne begins. It is about 750 metres from the Arc de Triomphe. The park boasts existing roadways, a number of lakes, two racecourses (Longchamp and Auteuil) and is adjacent to the Stade Roland Garros (home of the French Open tennis competition) and the Parc des Princes stadium. The park is served by a string of Metro stations, features the dramatic Fondation Louis Vuitton building (the most interesting new building in France since the Pompidou Centre, and the park exists for the enjoyment of the citizens of Paris.

From a motorsport point of view, it has heritage as the world's first motor race, the Paris-Rouen Trial of 1894, started at the Porte Maillot. The first motor race after War World II, known as the Grand Prix de la Libération, took place in the park. It is easy to see such an event as a French version of Albert Park. The problem is that everyone thinks it would be a nightmare to organise. That is probably true but if the President was behind it, and the CEOs of the CAC 40, the biggest problem is really the mayor of Paris. Her name is Anne Hidalgo and she is opposed to automobiles. However, she believed all the gumph about Formula E and allowed the series to race on the streets. F1 has long had a habit of screwing up its environmental messaging but if it can get that right (and the signs are that this is now happening), Ms Hidalgo will struggle to find a good argument against it and should therefore embrace it with fervour. Having said that, she is a socialist and would not be too keen to agree with Macron, but given that her recent presidential bid, as the Socialist Party candidate against Macron was little short of a disaster, it might be wise for her to cuddle up to the President.

Anyway, the idea of city racing, which Grand Prix racing began in 1929 with Monaco, is still a popular idea. The latest racing series to leap on the bandwagon is NASCAR which has just announced that it intends to run its big stock car around the street of Chicago. It is an interesting idea, particularly as the race will be part of the July 4 Independence Day holiday. It all sounds great but I am slightly worried that big heavy stock cars (which weigh 1,450 kg but are very powerful) might be a little too much for the usual concrete barriers to handle. F1 cars tend to bounce off concrete blocks, but when it comes to NASCAR, I fear that the concrete blocks will be bouncing off the cars...

Because it is not overly popular with Beautiful People and the weather was hot, the French GP was a little short of good gossip. Things were booted a little by news from Germany that Herbert Diess is to be removed as the head of Volkswagen. His role will now go to the Porsche CEO Oliver Blume. The good news for F1 is that Blume is very keen on what F1 can offer the industry and he already has a deal (yet to be confirmed) that Porsche will part with Red Bull Racing in 2026. At the moment, F1 is waiting for an announcement but this is expected as soon as the FIA gets its act together and publishes the 2026 rules.

It is expected that Audi (a VW brand) will also then announce that it is buying Sauber is a phased deal over three years. This will mean that Alfa Romeo will get squeezed out, but as the Italian brand is getting a cheap ride in the sport, as it sponsors the team which uses Ferrari engines, no-one is particularly bothered if Alfa Romeo disappears. It isn't a proper factory team....

When it comes to engines in the future, the word is that Honda may be looking to do a sponsorship deal with Red Bull Racing, in order to take advantage of the ongoing success of the team. This could only be a sponsorship and engine-badging deal and it would end, by necessity, in 2025 when Red Bull is (expected to be) committed to Porsche. It seems that Honda, which always makes bad decisions when it comes to F1, now thinks it might be good to get back into the sport in 2026. But it cannot leap back into bed with Red Bull after 2025 as the team will be working with Porsche. Honda's timing in F1 terms has often been poor and this is all in the traditions of the firm. It joined forces with Red Bull Racing in 2019, just after the team had done a title sponsorship with Aston Martin so it was not until 2020 that the team became known as Red Bull Racing Honda in 2020. And then Honda decided to end the relationship at the end of 2021, although a deal was struck for Red Bull to continue to use the engines. After the Honda announcement, Red Bull went out and sold its title sponsorship to Oracle. The team would become Oracle Red Bull Racing Honda in 2023 with the engines switching from being called Red Bulls to being Hondas again, but the firm then needs to decide rapidly if it wants to stay in F1 beyond 2025 and what form that programme might take. The options include engine supplier to a different team, or buying a team...

Talking of buying and selling teams, Alpine is definitely selling a portion of its F1 team, but has no intention of losing control of the operation. This might sound odd given that the team bought Genii Capital's minority shareholding at the start of this year, but the truth is that the team wants a different kind of partner. The team has tight budgets but feels that it needs to improve facilities and increase staff in order to be fully competitive. Both the Enstone and Viry-Chatillon have been expanded and modernised in recent years and Renault is looking for at least one engine customer for the future, although it makes little sense for teams to change before the new engine formula begins in 2026. The engines are now fairly similar in terms of performance and the disruption of an engine change today means that it takes at least a year to get up to speed.

The decision to sell some of the shares is the result of a desire to invest more, while at the same time giving the team a concrete value. New shareholders would obviously benefit from any profits that are made in the future and from the increase in the enterprise value, but they could also be called upon to help funding if the team requires more money, so it is a bit of an insurance policy as well. Perhaps there would also be an option to buy more in the future if Renault one day decides to offload the team again...

Money is important at Alpine and thus negotiating a new deal with Fernando Alonso has been quite complex as the Spaniard has ideas of his own worth which are, how shall we say, impressive. However, the threat of the team signing up a talented youngster called Oscar Piastri was obviously helpful in the negotiations. Anyway, the word is that Fernando now has a new two year deal (perhaps one plus one) and this will be announced after August 1 when an option date will pass. This, of course, means that the team will have to release Oscar Piastri unless it can convince him to join Williams for a year or two. However, it seems that Oscar is more interested in an offer from McLaren that would require him ceasing to be part of the Alpine Academy.

Of course, this would be complicated at McLaren as the Woking team appears to have contracts with Lando Norris and Daniel Ricciardo in 2023 – and has a testing programme going on with Colton Herta, with the goal being to have an American driver in the future. Ricciardo says he is staying where he is, so if the Piastri deal is to happen, Daniel has to go. That would require a contract settlement, and while it is fair to say that his performances over the last two years have not been what was expected, there does not appear to be a specific performance clause in the contract, so the situation could get messy.

There are options for the team to offer Daniel a deal with the McLaren IndyCar team. This seems pretty confusing at the moment as Pato O'Ward and Alex Rossi could be joined by Felix Rosenqvist. The team also announced a deal with 2021 IndyCar champion Alex Palou. This has turned very messy with Palou's employer Ganassi saying that he cannot leave because it has an option on his services and that this has been taken up. Rosenqvist can be offloaded into the McLaren Formula E team while the Palou deal seems ugly with the team filing a law suit against the driver. Mclaren says that it won't pay for Palou to get out of a deal it did not know about. Oh boy...

Williams, in the meantime, appears to be focussing on Logan Sargent. The 21-year-old Florida driver has come good in recent races with Carlin and won feature races in Silverstone and Red Bull Ring. He is the best rookie in the series this year and currently third behind the more experienced Felipe Drugovich and Théo Pourchaire.

If Piastri does decide to leave Alpine, it still has Jack Doohan and Victor Martins on the books for the future, while Alonso could transition into Alpine LMDh team in the longer term. The driver market might get a bit more lively in Budapest. We still need to find out whether Sebastian Vettel will retire... to be replaced at Aston Martin by Mick Schumacher.

It is all bubbling away in the pot at the moment... in the interim everyone is looking forward to the summer break, after four races in five weekends.

From Mosonmagyaróvár

2 August 2022

The sun is coming up in Mosonmagyaróvár, or perhaps it is better to say that the skies are lightening across the Pannonian Plain. You can tell already that it is going to be a blisteringly hot day across Europe, but the sun will not make an appearance until about five thirty. By then I hope to be across the Austrian border and wiggling through the Wienerwald, where Johann Strauss wrote waltzes and where today the Vienna ring road helps one avoid traffic jams in the city. I am glad that I am not driving east, but I know that by evening I will be heading straight into the setting sun, which will make things a bit more complicated in the final few miles, when I will be closer to home, in country lanes, with a million dead bugs on the windscreen.

I know it doesn't sound very sensible to set off to drive 994 miles after a night without sleep but there are times when you do what you have to do, no matter what it takes. And I am used to long drives when I am tired. It's my wife's birthday and it's never nice to celebrate alone, so I'm heading home to start the summer break a day earlier than planned – and I haven't told her and I have cursed the calendar-makers of F1 for putting the race on the wrong weekend, so it will all be a big surprise…

I've already covered a couple of hundred kilometres, but home is still 870 miles away. The journey will take me by way of Linz, Munich, Stuttgart, Metz and Reims. If I drive all day, I should be home before the sun sets.

The Formula 1 summer holiday has begun and the idea of spending time at home is most appealing, particularly after four races in five weekends. I drive because I no longer want the stress of airports and planes at a time when everything is up the creek following the Covid pandemic. At every race I hear the tales of travel horrors from those who are condemned to fly everywhere, of missing bags and queues as far as the eye can see. Driving may not always be easy, but at least you are in control of your own destiny – and you can leave a queue and find another way to get home. That sense of freedom and the lack of stress makes it worthwhile. Stress, as the old F1 doctor Sid Watkins always used to say, kills more people than other things – and so I take Sid's advice and make new discoveries every day.

When I crossed the Austro-Hungarian border on the way out to Budapest, I did what I always do and switched the radio to a local station. You learn a lot just by listening to a language and these days I can understand far more languages than used to be the case, thanks to listening to traffic reports and news bulletins. But I am convinced that I will never understand a single word of Hungarian. I was impressed by the road signs that screamed "Tartson Jobbra!", which sounded vaguely rude, but I learned means "Keep right".

After a while, I realised I had some time to spare and decided to have a bit of a wander around and headed down Route 82, which goes from Györ to Veszprem, over the Bakony mountains, which run diagonally across the western part of the country, splitting the Great Hungarian Plain from the Little Hungarian Plain. It was not long before I encountered a horse and cart... Then the magnificent Castle of Csesznek, or at least the ruins of it, appeared. I guess it lies in ruins because of battles between the feuding clans of Hungary, but in truth I was more interested in the fact that the town of Papa is about 50 miles from the village of Dad, by way of a lot of villages that would score very highly when playing Scrabble. I did however discover that Veszprém will be the European Capital of Culture in 2023, which means that they are digging up all the roads at the moment and their signposting is so poor that I ended up in a place called Marko and wondered if the family of the good doctor of Red Bull fame might have hailed from these parts.

Anyway, all of this gave me plenty of time to think about the F1 calendar and what a difficult beast it is to tame. In a normal year, there would be a draft of next season's calendar before the summer break and the folks at Liberty Media, while still wet behind the ears, talked of producing calendars earlier and more regionalised than used to be the case in the Ecclestone Era. This was commendable, but the desire for more dates means that things are much more complicated. Race promoters have their own ideas about what they want and they do not much care about other races – except to avoid them, if they consider another Grand Prix will take away some of their spectators. Having a better calendar would also help F1 in its desire to reduce emissions, which is one of the goals that the sport has set itself, in order to stay out of trouble with activist environmental groups.

The last couple of weeks have seen me driving nearly 3,106 miles, with another 2,485 in the fortnight before that. This could hardly be described as environmentally-friendly, particularly when one considers that the F1 circus requires around 300 big thirsty trucks to go from place to place. They always look nice and shiny, which is a good advert for the sport, but they pump out fumes aplenty. This fleet has gone from Britain to Austria then back to France and then back to Hungary before heading home for the break. This means a great deal of needless emissions for which F1 gets the blame, although to be fair it is because the race promoters in Austria and Hungary think the races are too close together (geographically) to be back-to-back. This is not a very sensible argument because some of the fans (mainly the Dutch) will go anywhere and will often combine two events with their summer holidays.

The biggest problem for F1's regionalisation programmes is that some of the promoters have the date of their races written into the contracts and are unwilling to change the terms of the deal. This means that F1 cannot change the dates unless compromises can be found.

This is particularly obvious with Miami and Montreal, one in May and the other in June. The two races are far enough apart on a map not to create a problem, but Montreal wants to stay on its June date, which it views as being key to its success, and Miami has a 10-year deal for early May, between its Miami Open tennis competition and the point at which the weather in Florida gets too hot. Moving Montreal into May would create the opposite problem because in Canada it can still be pretty wintry at that point. So F1 has to go backwards and forwards across the Atlantic twice in the spring.

One has to add the fact that (quite rightly) the teams do not want triple-headers (because F1 people need lives as well), plus the freight difficulties and the usual desires to have a race fitting in with a local holiday, such as Mexico's Day of the Dead. And, on top of all this, there are other sports events that are best avoided. These days one has Covid problems as well because China and Japan have not got it sorted yet and then there are ego problems with Monaco and money to be found in South Africa.

In short, it is a complete nightmare. There are various different draft calendars at the moment, each dependent on which race agrees to go where. Until recently it looked like the start of 2023 was sorted out, with the first race being in Bahrain on March 5 with a break and Saudi Arabia back-to-back with Australia, on March 19 and March 26. However, it now seems that this has been vetoed, although I did note the presence of the race promoters from Australia and Saudi Arabia in Budapest. For now, it seems that there will be a weekend off between Saudi and Australia (and thus more people flying out and back and out and back). Australia was then going to go back-to-back with South Africa, but the Kyalami contract is not yet signed off because of money (or rather the lack of it). We also hear that Qatar has now decided that it does not want to be twinned with Abu Dhabi and would prefer a spring date... and, of course, Doha is paying a lot of money.

As an aside, I also discovered that the plan to have a waterfront event in Doha has evaporated and the Qataris now think it is better to upgrade the Losail facility. I am not quite sure why a track surrounded by sand will sell the country better than a track along a waterfront, but perhaps it is because Qatar does not want to be seen to be copying Saudi Arabia. Oddly enough, however, the Saudis are still planning on moving their race from the Jeddah Corniche Circuit to a wadi near Riyadh, so maybe the Qataris will change their mind once the Saudis have finished that...

The inclusion of the Belgian GP seems to be conditional on China and/or South Africa not happening, but no-one seems sure about where Imola, Barcelona or Baku will fall, nor whether Monaco will happen. Is there any part of the calendar that is actually settled? Well, difficult to say, but I hear that the crazy Britain-Austria-France-Hungary leg will become Austria-Britain-Something-Hungary, which makes a bit more sense. The something could be one of the above...

I am pretty sure that the Dutch GP will be at the end of August, with the Italian GP a week later and the Singapore-Japan back-to-back will be in September, although China will be moving to the autumn, if it happens at all. I also hear that Austin, Mexico and Brazil will be a triple-header, and that Vegas will go back-to-back with Abu Dhabi. The good news, however, is that it looks like the season will be finished by the end of November which means that F1 families should be happy as there will be some time for Christmas shopping...

What I can tell you with confidence (as much as you can with anything in F1) is that the Australian Grand Prix will be the opening race of the FIA Formula 1 World Championship in 2024 and 2025, because the Middle Eastern races need to take place later because of Ramadan.

Still, in F1 one needs to be wary of "certainties". I was just a tad irritated when I heard that Fernando Alonso had signed for Aston Martin, because it was clear before that came that he would be staying at Alpine in 2023. It was a big surprise in that it is utterly illogical (except from a financial point of view) and it came as a shock to everyone, even Alpine boss Otmar Szafnauer. This made me feel a little better as a few hours earlier I had written confidently in my JSBM newsletter that Alonso would stay, based on the fact that all my sources who know these things were agreed on it. The newsletter also included a lot of detail about Oscar Piastri joining McLaren and how that might be possible.

What was clear was that Oscar could not afford to sit out another year without racing and Alpine had to decide whether to keep Alonso, who is doing a great job, or dropping the old lion and putting in a feisty pup. It was a tough call but teams always want to avoid the bad publicity that comes with dubious contractual behaviour, although history relates that all contacts can be broken if a team is desperate enough – and rich enough.

On paper, of course, McLaren has contracts with Lando Norris and Daniel Ricciardo – and has a testing programme going on with Colton Herta. Piastri is seen as being a bit special and, with Alpine in a difficult spot, it seems like McLaren saw a chance to grab him. Piastri has a contact with Alpine (so they say) which guarantees him a race seat in 2023. This may not say which team that seat would be with, and the word is that Alpine offered to put Oscar into Williams. This is not a good choice for him. The rest of the story depends on the wording of contracts, which we are never privy to.

Ricciardo has a contract for next year but, popular though he is, Daniel has been disappointing in his time with McLaren, except that he won a race last year. Lando has yet to win, but clearly has the advantage at the moment. Ricciardo is saying that he has no intention of moving, but one can see why McLaren might want to off-load him and grab Piastri. Pushing Daniel out of the way would require a contract settlement and how this could be achieved is unclear because money is not the only thing. Without a McLaren drive, Ricciardo's F1 future is not looking great. McLaren seems to have got itself into a similar mess over the US where the Indycar team appears to be overstocked with drivers with Pato O'Ward, Alex Rossi and Felix Rosenqvist on the books – and some kind of deal going down with Alex Palou.

The Spanish driver's current employer Chip Ganassi says he has a valid option with Palou and it all seems to be heading into the hands of lawyers. This is all a little strange. The problem between Palou and Ganassi is clearly money. Chip made him a star and now wants a third season cheap. There is an option (wording unknown) but Palou thinks he can get out. Ganassi thinks Palou has to stay.

One imaginative solution (which perhaps McLaren has thought about) is for McLaren to offer Ganassi Ricciardo in place of Palou, particularly if McLaren agreed to pay him a suitable salary (which means a lot less than F1). This would put Daniel into a top IndyCar drive, would leave McLaren with enough to pay Piastri and to see Palou racing IndyCars with the team and secure two hot talents at the same time. Rosenqvist would then be shunted into Formula E.

The downside of all of this is that there would be no room at McLaren for Herta. He has, in any case, a contract with Andretti to race IndyCars until the end of 2023 and he does not have the super licence required to race in F1, so he could not join McLaren until 2024 at the earliest, although with Piastri and Norris there would be no room for him until 2026.

One can perhaps also argue that the testing deal that Herta has with McLaren could be designed to help Michael Andretti developing a driver for a possible Formula 1 team – if that ever comes to fruition.

Losing Daniel would be a loss for F1 but might be best for him, better for McLaren, great for Ganassi and perfect for Palou. And Zak Brown would look very clever for having put it all together.

As I write this Notebook, an email has arrived from Alpine announcing Piastri. This was a surprise and it was immediately suspect when I saw that there was no quote from Oscar. Every new driver press release has a quote from the driver saying that he is "delighted to be joining etc etc". No quote, for me, means no agreement or at worst a bad start to the relationship.

One might also ask why Alonso wants to join Aston Martin, given the team's lack of performance. There is, of course, the chance of a longer contract, more money, a team-mate who might not be too difficult to beat and one day a better car, but it is an odd move in many respects. Alpine probably thought that Alonso would reduce his salary demands to stay on and so the team would be getting a good deal. Perhaps. Perhaps, also, Alpine annoyed Fernando over this question.

Will Alonso and Aston Martin be a match made in heaven? Probably not. Fernando is not easy (although he is more relaxed these days). Lawrence Stroll is not known for being an easy companion. What he is known for is his belief that Lance is an undiscovered genius, capable of winning World Championships. Being a racing dad and a team owner is not a good combination and one wonders what will happen when Alonso beats Lance every weekend.

Fernando is smart, but he is not ever going to say "After you Lance…"

It has all the makings of a disaster ahead… but let's wait and see. Lawrence seems to think that all is well with the car company, but reality checks in from time to time. Last week Aston Martin reported first half losses for 2022 of £285.4 million, saying that supply chain shortages hit production which meant that it could not meet the demand for its cars.

Let's not dwell on that…

Elsewhere, Williams was hoping that Piastri might come its way but has been in deep discussions with Nyck de Vries, the Dutch Formula E World Champion. Nyck has a couple of drives up his sleeve which have yet to be announced in WEC and Formula E and he must soon decide whether to give it all up to become an F1 driver. He's a little older than your average F1 debutant and so might conclude that it is a bit late to dream of glory in F1 and better to take winning drives (and a chunk of cash) elsewhere. Nyck must decide at some point but Williams is in a difficult situation in that the choice of its test driver Logan Sargeant is not a bad idea as the 21-year-old Floridian driver might unlock the doors to US sponsorships as F1 grows in America. The problem is that Logan does not have a super licence and the F2 championship is quite close and so confirmation of the licence might come too late for the team to rely on it. And if de Vries signs elsewhere and Sargeant misses out…

Oh dear.

The details of the yet-to-be-announced Porsche-Red Bull alliance have emerged from the unlikely source of the Moroccan government's competition authority in Rabat, which says it is considering the deal on the grounds of competition questions. It is hard to imagine how this might be he case, but the paperwork does include details of the planned transaction in order to get clearance for the deal. It is unlikely that any F1 journalist would have considered looking for competition clearance for a deal in Morocco and so it is most likely to have been a leak. One might speculate that such news would do no harm at all to the Porsche share price as the firm prepares an IPO. Anyway, the document reveals a joint venture between Porsche AG and Red Bull GmbH and the purchase of 50 percent of Red Bull Technology Ltd shares by Porsche. It is interesting that neither party seems to have control, although that could depend on who the chairman of the board would be, even in such a situation one can have a different chairman at each meeting. The danger with 50-50 partnerships is that they can become deadlocked if the parties do not agree on their strategy, unless there are clear rules about who makes the decisions. One should also note that the world has changed a little since the documents were filed with Herbert Diess being replaced as the head of the Volkswagen Group, with the role going to the Porsche CEO Oliver Blume. This might impact on Audi's plan to enter F1 as the brand is also owned by Volkswagen. Audi boss Markus Duesmann was a rival to Blume for the VW role and he may now decide to move elsewhere. Duesmann is a former F1 engineer from BMW who believes that the sport is the best way to sell cars and to develop new technology. His plan to make Audi more successful rests on the idea that the firm will get rid of its smaller cars and focus more on the lucrative luxury segment, which he wants to expand.

Much of this depends on the 2026 regulations but the word is that the F1 Commission will vote on this shortly and the rules will be published after the FIA World Motor Sport Council has an electronic vote.

The goal then is to have 50-50 super-efficient ICE-electric power units, with synthetic fuels. Formula E may have painted itself green more successfully than F1 has done, but the world is beginning to realise that F1 engines are a better long-term option and astonishing pieces of kit. My favourite statistic in this respect is thermal efficiency (the percentage of energy in the fuel that makes it to become energy in the rear wheels) because it really shows what F1 has done. If one considers that the first practical automobile powered by an internal-combustion engine arrived in 1885 and in the 128 years that followed the best that generations of brilliant engineers could achieve was a rather disappointing 35 percent thermal efficiency, which meant that a huge amount of energy was being wasted. In the nine years since 2013 F1 has driven that figure up to around 52 percent.

Synthetic fuel is interesting but in the rush of recent races I noted that Mercedes-AMG Petronas has announced that it is becoming the first global sports team to invest in Sustainable Aviation Fuel (SAF). The team says that it uses a lot of fuel flying around and wants to reduce its global footprint but of course it might also want to make some money and what is required in SAF is not very different to what is required (or will be required) in F1 fuels.

"We aim to be on the cutting edge of change, using our global motorsport platform as a model for a more sustainable and diversified future," said Toto Wolff, a man who has made a few quid over the years by betting on new ideas.

And on that green (as in greenbacks) note, I will sign off for the summer break.

From Oudenaarde

31 August 2022

Memory is an amazing thing. As I drove past a sign to the village of Oudenaarde, bells rang in dusty corridor in my brain and a messenger came running along shouting the words: "Marlborough" and muttered something about Spaniards and Austrians. It has been a while since I last heard the name – about half a century – and I had no idea exactly why the Duke of Marlborough was marching armies around a very flat part of Belgium, but I concluded it was something all to do with quibbling European nations and Kings with boots too big for their feet. And I pondered that in the overall scheme of things, little has changed since then (whenever then was) and that the world remains driven by greed, ambition and, of course, sex. I had a conversation on this very subject with an Alpine PR man in Spa, who was trying to convince me that the Oscar Piastri business was all about money.

I argued that it was probably not because ambitious young drivers often break contracts in order to get into a place they consider better than previous choices. It is normal behaviour and one can say the same thing about Alain Prost, Ayrton Senna and Michael Schumacher. They all did things which resulted in tut-tutting in the F1 Paddock, but they got where they wanted to be.

Whether the choice of McLaren over Alpine is ultimately the right things to do remains to be seen, but it is probably a wiser choice than leaping from Alpine to Aston Martin. Still, when it comes to career moves, there is a reason that Fernando Alonso won fewer championships than the eminent list above...

Anyway, Spaniards and Austrians were much in discussion in the Paddock in Spa, with regard to the F1 silly season, rather than the impact of said countries in Belgian history. Of course, when it comes to simplicity, Belgian does not win many prizes. Still, it is an amazing country. In 2020, it broke its own record for the longest period for a country without an elected government after 592 days. The record had previously stood at 541 days back in 2010 and 2011. Is it any wonder that organising a sensible traffic plan around Spa-Francorchamps is a bit of a challenge. Of course, in addition to Belgium's three federal police forces, there are 185 local police forces – the latter being in charge of maintaining public order and traffic for big events. Who knows how many police commissioners were involved in Spa's traffic plans. It does not really matter because none of it worked (again). I am advocate of posting the local police chief(s) to Outer Mongolia (on a permanent basis) to help with law and order there and asking the Mongolians to work on a new traffic plan for Francorchamps, as they can hardly do a worse job.

This seems to be the primary reason that F1 decided that it had had enough of Spa, particularly after the non-race mud-bath of 2021. The race promoters seem to have found the cash to keep the race and have invested a fortune in upgrading the circuit, to allow for MotoGP events, but no-one thought that it might be wise to drive a four-lane highway straight into the circuit. Having spent my weekend driving through winding forests, going backwards and forwards to a hotel in Germany, there does not seem to be a problem with cutting down trees...

The reason I was staying in Germany was that there has been a very nasty outbreak of naked greed in the Spa region and hotel prices have reached insane levels. The same is happening with lots of race at the moment but the Walloons are really gouging their visitors. Yes, I know, it's supply and demand and that is why I went to Germany: to give them some money and not spend it in Belgium. This meant that, by the end of the weekend, I was rather weary as I was setting off each morning in the dark and returning each evening in the dark, the only way to avoid wasting time and polluting the universe by being part of a traffic jam. I did at one point consider stealing an old tank that was sitting in the middle of a roundabout in Butgenbach and driving it through the forest to the paddock, thus creating the path for a new road, although I suspect some folks might say this would be a horrible thing to do.

Anyway, it was worth noting the appearance of Belgian Prime Minister Alexander De Croo on the grid (and podium) on Sunday. This was a first and very significant. De Croo is Flemish. The race is in Wallonia. These things matter in Belgium... One wonders what brought him to Spa, but I suspect that a new five-year deal is in the pipeline and Belgium will remain an F1 nation if the PM agrees to do all the right things, whatever they may be...

The F1 calendar is proving complicated this year, which is what happens when you try to squeeze things into a small space. Each promoter has its own wishes and requirements, some of them written into contracts. Others have ambitions that they cannot meet, or bosses they cannot control. It is clear that Belgium is back on the calendar in 2023 because South Africa is gone. It remains to be seen if a race can be put together in South Africa in 2024 but otherwise F1 is going to start looking at other options in Africa.

The word is that Belgium will take the July 23 slot, fitting in the week before Hungary (July 30). This will follow on from a double-header in Britain (July 2) and Austria (July 9). The Dutch will take over the current Belgian date (August 27) and Italy will follow on September 3. Singapore will have its usual September 17 date and logically Japan would be a week later.

The front end of the calendar seems settled now with Bahrain opening the season on March 6, followed by Saudi Arabia on March 19 with Australia a week after that (March 26). April is complicated with Imola and Baku likely, but the possibility of China is still floating. Qatar did want to be up front as well but it has just demolished the pits at Losail and the new buildings will not be ready until the autumn. This is clear conformation that the planned street race in Doha is history (at least for now). Why? Who knows? Perhaps Doha did not want to be seen copying what Jeddah had done... Doha will probably follow on from Singapore and Japan. There will then be the races in Austin, Mexico, Sao Paulo (a triple header?) and Las Vegas, with the season ending on the last weekend of November in Abu Dhabi.

Canada will have its usual June date and Miami will stick with its May 5 date, and Monaco (if t happens) looks like being part of a triple-header involving Imola and Spain. But how it all fits together with the floating races remains to be seen. Draft calenders were flying around all weekend, like confetti in June.

Talking of confusions, the announcement that Audi will be entering F1 as an engine supplier in 2026 was celebrated by the German firm's CEO standing next to an Audi-branded car, which was a massive piece of mixed messaging, suggesting that Audi is not just planning engines but also a full factory operation. Given that soon after the Audi announcement Alfa Romeo announced it is giving up the title sponsorship of Sauber at the end of 2023 pretty much confirmed what will happen.

By the start of 2024, Audi will own 50 percent of Sauber, according to my sources, and so Alfa Romeo will no longer be welcome. All things considered the Audi announcement was pretty odd as Audi's sister brand Porsche is also planning to race in F1 and that the Audi announcement came just a few days before Porsche boss Oliver Blume takes over as chief executive of the entire Volkswagen Group, Audi's parent company.

Duesmann was a rival for that job, but in the end lost out. It may just be a coincidence that the Audi F1 announcement came just a few days before Duesmann got his new boss...

It has been rumoured for a long time that Volkswagen would have two brands in Formula 1, although on paper that is strange when the automotive industry is always focussed on creating synergies and saving costs, but the announcement of the Porsche IPO should come in the next few days and the word is that this will raise $85 billion, so there will be some money sloshing about.

However, there have been whispers inside and outside the paddock that Porsche and Red Bull may not go ahead as planned because Red Bull might have got a better offer from Honda. In one of his answers in Spa, Duesmann said something interesting (not much of it was). "We will have completely separate operations," he said. "We will have our operations in Germany and, if Porsche enters, they will have their operations in the UK." Duesmann thus confirmed the Porsche project, but at the same time cast doubt on it with the word "if". Given that he is neither the boss of Porsche nor the VW Group, this is strange behaviour although the Audi contingent present at Spa were keen to bang the drum that all is perfectly harmonious in the VW empire. It does not feel that way. Still, I guess we will find out soon enough. Tomorrow Blume ceases to be Duesmann's rival and becomes his boss... One wonders if there will be some fireworks...

Talking of fireworks, one place where there were none at all was in the McLaren company's half-year results, up to June 30. This made pretty grim reading with sales and revenues significantly lower than the same period last year. The firm blamed this on semi-conductor shortages but sales of only 850 cars – down 24 percent – is not great. Revenues were down 23 percent from £350 million in 2021 to £258 million this year. The company thus booked a loss. However, McLaren did get a new CEO in Michael Leiters, who joined in July. He is believed to be planning to follow the current trend for such companies and create a McLaren SUV.

Talking of McLaren, it is clear that fairly soon the company will announce that Oscar Piastri is joining the team. The Contract Recognition Board met on Monday and there will be a result by now, but these things are secret and so the first the world will know is when either McLaren confirms Oscar, or Alpine signs someone else. The result of the CRB is really only to establish whether Alpine should be compensated, although the board does not deal with money. That is up to the teams. The word I heard was that while Alpine says Piastri signed a contract in November last year. He may not have actually signed a long form contract. This would explain why Alpine says he signed a deal and Piastri and his management say there is nothing binding. He signed a McLaren contract on July 4 and so clearly believed he was free to do so. One can perhaps theorise that Oscar signed a "heads of agreement" document but this is, by nature, a tentative document, which is usually considered non-binding... It could also be a question of wording, but whatever Oscar signed it could not have been to race for Alpine in 2023 because the team at that point did not have a seat available to commit to Piastri. Thus the wording of any deal would have had to be a commitment to provide Piastri with "a Formula 1 drive" or something along those lines. If the car was not specified, there is an argument that this could be deemed unfair in a regular commercial court... As we do not know these things, we can only guess. What we do know is that the relationship with Alpine is broken. In fact, McLaren may end up in a stronger financial position now that a settlement has been agreed with Daniel Ricciardo. The team was due to pay Daniel $16 million in 2023 but the whisper in the paddock was that a settlement was reached at $10 million. That sounds about right. However, it does mean that McLaren will have $6 million more to spend on driver budgets... Piastri will be cheaper than that for a while and so there might even be some cash left over to sort out the mess in Indycar where the team has a problem securing the services of Alex Palou. A couple of million might help convince Ganassi that a bird in the bush is worth more than one in the hand. Still, these kinds of dealings do not help to foster trusting relationships...

So who will Alpine get? Good question without an obvious answer. There has been much talk of Pierre Gasly but this may just have been because Alpine went asking around about who was available. Red Bull's Helmut Marko is not averse to stirring up excitement in the media, either just for fun or to make noise at a time when there are other things going on. It's a classic F1 strategy: make a large bang and when the media runs off towards it, do whatever you are trying to do without anyone noticing. That was a favourite trick of Mr Bernie Ecclestone. It does not always work with judges...

The Gasly theory is sensible in that he is the best option, given that Ricciardo is disheartened and Alex Albon has been quickly re-signed by Williams. Esteban Ocon says he would like to see Mick Schumacher in the team but that seems pretty unlikely given that Ferrari and Haas have made it clear that they are not interested in him. It is hard to imagine that Red Bull would be.

There is also no reason why Red Bull would want to let Gasly go early unless there is a suitable replacement. Pierre was confirmed in June on this basis and nothing has much changed. He is there if he is needed. He does a decent job for AlphaTauri but he is not part of the long-term Red Bull plan.

Still it is better to have him on the books, rather than letting a rival team take him. Marko does not seem overly impressed with his current crop of youngsters in F2. Most have been disappointing this season, although Ayumu Iwasa has generally made a good impression. Marko's latest focus seems to be on F3 racer Isack Hadjar, who has been fighting for the FIA F3 title in his first season. He will move up into F2 next year.

The other difficult problem with Gasly is that while some folks say he does not get on with Ocon, they fail to understand the level of friction between the pair. Ocon bought his first kart from Pierre's brother and, at the age of eight or nine, they were rivals and best friends. The problem was that they fell out at about 11 and while both can be professional and say the right things, the hurt is still there and the relationship could crumble quite easily. There is also the question of Alpine marketing goals. Car companies go racing to sell cars. Alpine is a Norman firm, based in Dieppe. Ocon and Gasly are Normans as well, one from Evreux, the other from Rouen. It will be great news for car sales in the region, but it is doubtful that Alpine will sell much in Outer Mongolia (unless the Belgian police chief wants one). It would be better to have someone most international… One possible option might be Nyck de Vries, although his is more likely to sign for Williams and ditch his WEC contract with Toyota and his Formula E drive with Maserati.

Alpine's next young driver is Jack Doohan, the Australian. He has qualified for a super licence and is starting to come good in F2. He would be a risky option for the team, but the aim of a junior team is to provide a cheap supply of drivers, who are integrated into the team's ways over time. Thus he should not be excluded as an option… If he can do more good things in F2 in the next weeks, perhaps he has a chance.

Perhaps the strangest of the Spa rumours was the one about Colton Herta becoming an AlphaTauri F1 driver. The Californian does not have a super licence, he has yet to prove himself in F1 terms and would obviously need time. He has a contract with Andretti Autosport in IndyCar and is one of the team's biggest assets. It is always possible that Marko might like the look of him, but getting him would not be easy.

Elsewhere, I did hear that Brazil's Felipe Drugovich is talking seriously to Aston Martin about a reserve driver deal and is believed to be supported by a Brazilian bank, while it has been also been suggested that Ricciardo's best move might be to become reserve driver at Mercedes, to help build up his confidence again…

One Alpine driver that has not been seriously considered by the rumour-mongers is no less a figure than Jacques Villeneuve. I am joking but Jacques, now a commentator, is to test a 2021 Alpine next week at Monza to give him an insight into how the modern cars are. JV has already been in the simulator and is excited about the chance.

While on the subject of unusual stories in Italy, Emerson Fittipaldi is going to be standing for election to the Italian Senate, as a candidate for the Fratelli d'Italia, a national-conservative and right-wing populist political party led by Giorgia Meloni, who is a sort of Italian version of Marine Le Pen…

On Monday after Spa, I did not – sadly – go pottering around Belgium, as the plan had originally been. Instead I went back to Paris because the Japanese decided that anyone who wants to go to the Grand Prix in Suzuka must now have a visa, which was never the case before. So rather than a leisurely life, I had to rush home to do lots of Japanese paperwork which the embassy looked out and handed back to me as being not relevant, and then headed north again…

…which is how I ended up in Oudenaarde.

From Crèvecœur-le-Grand

7 September 2022

Driving home from Zandvoort, I passed through Crèvecœur-le-Grand, a town in the Oise département in France, surrounded these days by dozens of aeolian wind turbines. I find these constructions rather elegant and something of great value, but I know others think they spoil the view. In rough translation, the name Crèvecœur-le-Grand means "The Big Heartbreak", which is an odd name, if only because I'm not sure if there is such a thing as a small heartbreak.

If you try to trace the derivation of the name, looking perhaps for a story like Romeo and Juliet, one finds only the mists of time. The town name may have come from an ancient aristocratic family, or perhaps the family name came from the town. It is hard to tell. There are several other Crèvecœurs in Normandy and, inevitably, the name landed on the beaches of Britain with William the Conqueror and ended up in America, where it was mangled into Croaker and Craker. And while this was going on, the town of Big Heartbreak was being flattened and rebuilt twice by German guns and bombs. It was not a lucky place.

Crèvecœur's biggest claim to fame, apart from its repeated destruction, is that it was where the exotic American dancer Josephine Baker married (for the fourth time), casting away her skirt made from bananas – it was all she wore while dancing on stage in Paris. Her husband, for the next 14 months, was Jean Lion, a wealthy local sugar broker and aviator. The ceremony that put Crèvecœur on the map was performed by the mayor, who enjoyed the strange name Jammy Schmidt, a lucky name for such an unfortunate place. Mrs Lion was splendidly eccentric and kept a perfumed pig in her nightclub in Paris. She was once photographed taking her pet swans for a walk in Budapest (on leashes, of course). As a result of this brief encounter, Josephine Baker became a French citizen and today rests in the Panthéon in Paris, alongside national heroes (and heroines) with the likes of Victor Hugo, Emile Zola, Voltaire, Jean-Jacques Rousseau, Pierre and Marie Curie, Louis Braille, Jean Moulin and sundry military and political types.

The name Crèvecœur is also employed to describe a rather exotic breed of chicken that was named after Crèvecœur-en-Auge in the Calvados region of Normandy. These heartbroken chickens were very popular (for dinner) with the bourgeoisie in the Nineteenth Century. The French, however, blame the invading Germans for eating nearly all of these succulent chucks, and the breed has been endangered ever since, although the do-gooders of today have been busy encouraging them to propagate so that future generations can enjoy the taste.

The point of all this local colour is that the story of Crèvecœur (and the chickens) mirrors the one of Zandvoort, where heartbreaking events have led to a similar resurrection. Zandvoort was once a very chic seaside resort, with Belle Epoque hotels and villas, where the celebrities of the day bathed in the North Sea. Alas, when the armies arrived from Germany in 1940, the generals felt threatened by the lovely beaches and so demolished the fashionable town in order to build coastal defences. They used the rubble as the foundations for roads to link the blockhouses.

After the war, the mayor of Zandvoort, a racing fan called Henri van Alphen, saw the opportunity to use the German roads to build a race track to promote the town. Today, Zandvoort is an ugly town, with cheap and nasty post-war apartment blocks, but it has a splendid race track, to which the Dutch now flock in vast numbers (and orange clothing) to watch Max Verstappen winning motor races. There is a certain magnificence in these vast orange crowds, particularly for older Dutch racing folk who never dreamed that such things might be possible.

Perhaps with time, the city will demolish all the horrible buildings and make Zandvoort beautiful again.

The Formula 1 Paddock in Zandvoort was bustling with the orange folk, not least McLaren team people who seemed very pleased when it emerged (not surprisingly) that they had secured the services of Oscar Piastri, following a discussion by the Contract Recognition Board, which ruled that Alpine's claims about having him under contract were fatally flawed. The details of how this came to pass remain confidential but I am told that the story was not very complex, as the contract registered by Alpine with the CRB was no more than what is called a heads of agreement. Why this strange situation could have occurred is because when Piastri agreed to stay with Alpine last November, the team could not offer guarantee which car he would drive in 2023 and could only commit to "a Formula 1 car". At the time the team was still discussing what to do in the future with Fernando Alonso and already had a deal with Esteban Ocon.

Alpine was in a difficult situation because it wanted to hire both Alonso and Piastri but could no do so. It could, in theory, have signed both and paid off Ocon, but that would have been very messy given that Esteban is French and won a race in 2021 (which was more than Alonso did). In any case, Ocon has been driving some super races of late, notably in Spa where he did a better job than the celebrated Fernando. To be doing that is quite an achievement given that Alonso is one of the finest F1 drivers in history and ended up with only two World Championships because of poor career decisions, bad management and having the reputation for being someone who damages racing teams. One can add Alpine to the list after recent events... He is a fabulous driver but his talent should have landed him five World Championships rather than just two. In any case, matching him and beating him on occasion makes Ocon a very valuable driver.

Alpine must now find replacements for Alonso and Piastri and the team must be aware that, when all is said and done, it was to blame for losing the pair. Such setbacks always provide good lessons for those new to F1 and so it is best for Alpine not to get into a panic and sign up the wrong people but rather wait, watch and make sensible decisions about what to do next. There is no great rush to do deals. Piastri was the team's future, but there are other drivers in the Alpine Academy, notably Jack Doohan, who is showing signs that he is good enough for F1. It is too early for him, and the best move would probably be to give him a year testing with older cars and becoming part of the team, rather than throwing him in at the deep end. Thus, Alpine needs a driver who is willing to do a one-year deal. Perhaps the team would do OK with a Mick Schumacher, a Nico Hülkenberg or a Nyck de Vries, but one-year deals can be fraught arrangements because a driver with no future in a team wants only to show what he can do, rather than how he can help the team.

Daniel Ricciardo looks like a man who needs to rest and get his head in gear, while Pierre Gasly would be a good choice were it not for the fact that he is French (and why would the team want two Frenchmen?). There is also the fact that he and Ocon do not get on. They are the worst kind of rivals. They were best friends when they were young, before they fell out. One should add that Pierre is also locked in a contract with Red Bull (to race for AlphaTauri) and it will cost money to get him out, as Red Bull really needs him in reserve in case something happens to one of the Red Bull drivers.

It is a bit odd that Dr Helmut Marko has got excited about Colton Herta and says that he will sell Gasly if he can get Herta. It looks from the outside like Marko is playing games to disrupt rival teams as it is a tough project to extract Herta from an IndyCar contract with Andretti Autosport in 2023, get him up to speed in F1 rapidly and try to get agreement for him to be given a super licence he has not earned. On can argue that the super licence rules should be tweaked in future to allow Indycar race winners to jump into Formula 1, but there should not be a precedent set that allows the rules to be bent. This will only lead to problems in the future. The rules exist to ensure that the quality of driving in F1 is maintained and while Herta may (or may not) have what it takes, there are others who might get in later, based on money rather than talents. A driver who earns a super licence (even a rich one) has still earned the right to race in F1. Undermining the super licence system would undermine the FIA's reputation in F1.

The argument that F1 needs an American driver is utterly flawed, unless the American is the right one. Right now, Williams is supporting the efforts of 21-year-old Florida driver Logan Sargeant, who is currently in the process of gaining a super licence in the prescribed way, and, despite some mishaps in Formula 2, is still in a position to have one next year. Herta is clearly talented, but neither he nor Marko should be helped to get him a licence. If he has the talent needed and the will to succeed, then he will find a way without help with the licence.

A driver's success in F1 is based so much these days on psychology that it is always best to find the right fit rather than trying to ram a driver who is a square peg trying to get into a round hole.

Ricciardo is a good example of a driver who has super ability but just does not fit in the team. No-one can figure out why and the Australian's confidence has been battered by what has happened. This does not mean that Daniel is useless and finished, it means he needs to rebuild, rethink his priorities and find a way to get back his missing mojo.

The latest word is that Daniel might take a year off in 2023 if he is not offered the Alpine drive. Then, as an experienced F1 winner, he could return to the sport as a reserve in 2024, helping to rebuild his confidence by measuring his performance against the top names. I hear he has been talking to Mercedes about such a role, which would put him in with a chance of a race drive in the future if Lewis Hamilton decides that he has had enough. That must happen eventually and while Mercedes has George Russell in place, it is waiting for the next big thing. This appears to be a 16-year-old youngster it manages called Andrea Kimi Antonelli, who is wowing everyone at the moment in Formula 4. He is at least three or four years away from F1, so there is likely to be a gap between Hamilton's departure and Antonelli's arrival...

It is tough getting a break into Formula 1, even if you are talented, and I have rather enjoyed rumours in recent days that Formula 2 champion-to-be Felipe Drugovich could be joining Aston Martin in 2023 as a test and reserve driver. This is smart thinking. Drugovich has dominated F2 this year but it is his third year in the formula and F1 teams tend not to look at such drivers. However, Drugovich is smart enough to realise that jumping straight into F1 will be almost impossible and going to Aston Martin is a decent gamble because Alonso and Lawrence Stroll may not get on, and even if they do, that will come at the expense of Lance Stroll, so one can wager that one or the other will be gone by 2024 and being integrated into the team, Drugovich would be a good bet as a replacement for one or the other... This would also be good for F1 as the sport could use another Brazilian...

On final thought on the subject of drivers, I heard that Marko could be stirring up a storm in the driver market because he does not want F1 scribblers focussing on Red Bull's other big story at the moment: the fact that its planned relationship with Porsche is coming undone and Porsche will not become a shareholder in the team.

It seems that Red Bull has concluded that it would rather stay as it is and run its own engine programme, rather than have other folk coming in and disrupting the successful squad that it is today. Red Bull now has its own engine programme – the first prototype ran recently on a dyno in Milton Keynes – and the firm does not really need Porsche, unless it wants money, which has never been Red Bull's problem...

The team can do as it pleases with its engines in 2026 and is happy to be independent and not have to answer to a partner or be dependent on an engine supplier. Red Bull can accept money from someone who is willing to pay to badge the engines, but it wishes to retain control. The whisper in F1 circles is that Red Bull was unimpressed by leaks about Porsche in the media as these were seen as being designed to boost the value of the Porsche IPO that will be happening in the next few weeks. This leaves Porsche in a complicated situation as it does not have the thing it needs to build F1 engines on its own. It does however want to use the sport to highlight its involvement in sustainable fuel development. The recent Audi announcement has similar problems because there is a lot to be done if Audi is to get a team competitive by 2026. And there is more politics to come within the VW empire (which owns both the Porsche and Audi brands).

Elsewhere in the car industry there is a very interesting development at Renault (which owns

Alpine) where the boss Luca de Meo is planning to revamp the whole company by making some dramatic changes. One of these is to lump together the company's traditional internal combustion businesses in a business based outside France and sell off much of the business. This will mean that Renault can claim to be an all-electric firm and he hopes that the electric side of the business, which is currently being labelled as Ampere, a similar independent firm, based in France, but with Renault keeping control, will attract more investors and the kind of valuation that Tesla has managed to achieve.

The traditional ICE business has been given the codename "Horse" and the word is that Renault will would keep only 40 percent with China's Geely taking another 40 percent and the Saudi Aramco oil company taking the remaining 20 percent.

Logically, Renault's motorsport engine design hub at Viry-Chatillon would become part of "Horse" and that would mean that the three shareholders might all be able to get hybrid F1 engines. Alpine could continue with Renault, Geely is the owner of Lotus and there is a strong argument that if one wants to expand Lotus road car sales, the best way to do it would be an F1 programme, given the heritage of the brand in the sport. And Aramco is the primary sponsor of Aston Martin Racing and wants to have an F1 engine so that it can show off its synthetic fuel programmes, and provide Aston Martin will its own brand engine...

Still, F1's relationship with China is less than easy and the Chinese are one of the problems that F1 has creating its 2023 calendar. Things are moving onwards with no resolution to the Miami and Montreal impasse, which means that F1 has to criss-cross the Atlantic twice in the spring. Monaco is still a problem and Baku is not happy about being asked to move from its June date. We know that South Africa has now dropped out of the running for 2023 because money did not arrive, that Doha is not moving to the front of the calendar (because they have demolished the pit buildings and these cannot be rebuilt in time for next spring). We know also that the British GP and Austria have switched dates in July with Silverstone on the second and Austria on the ninth. We also know that Zandvoort is taking Spa's date on August 27 and that Spa is jumping back into the calendar on July 23. But what we don't know is what happens with China as it is unclear whether the country can commit to a race because of its Covid-19 policies. At the moment, the government continues to try to maintain a zero Covid policy and in recent days has shut down the cities of Shenzhen and Chengdu. It is difficult for any sport to plan around such decisions and a string of big international events have been postponed or cancelled in recent weeks. The policies may change after the National Congress of the Chinese Communist Party, which happens only once every five years. This decides the country's leadership and thus the policies for the next five years. This happens in late October, but F1 wants a calendar before then. Once China is settled on a date, the other races can slot into the available slots.

Once that is done, the F1 group can start worrying about what to do in 2024...

One race that will be up for renegotiation is Zandvoort... which will have ended its initial three-year deal.

From a State of Confusion

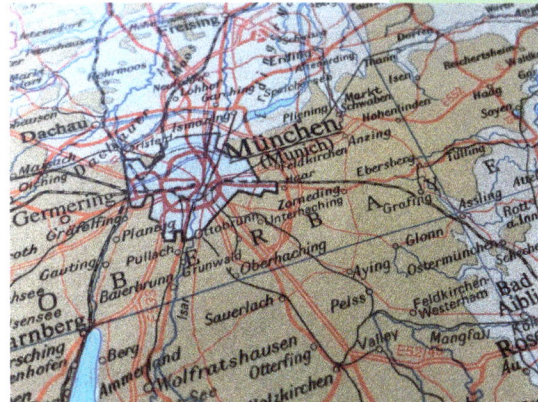

14 September 2022

The last three weeks have been a bit of a blur of European countries. I've driven close to 3,106 miles since setting off to go to Spa and in the interim I have been to various countries, including Belgium, Germany, France, the Netherlands and Italy and I've driven along the Swiss border a couple of times on the way to the Mont Blanc tunnel. Driving a lot gives one plenty of time for thought and it struck me that such travels can be very confusing for those embarking on such voyages for the first time because of the strange European habit of having cities called by different names. To use technical terms, there are toponyms (place names), but these can be endonyms (which is what the locals call a place) and exonyms (which is what other people call it). As an example, I once caught a train from Milan to go to Monaco and found myself en route to Munich. Italians call Munich Monaco, while the Germans, who should know best, call it München. Still, as the Bavarians call it Minga and the Czechs call it Mnichov one can fully understand why the Pole call the city Monachium. Still, the German called Milan Mailand – probably to get their own back.

When it comes to places like Belgium, where they have several languages, things get really confusing. The city which the English call Ghent, is Gent to the Flemish and Dutch, but Gand for the French and Walloons. Lille is Rijsel for the Flemish. And then there's Liège: the locals call it Lidje, the Flemish Luik and the Germans Luttich. If you ask a Frenchman for directions to Aix-la-Chapelle, you'll end up in Aachen, if both parties got things right, although a local will call it Oche. Antwerp is also known as Anvers and Eupen as Neau. When you cross the border to Holland (as the English call Nederland) things can become really confused as the port of Vlissingen is called Flushing by the English. If you go to den Haag, you will find some folk who call it s-Gravenhage, but the French call it La Haye. Logically the English should call it The Hedge, which is the literal translation, but they insist on The Hague. Go figure...

In motor racing there have been a few people who went to Nürnberg rather than Nürburg. This is a big mistake. Nürnberg is the German name for Nuremberg, where there is a race track called the Norisring, but Nürburg has a rather famous Ring called the Nürburgring. And if anyone mentions the Nuremberg Rallies or the Nuremberg Trials, they are not talking about motorsport events. I could go on at length about these strange habits: Styria in Austria, is Steiermark, Cologne in Germany is Köln, Trier is also known as Trèves and Napoli as Naples. The Italians call Paris Parigi, and Nice Nizza. Lakes and rivers have similar problems: Lac Léman is Lake Geneva while Lake Constance is Bodensee. The Danube is the Donau in Germany and the Duna in Hungary. Rivers, of course, pass through various countries, but what amount of arrogance is required to call a city by a name you like, rather than what the locals want you to call it? Yes, I know, in the

Polish version of Scrabble, the letter Z is worth only one point, but one can at least try to say Ostrowiec Świętokrzyski or Tomaszów Mazowiecki. Of course, there also have been bits that were once invaded and so the Aosta Valley in Italy is full of places with French names and the east of France, which has been regularly invaded by their neighbours, has lots of places with names such as Krautergersheim.

All things considered, one can get hopelessly lost in Europe, even if you follow the road signs.

All this is a bit like trying to figure out the Formula 1 calendar for 2023. Each week we try again and each week there are things that have changed – or changed back. The fleeting appearance of Prince Albert of Monaco in company with the Automobile Club de Monaco President Michel Boeri may have escaped most people because they were not trying to be noticed, while the likes of Sylvester Stallone were only too keen to be on camera. This led to reports that a deal has been struck with Monaco. At the time of writing (6pm on Wednesday), this was not true but it might easily be true by 6.05pm. Both sides want to agree terms, but neither wants to give way in the negotiations, so we get into a Liege/Luik situation. The question is not about money (at least not totally), its also about TV coverage, trackside signage, hospitality rights and track design. There is also the question of attitude at the ACM, which seems to upset most people who are not members (and some who are), although to be fair the organisers of the Italian GP at Monza also seem to think that because their race has been around a long time, they know how to organise races better than anyone else. But I guess if you want to have paddocks that smell of overflowing drains, one should follow their lead.

Anyway, the Italians have a strong tradition of complicated and slow-moving bureaucracy, although they do seem to be pretty hot when it comes to building permits. It would be useful if they turn this speed into rebuilding Monza access roads. The Formula 1 group (no less) ran into trouble this year with its plans to construct a Fan Zone behind the main grandstand at Monza. Work had to be stopped until a permit was granted and as a consequence, things were still being finished when the race meeting began. A little further down the main straight, a group of 80 Dutch fans decided on an odd idea for the famous campsite that is located next to the first chicane. They arrived from Holland (or should I say Nederland) with tents, orange shorts, flares and copious amounts of beer –and tons of scaffolding. Having staked out their plots,

they then began to build their own grandstand. This drew them to the attention of the local police and at vast speed they were ordered to disassemble their structure.

The Dutch are beginning to make the tifosi look sane and sober, although I did spot a few red flares on Sunday at Monza. The good news, however, is that Monza remains on the calendar for now, despite the encroaching Imolese... And long may that be the case. Monza is 100 years old and wonderful and should always be on the F1 calendar.

The calendar problems are caused not only by Monaco but also by the Chinese. They want to get back onto F1 calendar, but they want a date in the autumn because they are still locking down cities every so often because someone tests positive to Covid-19. The problem with this theory is that the only date available is October 8 and that is also the only date that Doha can manage because the Losail circuit is currently rebuilding its pits and cannot be ready in the spring, where it really wants to be. There is also a problem with Baku not wanting an April date – and insisting on a race in June (presumably because drains smell less at that time of year). This all means that races which can slot in anywhere are just floating about at the moment, so we don't really know what will happen with Imola and Spain until the other problems are solved.

But then we have races that want to change their dates with one another and we have had two them now with the British and Austrian GPs having agreed to switch: Austria moving to July 2, with Britain to July 9. This is something to do with tennis. The Belgian and Hungarian GPs, which were scheduled for July 23 and July 30, have also agreed to switch, in order to avoid a clash of the Belgian race with the country's National Day on July 21. This means that the annual Spa 24 Hours, scheduled for July 30, will now have to move elsewhere.

However, when you boil it all down, there is a very simple reason for the problem. There are too many pieces trying to be fitted into a complex jigsaw puzzle and it might be wise to throw a couple of pieces away so that it all fits nicely...

There seems to be a similar (but not unusual) problem of there being too many drivers for the number of available drives. The German media is spending much of its time trying to work out what will happen with Mick Schumacher and is ignoring that he has not done enough to be retained by Ferrari and thus has no real possibility at Haas, as the team is looking for an experienced driver, such as Giovinazzi or Nico Hülkenberg. There is speculation that Schumacher could sit out a year before joining Sauber when it comes under Audi ownership in 2025. The argument is that the sport needs a German driver, now that Sebastian Vettel is retiring but, if Mick had done enough, Ferrari would still be interested...

Much of the ongoing driver gossip relates to the situation at Alpine where Fernando Alonso is departing to join Aston Martin and Oscar Piastri will join McLaren. Esteban Ocon has a three-year contract until the end of 2024 and has been doing a good job, up against Alonso, but the team must now decide what to do next. Alpine boss Laurent Rossi says he is in no rush to make a decision. There are some in the team who understand that a Gasly-Ocon line-up would be too risky given the history of the two men, and Doohan is considered too risky because he needs more time to develop. Alpine had planned to put Piastri into a Williams for a year or two, but he was not interested in that and so ran off to McLaren.

Williams is not too keen on taking on those who are contracted elsewhere and so de Vries is a good fit, as he has to give up a Toyota WEC contract and a deal to race for Maserati in Formula E if he wants to be an F1 driver. Having said that, he did a great job at Monza to score points on his F1 debut, when he stepped in at the last minute for Alex Albon. If anything, this drive was the evidence (if it was ever needed) that Nicholas Latifi needs to look for other things to do in the future.

With Albon and de Vries, Williams would have a great driver pairing. Of course, the team has a young driver programme as well which could mean that American Logan Sargeant might step into F1 next year, but it would be a little early for him... The same is pretty much true at Alpine where the team has Jack Doohan keen to land the empty Alpine seat. If one was looking for ironies, it was rather extraordinary when Doohan and Sargeant tangled in the Formula 2 race on Sunday and dented one another's F1 ambitions... although to be fair, neither was really to blame.

The guy who does seem to have it all sorted is the new Aston Martin reserve driver, F2 champion-in-waiting Felipe Drugovich. Aston Martin might not be the obvious choice at the moment but Drugovich is bargaining on two things to happen: the car has to be better than this year's car (it could not be much worse) and the team's new signing Fernando Alonso and current incumbent Lance Stroll are going to produce fireworks, one way or the other, as Stroll's dad is going to run into grief whatever happens because one driver is inevitably going to be faster than the other...

The next big thing in the silly season is a private Alpine test, using an old car, in Budapest later this month. The team is not saying who is driving but it is being billed as a shootout between de Vries, Doohan, Colton Herta, and Schumacher. Whether they all appear remains to be seen.

There are some who think that the whole Colton Herta business is a giant smokescreen to keep the media amused while Porsche and Red Bull fall out of bed with one another. Without all the speculation about Gasly and Herta, the Porsche and Red Bull relationship (which looks like a fling that ran out of steam quite quickly after Red Bull met Porsche's parents) would have been front page news. Now it isn't.

The Gasly-Herta shuffle was all rather unlikely with Herta under contract to Andretti next year, only 10th in the championship this year and not the holder of a super licence. Trying to change the super licence rules makes no sense at all because F1 does not want to create precedents and undermine the structure that means that the sport has more top quality drivers than ever before.

Anyway, Porsche now needs to look at other alternatives, but these are thin on the ground. The Red Bull engine programme was always going to be a badging exercise using Red Bull Powertrains power trains and so Porsche was not going to invest in its own engine programme. The obvious thing now, if Porsche really does still want to join F1, would be to work with Audi and share technology with Audi, which is already publicly committed to F1 in 2026 but it has been working on the programme for some time and has laid the groundwork for such a project, by buying dynos and doing a (supposedly secret) deal with Sauber. Porsche has done some design studies into F1 engines, but there is a big difference between building prototypes and manufacturing competitive engines.

There are good reasons for Porsche to want to be involved in F1, specifically because of the firm's interest in synthetic fuels, which F1 will adopt. Sharing technology between different brands makes total sense in the modern automotive world where it happens all the time between sister brands. The two brands already share a couple of automotive "platforms" in an effort to save money... However, things will go quiet for a while now until the Porsche IPO is out of the way.

The Renault group is also likely to share its F1 engine platform in the years ahead, or at least it is open to do so. The firm's own brand is Alpine and there are big plans to develop this into a wider technology firm. I hear that Viry-Châtillon, where Renault designs and develops its F1 engines, will not be hived off into or other of the planned production power unit divisions (known as Horse and Ampere) but will stay as part of the expanding Alpine unit. However, Renault is happy to share its technology with the new partners in Horse – Geely, the Chinese firm that owns Lotus – and Aramco, the oil company that is in bed with Aston Martin with the plan to build engines together.

Elsewhere, I hear that Alfa Romeo bods have been banging on the door at Haas, offering the team the same deal that Sauber has had, which is sponsorship to go with a Ferrari engine. I am not sure that this will happen because I also hear that there is a massive title sponsorship deal coming soon for Haas from a big American corporation, which will fund the team for at least the next three seasons and perhaps beyond that. One can only guess who this will be but I don't believe it is a OEM.

Alfa Romeo's parent Stellantis (the merged PSA Peugeot-Fiat Chrysler with a fancy marketing name) has a lot of shareholders in common with Ferrari. The Ferrari President John Elkann is also President of Stellantis and so one can imagine some badge engineering going with Ferrari technology as well, which makes sense. Alfa Romeo is being pushed upmarket by Stellantis and is aiming to make a dent in the luxury sporting market sector, taking on BMWs, Audis and Mercedes. Cynics may say that trying to crash into that market might dent Alfa Romeo more than it dents to market. But if there was a real (pretend) F1 programme, it might help. Who know what will happen? Car company executives are a strange breed (based on some of the characters who have gone before). Experience has taught me that quite often, when someone expresses confidence in someone else, it usually means that they have no confidence at all and that the person is about to be ousted.

Thus, if I were Mattia Binotto, I might be looking over my shoulder because Ferrari chairman John Elkann felt the need before of Monza to say that: "We have great faith in Mattia Binotto". Given that Ferrari screw-ups this year have not been in short supply, and Max Verstappen is in a situation where he can win the World Championship in Singapore, if I were Binotto, I would be taking occasional glances in the mirror to make sure no-one with an axe is anywhere close.

But then again, maybe Elkann is different…

Right, I'm off to Parigi…

From the Dead Sea

29 September 2022

No, it's true, I'm not visiting the Dead Sea, at least not THAT Dead Sea. However, not far from where I live in Normandy there is a place called Mortemer, which in English means Dead Sea... The name comes from the Middle Ages when, I guess, the valley in question was a worthless flooded marsh. Then someone worked out how to drain the place and soon there were fish-filled ponds and a rather grand Cistercian Abbey was constructed.

England's King Henry I liked the area (he was also the Duke of Normandy) and came often to hunt. Alas one day he ate too many nasty-looking fish called lampreys in a village nearby and shuffled off his regal coil. His funeral procession went from there to Reading in Berkshire – which was quite an achievement in 1185...

Anyway, to sum up the next 850 years in two sentences: the monks had a grand old time until they were massacred by French revolutionaries, at which point the abbey became a splendid ruin and the murdered monks haunted the place enthusiastically. There is even a story of a ghostly monk emerging from the forests to guide a downed RAF man to (relative) safety in World War II.

I could go on telling stories about the area for a while yet, but you have come to this blog to read of motor racing and so we must wind our way down the valley of the stream they call the Fouillebroc to the village of Lisors.

Until recently, one of the locals used to fly a Red Bull Racing flag in his (or her) garden, although I never stopped to ask why there was such passion for the Austrian fizzy drink team. Perhaps the home belongs to a Pierre Gasly fan, as the AlphaTauri driver comes from Rouen, just 20 miles to the west. Jean-Eric Vergne (once a Red Bull driver) is also quite local, having grown up 30 miles to the east, while Esteban Ocon, who has never been blessed with Red Bull cash, spent his childhood in Evreux, 35 miles to the south-west. So, the point I am trying to make here is that this is racing country, at least in the modern era. Obviously it isn't far either from the old home of the French Grand Prix at Rouen Les Essarts.

One could also mention that Dieppe is not far away (to the north) but that might get us into a discussion about whether it is a good idea to pair Gasly and Ocon at Alpine in 2023... which seems to be under intense discussion in Alpineland. The duo were best buddies when they were eight, but fell out at the age of about 12 and have been rivals ever since. There are scandalous tales of family punch-ups and the like, although I don't know if these are true, but there is obviously a risk of trouble (or at least disunity) if Alpine decides to go fully Norman.

Those who don't know might argue that the French will choose French drivers because the apocryphal Monsieur Chauvin (after whom chauvinism was named) came from France, but when one looks closely at the Alpine team it is about as French as an Eccles Cake, with Otmar Szafnauer being a Romanian who grew up in Detroit and the only French words that are widely known at Enstone are "bonjour" and "merde". We will see soon enough what Alpine decides. Last week the team held a private test in Hungary for Nyck de Vries, Antonio Giovinazzi and Jack Doohan, although the tub-thumpers in the French media continue to insist that Gasly is the man.

Anyway, back to Lisors... It's a picturesque spot with a village green, a duck pond and a pretty church. Beside the church is an old farm from where one can buy proper old school charcuterie. It is not exactly a motorsport mecca... except that Lisors is also the home of the Circuit de Grosse Haie, or the Big Hedge Circuit if you wish to ruin the romance and translate the words into English.

This, however, is a good description of the circuit, because it really is hidden behind a very big hedge.

This is the home track of the Auto Rodeo Club of Lisors (ARCL) and for years I've been meaning to go along to see what happens behind the hedge. The other day, seeing that they had an event and I was not in Russia (as had once been planned) we paid €7 a head to go and see whatever action there was to be found. It's not that I was missing racing after two weekends off – an F1 calendar these days gives one plenty of races to watch – but rather it was out of curiosity.

Every now and then, I think it is good to go and see something other than F1... to remind oneself that there is more to the sport than Grand Prix racing. F1 is sometimes a place that floats along on its own cloud, up where the cuckoos fly, and it has been a while since I went to a local hillclimb, or to a minor formula race. If nothing else, it reminds one that the sport is about passion.

The racing, it said on the sign in front of the hedge, was "Fun-Cars". The track, I knew from Google Earth, was a basic 600 metres of wiggly dirt, although

I hadn't realised that the surface of the circuit was actually embedded into the landscape, so that the cars were basically racing along between walls of earth. This made spectating a bit of a challenge, but it was clear that it was pretty safe as getting a car to jump out of "the ditch" would be quite an achievement.

To be quite honest, the first impression was not great. These were not the shiny and polished machinery that one is used to seeing at Grands Prix. Far from it. Most of them looked like real wrecks with much-beaten metal panels daubed with whatever paint might have come to hand. The only sponsorship came from the local butcher and similar such establishments.

But, after watching a string of five-lap heats in quick succession, the conclusion was that Fun-Car lived up to its name. It was not about composites, aerodynamics and tyre compounds. It was all about tuning up an engine, sticking it into what at some point used to be a car and then going racing, fiddling with the suspension a little to make the machine ride the bumps – and then just going for it. In theory contact is frowned upon, but in reality the cars were bouncing off one another all the time, and most of them bore the scars of their fights (and the subsequent repairs).

What I can say beyond that is that if there was any paddock gossip behind the big hedge, it certainly wasn't about F1.

On to Singapore...

From Manila

4 October 2022

It's four in the morning and it's already Christmas in Manila. OK, that seems a little odd in October, but the decorations are up and the halls of the darkened airport are decked with boughs of holly. There are no bells jingling, no children listening, nor any treetops glistening and if there are snowmen somewhere, they will not be frosty because it is too damned hot.

Still, this is an eccentric part of the world. On the flight across the South China Sea from Singapore, the plane passed over the much-disputed Spratly Islands, which multiple countries wish to control, presumably because they find it useful to have unlimited supplies of guano (excrement of seabirds). The Chinese have even built some air bases so that they will have squadrons of fighters ready to be scrambled, to defend their guano from evil foreign invaders.

We live in a bizarre world at the moment. In the airport in Manila there are kiosks selling food (cash only) which include several culinary crimes against humanity: croissants with sausages inside them and pizzas topped with roast beef and bacon (together). Yet no-one here seems to be perturbed by such atrocities. They would prefer to argue over guano.

For reasons that I cannot quite explain, Manila reminded me of a sinister American counter-insurgency expert called Edward G Lansdale, about whom I studied many years ago. Lansdale was a man of his era, convinced that Communists wanted to rule the world and he was intent on stopping them. In his quest to discombobulate the Reds, he effectively invented psychological warfare, using local superstitions and folklore tales to terrify anyone who was supporting communist rebels in the Philippines. He did have some odd ideas, including flying quiet planes over rebel areas on cloudy days, with loudspeakers blasting out curses in the Tagalog language to convince the locals that the gods were unhappy with them. He had teams of graffiti artists who went out at night and painted evil eyes on the walls of houses belonging to supporters of the rebels.

My particular favourite was when he discovered the legend of the aswang, a blood-drinking vampire-like creature that lived in the forests of Luzon. He decided it would be good to liquidate a few captured rebels, drain their blood and make holes in their necks, and by doing so convince others not to go into the forests...

At one point, however, he went a little far when he suggested that they could simulate the second coming, using phosphorous flares to create celestial light, in order to show the god-less locals that Christianity was the right path. He was sent into retirement in La-La Land.

Still, Lansdale had a point. In South East Asia some of the people believe some very odd things (such as the Spratly Islands having any value).

It rained rather a lot in Singapore on Sunday night, delaying the start of the Grand Prix. It was the first time that this had happened in the history of the race, despite the fact that it has been going since 2008 and is always held in the typhoon season, when there is rarely a day without a big storm. My source for the following story is highly reliable, but I will leave it to you decide if it is credible. The Singapore Grand Prix, so they say, employed a local witch doctor to cast spells to ensure that rain did not fall when the races were on. Along came the pandemic and Singapore disappeared from F1 for three years. When the race was revived this year, the Grand Prix called up the witch doctor and discovered that the old fellow had gone to the great witch surgery in the sky and so a new witch doctor was required. A suitable replacement was found but no-one was quite sure if his magic would work. It didn't.

If you don't believe a word of this, I am not surprised, but while researching the idea I did stumble on the fact that there is a shopping mall in Singapore, called the Fu Lu Shou Complex, which specialises in mystical and magical products. I also read a wonderful story of a Singaporean lady called Bambi, who says that she earns $50,000 a month casting spells, selling haunted dolls, reading tarot cards and making candles in the form of genitalia, which are popular because they are supposed to aid reproduction when you light them.

Perhaps she could earn more if she bundled the candles with bottles of Champagne as candlelight and bubbles have often worked in these matters in the past...

F1 seems to be in the thrall of Asia at the moment (probably because the travelling circus is currently over there) and the paddock in Singapore was a busy place – when it was not raining. The topics were much as normal, although there was the added conundrum of whether Dietrich Mateschitz, the force behind Red Bull, was dead (as some insisted), or whether he was still alive and people (for reasons unknown) were trying to hide this fact. I honestly cannot see why anyone would want to do that, but there is no question that the sources were at odds. This would probably amuse Mateschitz (in the past or present tense) because he always liked to be rather secretive.

Th paddock had a few visitors with ambitions to run Formula 1 races in the future (which is not unusual). The most interesting for me was the delegation from Osaka. For those who don't know the difference between Fukui and Fukuoka, or that Kyoto is an anagram of Tokyo, it is best to say that Osaka is 500 miles to the west of Tokyo, on the shores of the Inland Sea. If you take the fastest Shinkansen "bullet train" (known as the Nozomi) it takes two and a half hours to travel the 300 miles or so between the two cities. Osaka is either the second or third largest city in Japan, depending on your interpretation of the country's complicated administrative boundaries.

Anyway, race fans will know that the home of F1 in Japan is Suzuka, the Honda-owned circuit located close to Ise Bay, south of Nagoya, which is between Tokyo and Osaka. Pretty much everyone likes Suzuka and it has always had a big crowd, although it is not an easy place to get to. F1 currently has a contract to continue to race there until the end of 2024 and will probably stay longer if Honda decides to remain active in F1. The Formula 1 group, however, might prefer somewhere else. The Japanese GP has been held at Mount Fuji in the past but this is prone to torrential rain and equally difficult to access. And neither venue is "a destination city".

Osaka is.

In 2025, the city will host the World Expo on an artificial island, called Yumeshima (literally "Dream Island"). The plans allow for 285,000 visitors a day, with a new station linked to the Osaka Metro. The big question is what happens to the site after the Expo. In recent days, MGM Resorts International has announced that it has agreement to develop Yumeshima into "an integrated resort" which will include three hotels, a casino, convention and exhibition space, banqueting halls, entertainment venues and so on. This will cost $9 billion and will aim to attract millions of visitors each year. It was interesting to see a number of people from the Osaka Convention & Tourism Bureau turning up in Singapore to discuss putting a circuit on the island. One of them even had a business card which said: 'F1 Business Development Manager".

Those who know about MGM might leap to the conclusion that this could all be linked to the ongoing F1 project in Las Vegas, but I am told it is a pure coincidence...

Talking of Vegas, F1 will soon be able to reveal its plans for its pit and paddock development in the city. It all seems quite impressive and I am told the big push will be to promote the facilities as being the most technologically-advanced building in the world. What this means is not entirely clear at the moment but it is certain to include unprecedented

– Joe Saward's 2022 Green Notebook –

levels of resource efficiency and intelligent features. This will be a useful promotional tool for the sport. I am told that it will not only be sustainable but will be so efficient that it will balance all emissions created during construction and even, perhaps, in the manufacturing of all materials required for the construction. It is all good for F1's sustainability programmes, although until the sport counts the emissions produced by spectators on their way to and from the track, it is all a bit airy-fairy. From what I hear, there will be a covered paddock, between the pit buildings and the team offices, and there will be bridges linking the two, so that VIPs can swan around without getting in the way as much as they currently do. The pit building will also feature a huge F1 logo, which will be flat on the roof, this will use dynamic digital illumination techniques to promote F1 day and night as it will visible from all planes going into and out of the airport. The facilities will include some form of permanent F1 exhibition space that will aim to draw visitors all through the year, helping to promote the sport and generate revenues at the same time.

Stefano Domenicali has been particularly busy in recent weeks with rumoured trips to Panama and Seoul. Both are interesting prospects. Panama is looking for ways to rebuild its tourist industry, which used to attract 2.5 million visitors a year but managed only 1.2 million in 2021.

Seoul is a great idea as well, although F1's history in Korea is not brilliant following the hopeless Korean Grand Prix, which was held in the marshes of Mokpo, 250 miles from the capital on the country's west coast. The idea was to build a city around the circuit and generate a tourist industry for the whole region. It was an expensive failure and the race stopped after four years. But Korea remains a big player in the global car industry, ranking fifth in automobile production behind China, the USA, Japan and India, but ahead of Germany. There is a new president who seems keen to use sport to promote the country and is currently bidding for the Asian Cup soccer competition in 2023, which was to be in China but was dumped by the Chinese because of the pandemic. Seoul has also recently played host to Formula E although few noticed that this was happening. Still, there is huge potential to build an Albert Park-like track in public parkland alongside the Hangang river, with easy access to the city's mass transit system. This is now a vital element in all new races because spectator emissions are a problem for all sports to which people drive. Mass transit systems are good. Cars are bad. Or that is the theory at the moment.

The failure of the South African GP to deliver the goods has led to new thinking in Africa. Kyalami is the only permanent track that is up to anything close to F1 standards, but there is the possibility of temporary or semi-permanent tracks in Johannesburg. It is worth noting that there were some street races in Soweto in 2008 and 2009 and these were followed by a number of F1 demonstration runs dating back to 2014 when Ferrari ran a big street event in Soweto with Marc Gené driving an old Ferrari F60 to the delight of thousands of spectators. Soweto is now quite a chic place and one of the primary tourist areas in Johannesburg. The district where the Ferrari demonstration took place is next to the FNB Stadium, alongside the Johannesburg Expo Centre, which might be a great venue, along the lines of the track at the Hard Rock Stadium in Miami.

There was a pleasant brunch involving Saudi Arabian GP figures and they were keen to discuss whatever we wanted to talk about, which provided some interesting discussion about the goings-on in the Saudi consulate in Istanbul a while ago, plus discussions about Houti missiles and the explosion on the Paris-Dakar Rally. This is actually a pretty good thing because talking about problems and perceptions in an open fashion is a step in the right direction. The Saudi Arabian Grand Prix, by the way, is likely to remain in Jeddah until 2028 because although work is progressing on the construction of a new circuit at Qiddiya, near Riyadh, and the recent announcement of a contract with MotoGP (without mention of a date or a venue), the aim is to bring the races to Qiddiya when the whole city is finished, because no-one wants to go racing on a building site.

There were a couple of big TV announcements in Singapore, notably about Sky renewing its deals in all three of its F1 markets: Britain, Germany and Italy. There was less coverage given to a deal that will see China Telecom acquiring the streaming rights for F1 in China for the remainder of the 2022 Formula 1 season. Chinese interest in F1 has not grown much despite the fact that my namesake Guanyu Zhou has had a promising first season, albeit hobbled somewhat by Alfa Romeo's unreliability. Without that, he and Valtteri Bottas would have looked a great deal better. Although the Chinese Grand Prix is on the calendar for 2023, you would be hard-pressed to find anyone who thinks it will happen. Much will depend on what happens with the 20th National Congress of the Chinese Communist Party, which is due to begin in Beijing on October 16. This will likely grant President Xi Jinping a third term as leader, but it will give him the opportunity to surround himself with new people and perhaps some new policies. The new leadership will set the tone for the country's foreign relations and will make decisions regarding China's Covid-19 policy. These might impact on F1 if Xi continues to make belligerent noises about Taiwan (and the Spratly Islands, for that matter), but it might also result in the race shifting from Shanghai to Beijing. The two cities are constantly trying to outdo one another (in the tradition of Sydney and Melbourne) and that would be a big win for Beijing. The word is that Xi would like to have a night race in the capital.

There was more Chinese news in the days before the Singapore race as Geely took a 7.6 percent stake in Aston Martin Lagonda, the troubled car company that Lawrence Stroll is trying to promote using the Aston Martin F1 team. This was yet another refinancing of a firm that Stroll keeps saying is fully-funded. It seems like there is some kind of hole in the bottom of the Aston Martin bucket because money just keeps draining away. Saudi Arabia's Public Investment Fund now owns 18.7 percent of the business, while Stroll's Yew Tree owns 19 percent.

There was some discussions about the F1 driver market but as things stand it looks like Alpine will soon announce that it has signed Pierre Gasly to partner Esteban Ocon. The team will probably have Jack Doohan as the reserve driver in 2023. Scuderia AlphaTauri is expected to take Nyck de Vries in place of Gasly. Williams is still working on a deal for Formula 2 driver Logan Sargeant, while Haas says it has not decided anything but the rumours suggest that Nico Hulkenberg is being considered as Kevin Magnussen's team-mate. Daniel Ricciardo looks set for a reserve driver role at Mercedes.

An awful lot of waffle was flying around about the Cost Cap with spin doctors doing their thing to stir up the media into a feeding frenzy on the subject. The message being peddled was that two teams have broken the cost cap limits for 2021 – and there was plenty of speculation about the FIA might do about it. The aim of all this seems to have been to make sure that topic remains in the spotlight so that it cannot be brushed swiftly beneath the carpet. The rules are actually fairly clear about what constitutes a breach and what the range of penalties there can be.

The vagueness of the penalties is something that can cause trouble and it might be wiser if the FIA rid itself of the uncertainty of the sanctions and simply introduced a system similar to some American sports, where there are spending restrictions in order to stop big teams spending too much. Teams ARE allowed to overspend but are then subject to a so-called "luxury tax", which is basically a surcharge when a team exceeds the allowable limits. This is usually a multiple of the amount overspent (perhaps three or five times the overspend) and this money is then put into a pot and divided up between the guilty team's rivals. It is a neat solution but, of course, it does not much matter if you are a team without any restrictions on spending.

Some of the more eccentric media have billed the matter as an attempt by interested parties to rearrange the result of the 2021 World Championship to allow Lewis Hamilton to win. I cannot say I believe a word of that – and it would be a very bad idea because some might then like to ask questions about other dubious championship outcomes in the history of the sport. Similarly, one does not want too much digging around about back room deals because that might leave a number of teams red-faced from past adventures.

If that was the thinking behind Cost Cap Gate, or whatever it is being called, then Edward G Lansdale would be proud of the spin doctors involved. Still, it's not Christmas, is it? So don't expect any such presents in the days ahead.

We have to get through the horrors of Halloween first.

From the Rapi:t

13 October 2022

Travelling in Japan is never dull, but the more you do it, the easier it becomes: you know where to go, and what to expect. For many in the F1 world, travelling in Japan means taking a train because it is more efficient (and cheaper) than chauffeurs or hire cars. This often means that one visits the station at Shiroko, which is on the Kintetsu Line, between Nagoya and Osaka. You then take the train in whichever direction you require, changing to the Tokaido Shinkansen at Nagoya, if you want to go to Tokyo.

The trick at Shiroko is to buy a ticket on a Limited Express. When you first hear that, you think that the Limited Express may not be as fast as an Express, but the reality is the opposite. The Limited Express is faster because the number of stops is limited.

It is one of those funny quirks one has to learn...

The ticket tells you all you need to know: exactly where you should sit, the departure and arrival times and the price. Japanese trains are never late and so you can get off with confidence at the station you want, based on the time on the ticket. In 37 years of visiting the country I've only ever been on one train that was late, which is something that railway workers in other countries really ought to consider.

Anyway, 90 minutes after the Kintetsu Limited Express for Osaka leaves Shiroko, it pulls into Namba station. The Tannoy plays some soothing music and a female voice says: "Namba desu", which translates as "This is Namba".

What she does not tell you is that Namba is not one station, but rather six, all linked by underground tunnels, escalators and stairways, with a multi-storey department store called Takashimaya and shopping malls called Namba Parks, Namba City and Namba SkyO, each of which have multiple levels. The result is a labyrinth that would warm the heart of even the most cold-hearted of moles. Somewhere in these tunnels you can find almost everything that a modern urban dweller could possibly want. Of course, for a gaijin (the word that the Japanese use for "foreigners" – although I have also seen it translated as "alien", which I much prefer) it can be a little overwhelming. This is to be expected if one comes from a world where stations are two-dimensional and trains line up side-by-side from Platform 1 to Platform 9 ¾.

Japan is not like that.

Perhaps you have heard of the Dutch artist MC Escher, who made the initials MC cool long before Mr Hammer (aka Stanley Burrell) rapped on the door of Celebrityville and they let him in. Escher created drawings of buildings that were impossible but looked right, using tricks with perspective. Escher may have designed Namba Station. The weird thing about it is that it becomes more complex the more you know about it. It is often flooded with streams of busy people, who all seem to know where they are going and who all seem to be travelling without any luggage. However, if one follows the signs and keeps calm it is not so bad. Trying to explain it to others is more complicated than teaching a German to understand the rules of cricket, but when you get to know Namba, you realise that it is quite brilliant. In Japan they don't have grimy railway arches, with lock-up garages inhabited by dubious folk. They have shiny shopping malls.

The goal when navigating Osaka Namba is usually to get to the Nankai Railway's Rapi:t service, which is an evil-looking train, which goes from Namba to Kansai International Airport (otherwise known as KIX). It is retro and at the same time futuristic. In fact, it looks like Darth Vader after he has fallen into a pot of dark metallic blue paint (which looks a little purple in some lights). It is fast and very convenient, although perhaps I should add that the name is pronounced "rapido" not "rapit" for reasons that were probably logical to Japanese people 30 years ago when Darth Train first rolled his wheels.

It has been three years since we were last in Japan and it seemed initially that a great deal had changed. The rush hour no longer seemed very rushed. Trains were half-empty. People were saying at home more. The whole place seemed a little unkempt and run down. Everyone was wearing masks, even if they are no longer compulsory. Without the bustle, Osaka seemed to be lacking energy, and I felt the same way when I got to Suzuka. There were still the eccentric fans (of course) but the Paddock did not have the zing one is used to. I couldn't work out why this was until a chance remark from someone in the F1 group came like a bolt of lightning. The problem at Suzuka was that Suzuka hasn't changed from three year ago. And F1 has. There are times when the endless throbbing music in the Paddock can get on your nerves, but it is energising. Suzuka had none of that energy. The other point I discovered is that Suzuka may not feel like a small event, but it is.

The media who attended the race were few in number, because of restrictions entering the country, but there was nothing to stop the Japanese fans buying tickets. The place seemed pretty full, but then you realise that the grandstands are concentrated in the same area and so it feels crowded, but the numbers do not bear out that impression. To give you an idea, the three-day attendance figures in recent months have been Canada (338,000), Silverstone (401,000), Austria (303,000), France (200,000), Hungary (290,000), Belgium (360,000), the Netherlands (305,000), Italy (336,000) and Singapore (302,000).

In Japan, with no reduced capacity and no requirement to wear masks outdoors, the total was only 190,000 over three days. Despite this, there were some pretty awful traffic jams during the weekend. It probably did not help that during the three pandemic years Suzuka Circuit Motopia, the amusement park alongside the track was closed. In an effort to cut down costs, the hotel at the track closed many of its facilities and quite a lot of rooms were demolished, which meant that people had to find alternative accommodation.

The whole complex is owned by Honda and while they are keen on F1 – particularly as they are winning the championship this year with Red Bull, it is clear that Suzuka is a pretty rural place. There are paddy fields between the houses and even stretches of open land, which is rare indeed on the flat in Japan.

Anyway, access to Suzuka is difficult and even if everyone loves it, the track is not keeping up with the way F1 is developing and while there are no serious rivals among the other Japanese circuits, there may soon be rivals because Japanese cities are waking up to the idea of hosting F1 races as a way of reviving visitor numbers (as noted in the last Green Notebook). It seems like Osaka is not the only city interested, and outside Japan there are a string of projects across Asia, all hoping to become part of the F1 circus – and willing to buy a stack of gambling chips to be allowed to sit at the F1 table. In many ways, this is a good thing because it means that F1 can be a little bit more choosy and more demanding. They can get more money and facilities they want to fit requirements, such as public transportation, which is now something essential for F1 as it seeks to be carbon neutral. The biggest problem for any sporting event these days is how people get to the venue. The crowd numbers mentioned above are only impressive if the fans all travel on mass transportation systems (or bicycles). F1 may be designed to sell cars, but it does not want people to use them…

In any case, the great circuits of old, the classic venues are not really fit-for-purpose these days. Monaco, Montreal, Albert Park, Singapore, Mexico, Zandvoort and even Baku are good. Monza, Suzuka and Barcelona do have railways that pass nearby (although the capacity is small in all cases). The Middle East tracks do not attract many spectators, but places like Silverstone, Austria, Paul Ricard, Spa,

Hockenheim, the Hungaroring and the Nürburgring are not much good. Such places can survive (perhaps) if they buy great chunks of Amazonia and do not cut down the trees, or they can do what Le Mans did and convince the local authorities to put in mass transit systems, but they need to do a lot in other respects to remain interesting.

One of the big talking points after the Japanese GP was that of recovery vehicles. It is not really surprising given that in 2014 Jules Bianchi died after colliding with a tractor at Suzuka. Recovery vehicles frequently share the track with racing cars when a race is running behind a Safety Car (as was the case in Suzuka) but this also requires the drivers to act in a responsible manner if they are not in the peloton behind the Safety Car. So, normally this would not be a problem. But if conditions are difficult and visibility poor, it is not a good idea to send out tractors until everyone is moving slowly.

After Bianchi's accident, the FIA appointed a panel to look at how to avoid the problem again. This was chaired by former F1 engineer Peter Wright, then the President of the Safety Commission. The panel, which produced a 396-page report, included Ross Brawn, Stefano Domenicali, Eduardo de Freitas and GPDA President Alex Wurz. They concluded that "it is imperative" to prevent a car ever hitting a service vehicle and made a number of recommendations, including avoiding races taking place during local rainy seasons. Their ultimate conclusion, however, was that the blame for the accident rested with Bianchi because he was driving too fast. There were many changes made after that crash, including the introduction of the Virtual Safety Car, but it was only good fortune that avoided a similar scenario in Suzuka this year.

So, it was correct to punish Pierre Gasly for exceeding 125 mph on "multiple occasions" and 155 on one occasion, but it is clear that other solutions must be found to stop any possibility of it happening again. The use of the red flag has increased in F1 (and it is not always popular) but the drivers have said that there should be no risk of such a thing happening in the future, which could increase the number of red flags. One understands why drivers want to minimise risk, but then watching them racing in those early laps after the restart (when they could see almost nothing) does make you wonder about their self-preservation instincts. It is a thorny question. However, it is safe to say that using big heavy tractors in such conditions is not smart. Using cranes is not really the solution because that adds to the risks for circuit workers and one might argue that perhaps the best idea is to not race at Suzuka in October. Still, there is little we can do to control the weather, unless we have indoor Grands Prix. Now there's an idea…

It is, of course, easy to blame the FIA for everything. This is the usual fall back position for folk who don't really understand the federation. To be fair, this attitude betrays a basic ignorance of what the FIA is and why things are happening. People do not understand how much work goes into trying to ensure that everything is safe, balanced, easy-to-understand and consistent. It is a real Sisyphean task and some might even suggest that anyone wanting to do it has masochistic tendencies (let's not dwell on that too much…), but it is a job that needs to be done, and it is not easy. Could it be done better? Of course, one can always improve things. That concept is at the very heart of F1 thinking, but so much depends on the people involved. Those who say that F1 should break away from the FIA and regulate itself (and few intelligent people in the teams do) simply do not understand what it takes. There are lots of people who think they know the answers, but many of their solutions have been tried before and are not used because they do not work. The idea of having a permanent steward is one such concept. That was tried and within a year teams were complaining about bias. Having a lot of different stewards meant that few knew all the rules and few had experience which is why the system of having a small pool of stewards in constant discussion is the best idea. There are of course differences of opinion, but that is normal among any group of referees.

Quite often, those who criticise do not even know the difference between the Race Director and the Stewards. They are not the same thing and have very different roles.

There was enormous confusion at the end of the Japanese Grand Prix about whether or not Max Verstappen has done enough to win the World Championship. Neither he, nor the Red Bull Racing team, was certain and for around 15 minutes after the chequered flag was waved no-one really knew. There were a string of different issues that caused this to happen. The first point is that new regulations were introduced this year, following the Belgian Grand Prix debacle last season. However, these changes were not included in the 2022 FIA Formula 1 Sporting Regulations at the start of the year, and did not appear until the end of April when "Issue 6 "of the rules was published. So you needed the right rulebook…

Secondly, you needed to remember that there were points awarded for the last four races, (thus a maximum of 104 points for four wins and four fastest laps) but a lot of folk forgot that one can also score points this year in the one remaining Sprint race...

And then there was the question of how many points should be awarded for the Suzuka race. Logically, there was a new sliding scale to cover various lengths of race. But these were ultimately irrelevant because the wording meant that if a race was red-flagged and then restarted, the event would be for full points – even if it lasted for only three laps without a Safety Car. So, the scales of points in the later version of the rulebook were all irrelevant because the race ended under a chequered flag (as opposed to a red one) because the time limit was reached. The Japanese GP ran to only 52 percent of the planned distance, but the wording meant that full points had to be awarded because the race had resumed after a red flag and had not ENDED under a red flag. This makes no sense at all, but it is what the rules say. How did that happen? Well, writing rules is not easy because one needs to imagine every possible scenario and if you miss something that could happen, you can be left with your trousers round your ankles. One must consider not only what the rules say, but also what they do not say.

So, yes, one can blame the FIA for a rule that did not cover what happened in Suzuka, although it should perhaps be added that the person who wrote the rule (whoever it was) has probably already gone from the federation because there has been a great deal of change since Mohammed Ben Sulayem was elected to the post of FIA President in December last year. Matters were not helped by the fallout from Abu Dhabi 2021, then the Ukraine Crisis, not to mention some fairly serious internal political battles within the FIA, not just between the old and the new. The new people who have been brought in since the change are still finding their feet, and not every call they have made has been right, nor has the federation communicated things well.

Rome wasn't built in a day and you cannot rebuild Rome in a day. Change is afoot but in the interim there is a state of flux that needs time to calm down. The signs are that there will be a new more egalitarian and sensible FIA in a year or so, but there must first be a vigorous flushing out of bureaucrats that Jean Todt loved to have around him. In my experience, most of the people who work for the federation in F1 (with a few exceptions) are very competent and work hard. They care about what they do. The stewards do it for free, but they are always working amongst themselves to make things better. They are constantly slighted and disrespected by almost everyone. They are an easy target.

When it comes to decisions about the F1 rules these days, most of them are made in close consultation with the teams. The budget cap rules took an age to finalise with all the legal people from the teams involved at every stage. The reason that the penalties are vague is that this is what it took to get the agreement through. The cost cap is an essential element for F1 and one which will bear fruit for the teams in the years ahead, but it is an agreement that still has some sharp edges that need to be rounded off. Like most things in life, a little time and work is required to get a perfect fit. And in case you wish to fire off accusations that I am defending the governing body because I am worried about keeping my permanent F1 pass, you can get lost. I'm simply trying to explain why things are difficult and how they came to be as they are.

The key point about the financial regulations is that they are doing what they were intended to do. Yes, there are some discussions about how Red Bull has defined certain things – and these have been creative. But if you look at the Mercedes AMG Petronas financial returns for 2021 which show that revenues rose from £355 million to £388 million, from additional F1 "prize money" and from additional sponsorship, which comes because the sport is growing. The team dropped its spending from £325 million to just under £300 million, reflecting the new budget cap rules despite an increase in the number of races. This meant that the design and engineering staff had to drop from 906 to 831 as the team sought to be more efficient. Some were redeployed in other parts of the empire, some took early-retirement, I believe. This meant that not only did Mercedes not have to put any money into the team (which makes it a slam dunk to keep going because of the value F1 brings (internally and externally) for the team. It also meant that the team made a profit of £68 million, a big hike. This meant that there was money to buy the land on which the factory is located from previous owner Adrian Reynard, thus removing rental costs in the future. This is why teams now have huge valuations and that the sport is so healthy. Anyone who is serious about getting into F1 needs to make an offer to an existing team that is impossible to refuse. There are a few teams that are overly laden with debt and need more cash, others where circumstances are changing. There is very little logic in starting a new team because it will cost more to get it to a competitive state than it will if one buys an existing team. There is a lot of delusional thinking going on amongst those who think they should be allowed to have entries. In many ways, they are being protected from themselves, just as the super licence rules exist as they do to stop people who are unqualified for the role of being an F1 driver being allowed to come in an embarrassing themselves.

Anyway, the driver market is all but done now and attention is beginning to turn to what could happen in 2024. Alpine has taken the plunge with two French drivers who have not always got on in the past. Time will tell if this is wise but I am told that, in an effort to keep friction to a minimum, both drivers have been informed that they can have family at only two events a year, and that the two families cannot attend the same races...

We have just two drives to settle (for now): the second Williams (which must wait until Abu Dhabi because of licence questions) and the second Haas, which will probably be announced in Austin, where Haas has a big event planned to reveal a new sponsor. It would be logical to name the second driver then...

From Jolly Cemetary

26 October 2022

Yes, I know that's not how you spell cemetery, but what can you do? That's the way it is. Mr Dunkin didn't know how to spell doughnuts, but that didn't stop money being made. Planet Earth somehow manages to keep on turning despite bad spelling and stray apostrophes. Whoever created the sign for this particular boneyard (see below), maybe 150 years ago, was rather better at carving than he was at spelling.

Jolly Cemetary is so-named not because it is a happy place (except perhaps at Halloween) but rather because it is in a place called Jollyville. Now you might think that this would mean it ought to be called Jollyville Cemetary, but a little research revealed why this is not the case. I assumed that Jollyville was a scenic place with a name derived from the French language, as "jolie" means "pretty", but I discovered that it is actually named after a former Confederate soldier from Tennessee named John Jolly.

He was looking for somewhere quiet to live after the war and found a large chunk of land in the middle of nowhere, away from humankind. The land was next to a trail that headed north and there were some passers-by and so he built a general store and opened a forge. Later he gave some of his land to build a school and a graveyard which was named after him, while the settlement became known as Jollyville. The trail became the Jollyville Road and went on to become US Highway 183, although it went nowhere interesting through Texas, Oklahoma, Kansas and Nebraska before stopping in a one horse town in South Dakota.

These days, Jollyville has been swallowed up the voracious city of Austin but the greedy hoteliers in the city have forced anyone without a trust fund to leave town and seek refuge in over-priced dives in the suburbs.

Until the 1960s, Jollyville was barely a village. It was quiet, a place with horse ranches and pecan plantations and plenty of old oak trees. Today it is very different and developers have made piles of money building houses. The area boasts a rather odd area where the streets are name after English things: there is Heathrow Drive, Shakespearean Way, Sherwood Forest and I even found Downing St.

The reason I know all this is because the dive in which we stayed backed on to Jollyville Road and the name sounded interesting. Readers of the Green Notebook will probably know that I love the United States, my son is actually a US citizen. I think of the States as an amazing country, but some of the people who live in this great place have very some strange views of the world. Having said that, I believe that something like 38 percent of all Americans have never had a passport and another 26 percent no longer have a valid passport which means that around 210 million Americans either never travel or have not travelled recently. This means that their

— Joe Saward's 2022 Green Notebook —

view of world is formed entirely by the media. I am not saying it is wrong not to travel if one is happy with one's own country, but it does lead to some odd attitudes and behaviours because the more one travels, the more one learns and the more tolerant one is to new ideas and different cultures.

This unworldliness was highlighted on Thursday when we went to check into the aforementioned hotel and were told that the fact that we had paperwork indicating that there were two rooms booked, confirmed and guaranteed was irrelevant because there was only one available and if we did not like it there was nothing that they could or would do about it.

After many years of travelling, I have had a few adventures with booking problems. My favourite (if one can have a favourite nightmare) was when I turned up one year for a weekend at Monza to discover that I had been booked into a place for three nights. The problem was that it was a restaurant, not a hotel...

On another occasion something had gone wrong and so the hotel staff converted their boardroom into a bedroom. They were people who cared about doing the job properly. The receptionist in the Jollyville dive – let's call her Brooke – was different. She said it was because there was an F1 race and there were few rooms available in town. Yes, we said, we are aware of this. It is why this booking confirmation was made many months ago. Not having a room was stressful, of course, but the worrying thing was that the only alternative would be to pay the going rate elsewhere – and that would be thousands of dollars. It is not unusual for unscrupulous hoteliers to cancel reservations in order to get more money, but you cannot cancel confirmed reservations that are guaranteed. Well, Brooke decided that she could. It was just tough. We should have come earlier. She accepted that the reservation did say that the rooms were confirmed, and guaranteed without pre-payment, but said these terms did not refer to the hotel. This was patent nonsense, of course.

It was clear that she had sold the room because someone else came along willing to pay more money and she figured that we could somehow be brow-beaten into accepting the situation. She even threatened to cancel the second room if I did not stop telling her that her behaviour was unprofessional. This, she said, was disrespectful. We pointed out that we too felt a lack of respect and made the point that two hard-bitten world travellers are not going to be bullied by some rank amateur and refused to accept such a situation. She had to fix it. At one point she slammed the door of the office in an act of frustration that we would not accept her diktats. She then decided to call the police, on the basis that we were being "rowdy". Our response was: "You're kidding!" The conclusion we reached while we waited for the police to arrive was that Brooke was completely out of her depth and not meant for a career in the hotel business. Officer Kim (number 6789) duly arrived and seemed a little astonished that rather than finding himself faced by gun-toting rednecks, there were two calm and lucid international visitors, who explained in a coherent fashion that the hotel was in breach of a contract and was unwilling to solve the problem. Officer Kim was an intelligent fellow and tried to find a solution although clearly there was none possible. So we ended up sharing the one available room for that night with no guarantees that we have two rooms for the weekend.

In the morning, within a matter of minutes, without Brooke, the problem was solved and apologies made. We did not see her again and hopefully she is now working in a job to which she is better-suited. Shovelling manure in a stable might be a good career path... but if she wants a reference for any job, I am very happy to give one, but she might not like what she gets.

This was all rather stressful and down at the Circuit of the Americas things were a little tiresome as well. The big story was the dull cost cap. Otherwise there was some vague interest when the Ferrari drivers put on cowboy hats, although it would have been fitting if other team members had been made to look like cowboys, given some of the team's adventures in recent years.

Daniel Ricciardo rode a horse (complete with a pass in the name of Horsey McHorse) into the pit lane, before riding off into the sunset...

Zak Brown and Mario Andretti drove old McLarens around, the old boy showing Zak that owning cars and driving them quickly are two entirely different things. Zak may have been feeling a little bit uncomfortable, not because fitting into the car was probably a bit of a challenge, but rather because a legal letter had landed on his desk from Red Bull, which was of the opinion that an open letter Brown had written to the FIA President was a direct public accusation of cheating. There were a couple of things amiss with the letter. Firstly, the FIA President should not be involved in any way in the cost cap discussions, so Zak's letter looked a lot like a PR stunt;

and secondly defamation is not limited to literal and obvious meanings but includes inference which an ordinary, reasonable reader would draw from the words. In his subsequent remarks to the media he was rather more circumspect, saying that he did not know the facts of the case and that his letter was based on the idea that 'if these types of things have happened' it would not be right. "I didn't mention any teams. It was a general response," he said.

Christian Horner was obviously not impressed, nor were Red Bull's lawyers. "It's tremendously disappointing. For a fellow competitor to be accusing you of cheating, to accuse you of fraudulent activity, is shocking," Horner said. "It's absolutely shocking that another competitor, without the facts, without any knowledge of the details, can be making that kind of accusation." He made the point that Red Bull had been on trial by the media and that this had been stirred up deliberately by rival teams.

My view is simple: how can one have a sensible opinion if no-one actually knows the details? They are confidential. The whole affair has been spun into a whirlwind of controversy, more of a dust devil than a tornado, but a lot more than the sport needs. We all want the sport to be fair, rules to be respected and to see punishments that fit crimes, but in this case there has been far too much spinning and briefing going on, and it looks like a serious attempt to undermine and discredit Red Bull, in order to weaken their challenge in the future, rather than being a discussion about what is right and wrong. They are angry about this, and you can understand why.

Most of what you will have read is information that is being leaked to a hungry media by people with agendas. Everyone sensible wants this issue to go away. It isn't good for the sport and it is fairly normal that there might be a few "grey areas" when there is a new regulation that is quite vague in terms of details. Interpretations can be different and so the accusation that this is all deliberate is really not helpful. The FIA has already said that the team has been cooperating all along the way, it is just that they do not agree on interpretations that have emerged since the accounts were submitted.

The good news is that there will not be any back room deals, as we have seen before (allegedly) because FIA President Mohammed Ben Sulayem campaigned on the basis that "transparency is vital to good governance and accountability". Most fans are really not interested in financial details: about differed corporation tax, how unused parts are categorised, argument over health benefits and catering costs. Dull stuff.

Far too much of the ongoing process has been conducted in public, when these are supposed to be confidential matters. What is important is to discover how other teams got to know what was in Red Bull's submissions. Somebody, somewhere has been leaking information. This is wrong. Similarly, using such information to create bad impressions is very dubious behaviour, particularly as the "facts" are very woolly. So there is work needed on getting the Cost Cap process properly defined and executed, although I am confident that things will be better in the future. Regulations often need tweaking.

This was a point that the FIA made in what was a very good report into the happenings at Suzuka, where no punches were pulled and good explanations given about what went wrong, who was at fault and how things can be fixed. Hopefully, this will become the norm in the future.

The big news was that Brad Pitt was wandering around. He looks good for a 58-year-old and if Tom Cruise (60) can play a Super Hornet F/A 18F pilot and Daniel Craig can still be James Bond a 54, there is no reason that Pitt cannot be a fictional F1 driver at his age, although it will make Fernando Alonso look like a spring chicken.

Brad and some of his crew met with F1 team bosses and others to explain their movie plans, which will feature Pitt as an old driver struggling against a young charger. The filming is due to start next year with the three US races likely to be heavily featured.

A successful F1 movie would, of course, be of enormous value to the sport as it gets cooler and cooler to US viewers. F1 is now so cool that I spotted Liberty Media boss Greg Maffei wearing an F1-branded shirt, which is something I've not seen before, as he likes to be incognito. The problem with movie-making is that sometimes films are not the hits that Hollywood folk think they will be and F1 really needs to avoid a Sylvester Stallone-like disaster 20-odd years ago when he produced an IndyCar film called "Drivel" – Oops, sorry, I meant "Driven". That film was truly awful although IndyCar has done better since then, notably with "Turbo", an animated feature about a radioactive snail who wants to win the Indy 500.

I know that sounds like a dead cert disaster, but for kids under the age of eight, radioactive snails are clearly very interesting as it has been a big hit.

– Joe Saward's 2022 Green Notebook –

I did hear an interesting story that Pitt was in town not only to chat and do some subtle promotion, but also because he is rather keen on Liberty Media kicking in some investment money for the movie. Given that Liberty recently spent $240 million to buy a plot of land in Les Vegas, on which to build a pit lane and paddock area for future Grands Prix, this is a pretty sensible thing to do, as F1 wants the movie to be made and they are never averse to a little profit if such a film becomes a success.

Pitt is a big star, but one got the impression that F1's new mega-star Guenther Steiner is nearly as big these days. Everyone wants a selfie with the bemused Steiner, who is still trying to figure out how he became a sex symbol. The Haas team produced some Guenther Steiner teeshirts for the weekend – the first team principal merchandising in the history of the sport, so they believe – and the website blew up as squillions of fans scrambled to get their hands on one...

The paddock was awash with money, with billionaires two-a-penny and mere millionaires being the new working class. There are reckoned to be more than 3,000 billionaires in the world today and, while I'm not a great celebrity watcher, nor indeed a Hello magazine reader, I would guess that there were dozens of them present in Texas. At one point I did see the bizarre sight of John Elkann, the chairman of Stellantis (the merged Fiat-Peugeot) and Ferrari, doing a selfie with someone I didn't recognise. I asked around and no-one seemed to know, but after a few moments I asked a passing billionaire who this person might be and was told that he was none other than Andrea Casiraghi, the son of Princess Caroline of Monaco, and fourth in line to the throne (or whatever it is that Princes sit on) of Monaco.

That was the kind of paddock Austin was with loads of rich people, some tubby social influencers with silly hats on, lots of school leaver-age people wearing shirts that said "F1 Experiences Expert Host" and a sprinkling of scruffy media types. I am not quite sure how one qualifies to be an "F1 Experiences Expert Host" but if there's money in it, I might have to offer my services...

There does seem to be piles of US money being spent in F1 these days and the new ESPN TV deal is a nice one for F1, as it is rumoured to be worth 16 times more than the current one. The new agreement will bring in around $4 million per Grand Prix with an average live US viewership at the moment of about 1.2 million. This is rising all the time while NASCAR'S numbers are sliding downwards from year to year. Nowadays, the American stock car series averages around 2.9 million live views a race, for which it earns in the region of $22 million per event. This is an interesting comparison because there is clearly potential for another massive hike when the new ESPN deal ends in 2025. Just suppose, if F1 earned half of what NASCAR does per race, the revenue from F1's US TV rights in 2026 could be $246 million a year...

This is why the deal is for only three years.

The other big announcement in Austin was Haas's new title sponsor for the next three years, MoneyGram International Inc, a money-transfer company which is in competition with similar firms such as PayPal, Western Union, Wise, Green Dot, WorldRemit, Remitly Global and Skrill. It's a tough market with plenty of competition. The F1 sponsorship is a major push from MoneyGram following its acquisition earlier this year by a private equity firm called Madison Dearborn Partners for $1.8 billion. This included paying off MoneyGram's debt of $800 million and taking it off the NASDAQ stock exchange, to allow the firm freedom to grow and not waste its energy on pleasing investors and reducing regulatory, governance and accounting rules and costs. How much of this was down to the Haas brand? And how much was thanks to the Guenther brand?

Dear God, we'll have Steiner-branded underwear and loo seat covers next...

There were various other smaller announcements including a McLaren deal with a company called Seamless Digital, which will introduce a system that will allow branding to change on parts of the cars DURING races. This is a clever idea which has been around since it was developed by the Media Laboratory at the Massachusetts Institute of Technology 20 years ago. It has never been used on F1 cars because of the weight of the film of "electronic paper" which can change where "electronic ink" appears. With the in-car cameras of today, McLaren is going to use it in very small areas, such as helmets and haloes, to get sponsorship that can change from one shot to another. It is still only available in black, white and shades of grey, but there are hopes that one day the concept will be able to change multi-coloured images.

Elsewhere, there are suggestions that F1 will come up with a scheme to replace the W Series in an effort to help develop young female racers. F1 is not keen on the idea of segregating women in their own championship, believing that it is better for them to sink or swim in the mainstream. It was offered the W Series several times, but declined to buy it for this reason. However, the sport does not want to be accused of not doing anything in this respect, as happened the other day when Lewis Hamilton started talking about how some of the money being generated by F1 should be used to "help out in that space". Rather than using the existing cars, the word is that F1 could make it compulsory for existing Formula 2 and Formula 3 teams to each run a pair of Formula 4 cars in order to create a championship that would run concurrently with F1 events. This would include an age restriction to avoid the problems that the W Series has of older drivers dominating but not being good enough to move on. This will provide women with track time when they need it most and potential role models for girls to be inspired by. Formula 1 people generally have a very open view on the subject and believe that if a women with the right skill-set comes along and is quick enough she will be welcomed in F1 with open arms. The problem is finding the right girl(s). The idea being floated seems to be a cost-effective way to continue the search.

The Chinese Communist Party Congress in Beijing, which has been taking place in the last few days, saw a very clear statement that the Chinese government is going to continue with its zero-Covid policy. This means that it is almost inconceivable for there to be a race in Shanghai in 2023 because of restrictions on spectators and, more importantly, the quarantine requirements that the F1 circus would face, which are currently impossible to fulfil. If the government makes an exception for F1, it will stir up discontent in the population, which the leaders want to avoid. In short, until the government eases off on restrictions it is unlikely that a race will happen. If it drops from the calendar in 2023, China will not be replaced.

And while it was a sad weekend for Red Bull, with the death of Dietrich Mateschitz, who has been a key member of the F1 world for many years, this all overshadowed the death of another man who had a similar impact in the sport half a century ago. Aleardo Buzzi, who died at the age of 92, was the man who called the tune at Marlboro from the very first stickers on Jo Siffert's March in 1970, to the successful times with McLaren and Ferrari, not to mention the funding dozens of young drivers, many who made it into F1. Buzzi retired from Marlboro in 1992.

People forget very quickly.

I guess if you want your name to live on after you go, the best thing to do is to have a cemetery named after you.

A Jolly good idea.

From the Islander Bar and Grill

3 November 2022

I bounce through Miami International Airport every now and then, and it always makes me smile when I see the airport code MIA. For me this acronym means Missing In Action. Quite often, one feels a little like that when one is jumping around between the time zones.

When I find myself in MIA with time to kill, I will walk through the terminal, which has crushed shells in the flooring (see below), presumably to make it more durable, as well as quite pretty to look at. When I get to Gate D4, I hide myself away in the Islander Bar and Grill. There's nothing special about the place but for reasons that I cannot quite fathom, it feels like a safe haven and one gets a hint of Caribbean life, with some dishes that originate from the islands. It used to serve conch and other such delicacies, but these days the menu is rather less Gulf Stream and a little more mainstream.

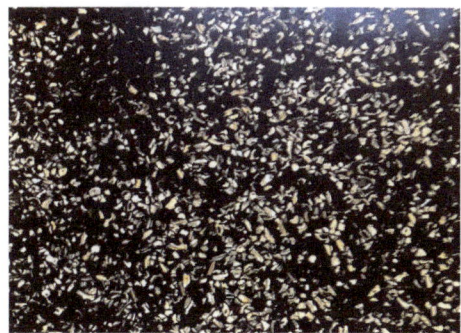

I had a few hours to kill in MIA on the return from Mexico City (it's cheaper when you do not fly direct) and I was pondering the Mexico F1 weekend, as I munched my way through some Cuban spring rolls. It struck me that Islander can be viewed as "I slander" and that one of the themes of the Grand Prix had been defamation, largely in relation to social media and how toxic a world it can be. This came up in the post-race press conference.

"I think it's just the sport is more popular so there are more people watching, so more people are writing," said Max Verstappen. "I think it's just that. It's not great that they are allowed to write these kinds of things so I hope we can come up with a kind of algorithm that stops people from being keyboard warriors. Because these kind of people... they will never come up to you and say these things in front of your face, because they're sitting in front of their desk or whatever at home, being upset, being frustrated, and they can write whatever they like because the platform allows you to. That can be really damaging and hurtful to some people and it's not how it should be. Social media is a very toxic place."

Lewis Hamilton was also quite vocal on the subject.

"Social media is getting more and more toxic as the years go on and we should all come off it, ultimately," he said. "Mental health is such a prominent thing right now. So many people are reading the comments, the stuff that people say, and it is hurtful. Fortunately I don't read it, but the media platforms need to do more to protect people, particularly young kids and women. At the moment they are not doing that so I think this will just continue."

And Sergio Perez agreed. "They don't understand that we are also human beings. And I think this has got to stop," he said. "And, obviously, as a sport, we need to also be responsible of what we post, by ourselves. We all have a lot of followers so it's very important that we try to get the sport in the right way because Formula 1, it's a great sport and has great values, but has to do more in that regard."

I could not agree more. One cannot post anything without someone taking offence, or gnashing their virtual teeth. The other day, I saw a tweet which suggested that researchers at Stanford University, a very fine institution, had come up with what they considered to be the image of God. It all sounded very unlikely and the image looked a lot like Fernando Alonso. In fact, it looked so like Fernando that I concluded that it was a fake story but, just to be sure, I did a little surfing on the web and discovered that the image had nothing to do with Stanford and was simply a 3D rendering of Alonso that one can buy on the web, if one feels the need to part with money to own a non-fungible token.

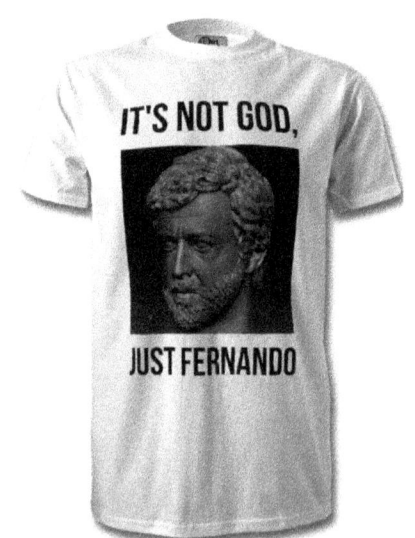

I have always struggled with NFTs because, while I understand that an image can be considered special and valuable, when you buy a virtual piece of art, you are getting absolutely nothing apart from an image that anyone who knows how to use a screen shot can also have at home. If you buy a painting you are at least getting some canvas, wood and paint.

I guess it is just about belief, similar to thinking that a bit of paper is as valuable as a piece of gold.

Anyway, I tweeted that it was an NFT and not some religious experiment that looked like Alonso and my phrase: "It's not God, it's just Fernando" soon appeared on a virtual teeshirt because Fernando fans thought this was a good meme. Then, of course, I got some responses from religious types saying that there is only one God and that it is disrespectful to compare Him (why not Her?) with Alonso because the bible is filled with exhortations to avoid and/or destroy gods other than the one mentioned in the "Good Book". Gods, in the wrong hands, are troublesome (I'd better © that one).

Anyway, Mexico City is all the fault of an Aztec deity with the easy-to-remember name of Huitzilopochtli, who said that the best place for the tribe to settle would be when they saw an eagle, perched on a prickly pear cactus – in a lake – and eating a snake.

Well, blow me down, this is exactly what some of the Aztecs saw in a swamp in the valley of Mexico. So they built a city called Tenochtitlan, created "floating gardens" on which to grow food and settled down to enjoy life, sacrificing people from time to time to stop the gods from making the ground shake, by ripping out the still-beating hearts of the victims. OK, they gave us popcorn and chewing gum as well, but the sacrificing stuff was not a very nice way of going about business.

Thanks to the hungry eagle, the settlement now known as Mexico City was founded (and the Mexican flag created), although in the modern world, the place is anything but perfect. It is in a flat valley at 7,000ft, surrounded by volcanoes that rise as high as 16,000ft. It is sheltered from winds but has no drainage so that when water descends from the mountains it has nowhere to go and causes floods. These conditions are not very helpful because a concept called temperature inversion means that air pollution is trapped and when the warm air near the ground does escape it creates violent thunder storms that cause more floods.

And that's without the earthquakes…

Despite these disadvantages, Mexico City has grown and grown. Today there are 22 million people living there (21.8 million of which are Checo Perez fans). Pollution used to be really horrible back in the 1980s but the Mexicans have done a decent clean-up job by building a very efficient mass transit system, although the traffic is still pretty awful. Mexico City is reckoned to be only the fifth most congested city in Latin America (avoid Bogota, Lima, Recive and Santiago) – but it is still a very crammed place. And yet visitors come to enjoy its cosmopolitan charms, its energy and its historical places. In the old days, everyone in F1 used to stay at the airport hotels because they were there to race and didn't care about the fancy hotels downtown. Today they want to stay in the wildly-expensive places and so have to spend additional money on police escorts and waste time getting through the traffic in their cars. One of my favourite stories of the Grand Prix weekend was that Carlos Slim Domit, the billionaire petrol head, who has funded much of Mexican motorsport in the last 20 years, and is largely responsible for Sergio Perez surviving long enough in F1 to get a decent seat, decided that he didn't want to sit in traffic and so took the metro to get to the circuit. Fortunately, this was so unexpected an act that nothing bad happened...

If you want to make friends in Mexico, you don't need to learn a lot of Spanish. If you can say "Checo" and give a thumbs-up, they will be happy and proud. However one gets the feeling that it isn't just Perez. Mexicans love racing. The support for Perez is spectacular but it is not quite the same as success-chasing supporters of Max Verstappen, who will fade one day if Max stops winning.

For Mexicans it seems that there is also plenty of national pride about the Grand Prix. It is a great event. It won the prize for being the best Grand Prix for five consecutive years between 2015 and 2019 (the award has not been made since), and the promoter has just signed a new three-year deal and the future looks rosy. The main focus these days is to build up the festival (ie money-making activities) around the event. Already it coincides with the colourful Día de Muertos (Day of the Dead) and so visitors can combine the two, which will bring more revenue to the city and thus enable F1 to ask for more money. This is exactly what Liberty Media's vision of F1 is – and it is working.

There is a developing problem, however, with the secondary market for tickets, which can get to daft prices because so many people want to come to the races. This presents a challenge for the organisers because if they sell cheap tickets these will end up nurturing touts. One can raise the prices to squeeze out the scalpers but if the demand is strong enough there will still be a margin for them.

The problem in Mexico City is that the Grand Prix cannot sell any more tickets and there is no space left for more grandstands. The logical thing to do in the circumstances is either to sit back and enjoy the situation, or to try and repeat the success elsewhere. With six races in the American time zones in 2023, there is probably still room for one more (which will mean one being lost in Europe) and although having two races in Mexico is not a realistic ambition, there is no reason why the promotions company cannot go elsewhere in the region and help out countries that do not know how to do it.

Anyway, the reason the new contract is short, is because there is an election in 2024 when the mayor of Mexico City Claudia Sheinbaum gets to the end of her term of office. It looks like she is going to stand for the presidency and so the Mexico City could get federal funding again and perhaps return to being the Mexican GP.

Perez is so popular in Mexico that his father Tonio thinks it could win him votes in he presidential election and he says he is standing for the role. This will not happen because he is in the same party – called MORENA – as Sheinbaum and Foreign Minister Marcelo Ebrard, who are probably a little more attractive to voters than Perez's dad, enthusiastic though he may be...

Mexico will at some point need to look for a new driver to support because Perez is coming up to 33 and while he is eight years younger than Fernando Alonso and could, in theory, go on forever in F1, there may come a point at which Red Bull will think that a youngster might do a better job. You can cheer until you are hoarse, but Sergio is nowhere close to Max's pace. He's solid, he's older and (perhaps) wiser, but there may come a day...

Mexico does have Pato O'Ward, who is nine years younger than Perez and a very bouncy individual. He is under contract to McLaren in IndyCar until the end of 2025 and is the same age as Lando Norris, which is two years old than Oscar Piastri, while Alex Palou is two years older. So, McLaren has an option that could one day make Mexico happy. A successful driver can make the sport very popular in their own country. We have seen that in Spain (with Alonso) and in Germany (with Michael Schumacher), but it doesn't always work because Sebastian Vettel never appealed to German fans in the way that Michael did. I have asked a lot of Germans about why this is the case and the answer seems to be a class thing. Michael was a working class hero, who rose to fame at a time when Germany needed figures to unite around. It all happened just after the reunification of East and West and, so they say, this is what made him such a huge phenomenon. That, and a lot of victories...

Today we have China's Guanyu Zhou but the Chinese are not yet getting excited. Things are a little complicated because I sense a new kind of caution in F1 about China. The 2023 race is going to be called off because of the zero-Covid policy. The Chinese leadership cannot let F1 bust all the rules without it stirring up trouble and that is the last thing that they want. So the race will have to go and maybe in 2024 they will get round to easing the lockdowns and getting on with life.. At the same time I feel that the view of China is changing. It is no longer viewed the investment opportunity it once was and lots of Western companies are winding down their operations. China's failure to condemn Russia's attack on Ukraine has not gone down well in the West and President Xi's combative attitude towards Taiwan is worrying. F1 cut all ties with Russia soon after the invasion of Ukraine – and would likely do the same if Taiwan was attacked. But, worse than that, there is a wariness about China that the leadership has created. I am sure they don't give a monkey's about F1, but it could mean that F1 will move its targets to places in Asia where it is easier to do business. Yes, China has 1.4 billion people, but India has about the same... Perhaps if the Indians can get rid of their red tape, F1 might look again. Perhaps not.

Next year, probably, we will have American Logan Sargeant trying to do the same thing with the USA. Colton Herta seems to have disappeared from the scene and I am told that he has just been signed to a vast new contract ($7 million) which is unheard of in Indycar. Perhaps if there is ever an Andretti F1 team, Herta might make F1, but right now it is all rather doubtful.

F1 continues to build in the US and this week at the SEMA Show in Las Vegas, the leading automotive trade show, Williams F1 is going to be present. Next weekend there will be a launch party for the Grand Prix in Las Vegas.

Sargeant's situation remains uncertain, which is a little ridiculous. The gap between the penultimate Formula 2 race meeting and the finale is a massive 10 weeks (from September 11 to November 20). This is one of number of flaws that Formula 2 suffers from: it is expensive and the cars are not always reliable and so the championship can be impacted by mechanical failures, which is not what you want when one is trying to develop the best drivers and technical issues distort the results. Secondly, the gap at the end of the year means that a number of current Formula 2 drivers need to wait until after the last race to see whether they qualify for an F1 super licence or not. They do not want to commit to returning to Formula 2 in 2023 because there is no real point in doing another season if one finishes well in the championship, but as they don't know where they will finish, they cannot commit. Felipe Drugovich has already won the 2022 title, having collected 241 points thus far. This means he cannot be caught by the second-placed Théo Pourchaire, who has only 164 points. There is maximum score of 39 points for an F2 weekend, which means that Pourchaire is not safe in second place because Sargeant (135), Jack Doohan (126), Jehan Daruvala (126) and Enzo Fittipaldi (126) could all beat him. There are five other drivers who might be able to overtake Sargeant for third place, if they score maximum points and he fails to score: Liam Lawson (123), Frederik Vesti (117), Ayumu Iwasa (114), Juri Vips (110) and Dennis Hauger (98).

So there are 10 drivers who could finish third in the championship. Sargeant needs to be fifth to qualify for his licence and thus be able to take up the Williams F1 drive that is on offer to him.

The problem with this is that while the drivers wait to see what will happen, the 2023 drives are beginning to fill up with drivers who know what they need to do. The same mistake is being made again in next year's calendar.

The paddock chatter in Mexico was largely about the cost cap, until the decisions were handed down, after which it ceased to be news and sank beneath silently the waves.

There was a bit of talk following the Audi announcement that it is jumping into bed with Sauber, a surprise to no-one. What is interesting about this is that the announcement said that Sauber will "undertake the planning and execution of all race operations during the 2026 Formula 1 season". Cutting through the waffle, this means that Audi is hedging its bets, but you can understand why. If a manufacturer comes in with full branding there is a risk that if it all goes wrong, the company will look bad. Toyota is a good example of how not to do it. Mercedes dived in head-first in 2010 when it acquired Brawn GP but Brawn was the World

Championship-winning team at the time, whereas Sauber is nowhere near achieving that.

Prior to that, back in the 1990s, Mercedes hid behind Sauber before becoming Sauber-Mercedes in 1994.

When Sauber was bought by BMW at the end of 2005, the team remained BMW Sauber, rather than being a straight BMW team, but if things had gone better it might have been transformed, but it seems that the sporting bosses had over-promised and the BMW board decided it was wasting its time and quit.

The other big question at the moment is what is going to happen with Audi's sister brand Porsche, which was hoping to enter F1 in league with Red Bull. In recent days, there have been rumours that Porsche could buy into Williams. This is not serious. Williams's owners have shown no intention, despite several approaches, to hand over control. Williams would like to have manufacturer support in 2026 – but Porsche does not have an engine and, so they say, does not currently have the capacity, the people nor the time to build an engine for 2026. Hence the Red Bull deal...

Porsche does have some knowledge of F1 engines because, back in 2017, the VW executive board commissioned the firm to build a prototype F1 engine. This was going to be used from 2021 onwards but the impact of the VW diesel scandal shifted the group towards electric motorsport. The dynos that Porsche had planned to use were sold to Red Bull.

When Audi announced its F1 plans, its boss Markus Duesmann was asked if Audi and Porsche could collaborate, the obvious thing to do if one is being cost-efficient. But that would be far too easy for a complex company like Volkswagen. Audi does not want to work with Porsche. It is a flimsy argument to say that they cannot because integrating chassis and engine is impossible. If you look at the technical regulations about power unit mountings, these must consist of six studs connecting to the survival cell. The precise nature of the rules includes coordinates of where the studs must be placed, which means that different engines can be used with different chassis. This was created to make it possible to change engines without huge costs being involved and so integration is a lot easier than it might appear.

Since Duesmann made these remarks a couple of months ago, much has changed: the Red Bull-Porsche deal has fallen apart, but Porsche boss Oliver Blume has taken over as the boss of VW Group, while still retaining his role at Porsche. This means that Blume is Duesmann's superior. Well, that's the theory. Logically, if he went to the VW board and suggested that Porsche and Audi share the same technology, it would be entirely logical for that to happen. You can argue that this is not the way Porsche does business, but then badging a Red Bull engine was not at all a Porsche kind of strategy.

Needs must.

The simple (but difficult) solution is for Porsche to be given whatever Audi has. One can stick a different badge on the cam covers and who will know the difference? Obviously Porsche would then need to invest in people and machinery so as to develop along its own path, but this might be a good starting point.

However, when it comes to VW politics, nothing is ever simple...

Money is not the issue.

Money is an issue in some parts of F1, notably the cryptocurrency firms, following on from the catastrophic loss of investor confidence in the sector last summer. Bitcoin has tumbled from $60,000 to $20,000, while Ferrari sponsor Velas has seen its market cap tumble from $1.2 billion in January to just under $100 million. F1 sponsor Crypto.com has also been suffering and has recently laid off around 30 percent of its staff and has cancelled a big sponsorship deal with UEFA.

Conversely, the more traditional money transfer businesses such as Haas's new sponsor MoneyGram or the likes of PayPal and Western Union are booming, along with a string of newer money transfer firms.

F1 is famous for looking at problems and finding solutions, so perhaps we will see some new names popping up soon.

The other day Alejandro Soberon, the race promoter in Mexico, came up with a brilliant concept about F1 and the environment. F1 is busy trying to convince everyone that it can reach zero emissions by 2030. This is a good idea, but it is pretty meaningless if one does not count the emissions created by F1's spectators. One can try to get people to use mass transportation systems (as Carlos Slim did in Mexico) or one can try to convince them to switch to emission-free cars. But, if one thinks about the problem, one can already argue that Formula 1 is carbon neutral. How? Well, Soberon argued, if one only counts the people attending events, you are missing a trick. F1 is responsible for them, sure. But F1 is also responsible for keeping people at home to watch races, rather than going out on Sundays to have drive in the country, picnics, shopping trips and so on. So one needs only to find a way to measure how many people stay at home because of F1 and work out the environmental damage avoided and one can quickly see that the number of spectators will quickly be outnumbered by the number of TV viewers.

Staying home is something that more and more media F1 media are now doing, which means that most of the coverage comes from people who use what is spoon-fed to them, or copy what those who still travel are producing, although obviously they do not pay for it. This means that the travellers foot the bills but publications won't pay what they used to. Anyone who travels the world at the moment knows that the costs are now horrendous. Flights are double what they used to be, hotels (particularly at F1 races) are off the clock. Hire car prices are bonkers. This is the cost of F1's success, the result of the pandemic and businesses trying to make back what they lost.

This can get you down sometimes. I see all the followers on my social media feeds and I ponder the fact that if all them were to purchase a subscription to the JSBM newsletter (http://flatoutpublishing.com/jsbm/) just once, not only would they get a unique news every week for a year – much more than appears in the Green Notebook – but I would then never have to worry about F1 costs again.

Ah, in a perfect world, where social media was a positive thing…

From Casablanca

16 November 2022

You must remember this... the last six weeks have been brutal on F1's travellers, with races in Singapore, Japan, Texas, Mexico and Brazil and all the other stopping off points along the way. Now, as we cycle backwards in mid-air (like Wile E. Coyote trying to reach the edge of a canyon) and head the other way through the time zones, we are all getting rather tired and so people are saying and doing strange things.

As my plane hurtles through the darkness, somewhere in the night sky above Casablanca, I can say without any need to reflect that I am a trifle weary, if only because I have watched too many bad inflight movies, of which there are plenty at the moment. Content is king, so they say, but good content seems thin on the ground and I am slightly worried about Brad Pitt making F1 movies as his latest hit, about a pacifist assassin called Ladybug (honestly) is set on a bullet train in Japan. Before I turned it off, I did begin to hope that the lethal serpent, which slithered about like an F1 reporter, might bite him and end the movie prematurely.

With this is mind, I see that Formula One has appointed a head of original content to help expand F1's production and to build up new relationships and partnerships within the movie and TV world. Isabelle Stewart has a long history as a fixer in this world, so we can look forward (hopefully) to some quality projects in the future. F1 is staying smart and is now working to find content that will drive the sport forward when Drive to Survive goes stale, as eventually it probably will. Having said that, people are a little strange about what they like and if The Archers, the radio show about "everyday country folk" is still going after 71 years, or the TV equivalent Coronation Street, set in a cobbled street in a Manchester suburb, has survived 62 years, a couple of years more that the US's General Hospital and the slightly younger Days of Our Lives, there really is no reason that the show cannot be going when Guenther Steiner is retired to a rocking chair on the shores of Lake Norman.

Anyway, we don't know for sure, but there is no harm in looking for ways to keep F1 in the spotlight in the US. There is plenty of room for racing movies and documentaries, but also potential for cartoons and content that will inspire younger fans to follow F1 in more than virtual form.

I also half-watched a movie about Elvis Presley, the message of which, it seemed, was that people are happy to be fleeced if they leave with a smile on their faces. This was the philosophy of Elvis's manager Colonel Tom Parker, who was not – inevitably – what he appeared to be. It seems that he was actually Dutch and his real name was Andreas van Kuijk.

In general terms, I like the Dutch, although I always laugh at the line from an Austin Powers movie: "There are only two things I can't stand in this world: People who are intolerant of other people's cultures, and the Dutch". I really didn't like Tom Hanks playing Colonel Parker… What can you do? There are people out there who see evil everything that Lewis Hamilton does, and others who think Max Verstappen is nasty. The virtual battles going on between their fans is ugly stuff.

It struck me as rather odd that Max did not give back the position that Sergio Perez had given him in the closing laps in Brazil. It seemed at face value a rather self-defeating thing to do. But it was clear from what Max said that there was a very specific reason for it, and that the team knew what it was.

It did not take long for a couple of Dutch reporters to claim that this was all because Sergio crashed deliberately in qualifying at Monaco and screwed Max's chance of taking pole position. At the time I have to admit that it did not seem suspicious but I did write that it was "ironic that Perez ended up third" and that Max was frustrated by his teammate's crash. History relates, of course, that Ferrari messed it all up with poorly-timed tyre changes and Perez was able to win and while Max was third in the end, he was not a happy bunny. I have no idea whether these claims are true, but it would explain Max's remarks after the race, and Red Bull's reticence to explain what he meant by them.

I think it would be wise for the FIA to do two things: investigate what happened and see if there is any evidence that could prove the claim (which is probably impossible because odd data can simply mean a mistake). The Singapore scandal of 2008 was something we suspected but could not prove and it only became fact when Nelson Piquet Jr admitted it to. Secondly, and more importantly, the FIA should adjust the rules so that one cannot profit if you crash on a final run in qualifying. The fastest lap time should be taken away, just in case it was a deliberate crash.

The Perez-Monaco story also includes elements of the other big story after Brazil which came out of Italy when the celebrated Gazzetta dello Sport reported that Mattia Binotto will soon be replaced because of all the disasters at Ferrari this year. This, one might understand, but the idea that Frédéric Vasseur would be a good replacement makes the story seem either ridiculous, or an indication that the high-ups at Ferrari are actually the real problem. You might think that this is harsh and Frédéric is the obvious choice, but I am afraid I really don't see that. As I wander the paddocks of the world, I have found that if one is looking for Vasseur the best place to find him is usually at Mercedes where – no doubt – the multiple World Championship-winning Toto Wolff is getting Fred's advice about how to best run a racing team. I cannot remember the exact details, but one of them was a witness at the other one's wedding, and so having the Ferrari team principal as the best buddy of the Mercedes F1 boss seems a wholly unlikely situation.

The key point, I fear, has nothing to with that. F1 is a numbers game when it comes to success. You are only as good as your last result and in the five years that Vasseur has been running the Sauber/Alfa Romeo team, with funding from one of the richest men in the world and from Alfa Romeo, the team has managed to collect just 181 points. That is 36 a season, which is 10 fewer points than Red Bull scores on a good F1 weekend.

Having said all of that, I think I have reached the conclusion that Ferrari could put Liz Truss in charge of the F1 team and it really would not matter. Despite not winning a World Championship title for 14 years and with all the mistakes that have been made this year, the company continues to sell cars and make pots of money. Ferrari has just published its Q3 results for 2022 and despite the world's car markets being at best dodgy, it reported earnings up 17 percent compared to last year, to an eye-watering $427 million. Ferrari expects to make about $1.7 billion this year. So, frankly, who cares who is running things in F1, if the performance has zero impact on the brand or the sales? To see Vasseur dress up in a red suit and jump into the bubbling cauldron with some vegetables and watch him turn into a pot-au-feu and be devoured by the Italian media, will be a spectacle that will keep fans amused while the other teams do the winning… as usual.

Quite how and why Ferrari is so successful is a mystery that Sherlock Holmes would struggle to solve, even with the help of Enola. And it is a risky business to think that one can emulate what Ferrari does. Some years ago, I heard Steve Wozniak talking about self-driving cars and artificial intelligence. He made a very good point: how can we hope to build artificial intelligence if we do not understand how the human brain works?

Aston Martin has been trying to do what Ferrari has done for 60 years longer than Ferrari has been in existence. It has declared bankruptcy no fewer than seven times (in 1924, 1925, 1932, 1947, 1974, 1981 and 2007) and each time it has been rescued by someone who believes that they can make the difference.

James Bond has been doing his best to help, but even 007 cannot fix this conundrum. Printing money is not a trick that many can achieve.

Lawrence Stroll and his Yew Tree consortium are brave to try and stubborn as well, but they seem committed, at least until it gets too painful to continue. Their position as the biggest shareholder in the firm has been undermined in recent months by refinancing, which has diluted the shareholdings of those involved. This as been done largely to try to reduce the company's debt load and to make sure there is sufficient cash to keep the doors from closing. Sales have been impacted for various reasons, notably the global pandemic and the resulting economic upheavals that have been impacting the car industry, with logistical problems and difficulties with parts supply chains. The firm is expected to suffer pre-tax losses that will be twice those in 2021 but they are standing by their ambitious long-term growth plans. Yew Tree's share was down to 19 percent, with Saudi Arabia's Public Investment Fund owning 18.7 percent and China's Geely having 7.6 percent. In order to stay in control, Yew Tree has now spent around $35 million to buy an additional 4.25 percent on the open market, admittedly because the share price is low, thus boosting its share to 23.3 percent and thus maintaining control. This matters only because Aston Martin Lagonda is reckoned to be paying around $28 million a year to the F1 team, although it is not owned by the company, of which the shareholders are rather different. If Aston Martin decided that the F1 investment was not worth it, that could cause considerable problems for the team.

I would argue that some things are just not fixable, at least not in any short-term fashion. I think Ferrari is a bit like Sao Paulo. When I first visited, back in 1990, it was a really horrible city. This was due to millions of Brazilians leaving the farms where they worked to move to the cities to find a better life. Many had no money and lived in shanty towns. These were everywhere. Because of poverty, crime was awful and it was dangerous to walk around in a lot of neighbourhoods. People used to joke that Brazil was a country with a great future – and always would be. But it was a city of life and passion and much of this was focussed on Ayrton Senna, a Paulista. Even after he was gone, the Brazilians kept on loving Formula 1 and the only thing that made the trip to Brazil each year worth the pain was to soak up the atmosphere and enjoy the wonderful races that Interlagos produced, some of the greatest we have ever seen. I hope we always come back for that reason alone.

Today Sao Paulo – like Ferrari – is still better than it used to be. Much has been done. The favelas have faded, transportation is better. There are leafy parks and cycle paths. There are bright shiny glass-fronted tower blocks and shopping centres. Today there are many more neighbourhoods where one feels safe, but you only need to go a block or two in the wrong direction and you find yourself back in a place you do not want to be. But the locals are proud when you say that it is better than it used to be. This is not to say that I am a fan of the largest city in the Southern Hemisphere, which now boasts around 22.4 million people. It has wonderful jacaranda trees and an energy that is hard to find elsewhere. There really is nowhere like it.

Most of F1 these days stays in the Morumbi area, where a large representation of a Christmas tree stands outside a glitzy shopping centre. It reminded us all that the end of the season is finally upon us. We are all tired. Stefano Domenicali spent much to the weekend without a voice and Lando Norris looked rather grey for most of the time. We all just want to get the season finished.

Morumbi is nice enough. It is where Senna is buried, if you can find the place.

The thing you need to know about it is that Brazilians use the letter r in a rather different way than the rest of the world and so Morumbi is pronounced Mohumbi, while you must say Hubens Bahichello if you want the Brazilian to understand who you are talking about. If you wish to go to the Autodromo by taxi, you have to say "Ow-toe-drome – Oh!", which sounds like you might have stubbed your foot. If you say Bom Dia (good morning) you have to say "bonjee-a". The language is complicated, but it is all still worth it, if you can get into Interlagos. Just for the passion.

It was nice to see Bernie Ecclestone wandering about, even if we are all supposed to tut-tut and say that he is horrid because he likes Vladimir Putin. Bernie is farming coffee in Brazil these days (or at least getting someone else to do it while he watches) but he's unbelievably sprightly for a man of 92. When I mentioned he was looking well, Mr E, gave a little twinkle and said that it was all down to his clean living ways... which made us both giggle. The ultimate laugh, however, was that Bernie was there not because of what he did for F1 for so many years, but rather because his wife Fabiana, was the highest-ranking FIA official at the event, now that she is the Vice President of Sport (Latin America). I have no doubt that Bernie ended up in the corner office...

The paddock gossip was minimal, with stories suggesting that Portugal could replace China in 2023. This is not going to happen. So, race fans, be prepared to have a four-week break from F1 next year between the Australian GP on April 2, and the Azerbaijan Grand Prix on April 30. It would be a good time to plan a holiday...

The Germans are rather worried that they are about to lose their two active F1 drivers, with the retirement of Sebastian Vettel and the fact that Mick Schumacher is about to be drop-kicked off the F1 playing field. The good news is that Nico Hulkenberg will be slipping into the cockpit of the second Haas. This will be confirmed at some point soon.

There has been chat for a while that Daniel Ricciardo will be joining Mercedes to help out. There is some logic in this, but the latest whispers in the wind are that Mercedes may be convinced that taking on Mick would be a good PR move. We shall see. Daniel has also been mentioned as a possible reserve at Red Bull, where he learned to be the character that he is. We will have to see about that. Other stories suggest that the role is going to be given to Norway's Dennis Hauger, who Red Bull hopes will become an F2 winner in 2023 after a rather average season in 2022. It seems also that Enzo Fittipaldi is joining the Red Bull flock (if the collective noun for Red Bulls is a flock, rather than a herd) and that he may also be named as Haas's reserve driver as his brother Pietro is hoping to go racing in the United States, where there is nice IndyCar drive going if one has the money to pay Chip Ganassi what he wants (which is rather a lot).

Anyway, now it's off to the onomatopoeic Abu Dhabi "do", where hopefully things will be less stressed than they were a year ago.

We will say goodbye to Vettel, who is planning a career saving the world and raising awareness for exploited folks and minorities by selling tee-shirts supporting his campaigns, at a thoroughly unreasonable €70 a pop. I'm all for good works and charitable gestures, but I am troubled by the idea of sending €70 for a tee-shirt, even if it miraculously turns into artichoke soup after being used a few times.

Still, Ferrari can demand such prices, so there is hope for the rest of us…

– Joe Saward's 2022 Green Notebook –

From the Land of Nod

23 November 2022

Those who read The Good Book, admittedly rather a small group in the Formula 1 world, may know that in Genesis one can discover that the Land of Nod is located east of Eden, and was where the nasty Cain was sent after murdering his brother Abel. It was probably not flowing with milk and honey. In Hebrew the word "nod" is linked to the verb "to wander", which means that heading off to the land of Nod can mean living the life of a vagrant in the desert. The English, however, purloined the expression centuries ago to use it to describe the warm and fluffy realm of sleep, where dreams can get pretty interesting. This is a curious use of a dismal concept but it appears to have derived from "nodding off".

Given that I have been wandering around in desert lands to the east of Eden, and I have been nodding off (or perhaps crashing out is a better description), I think the location for this Green Notebook fits the bill in several different ways.

Abu Dhabi was a tough weekend for those who have toiled from Singapore to Japan to Austin to Mexico to Brazil and to Abu Dhabi (and various points in between) in the last month and a bit. It has been pretty brutal. Things were made a little sillier in Abu Dhabi because the only people who could afford to stay in decent hotels were those who have trust funds, or oil wells in their back garden. Fortunately for the teams, they left flights and hotels out of the cost cap (go figure) so they won't have to move out of their wildly-overpriced digs for fear that it will impact on their spending...

Hotel prices in Abu Dhabi are now so silly that more than a few of us stayed in Dubai, which is 64 miles to the north-east of Yas Island, on a decent road across the desert, with a speed limit of 86 mph for most of the route. Doing this each morning and each evening is a little tiresome but needs must. The last trip, at about two in the morning on Monday, was the easiest and we arrived at Dubai International Airport without any drama. An empty airport is once again a thing of beauty now that the world has started to travel again. The following hours were spent in the lounge, finishing off and filing stories, trying to stay awake and then, as dawn was breaking, it was time to hop on to a plane home. I was asleep 30 seconds after hitting the seat.

When I walked in the door at home nine hours later, I was soon gone again for another four or five hours, and then, after waking up for dinner, I slept through Monday night as well, which was quite an achievement given the time confusions of recent months. The end of the F1 season really is like that, particularly this year.

There was a graphic on the world TV feed that claimed that 2022 was the longest ever Formula 1 season. I have not checked the numbers, but I am not sure that is true given that in the 1950s and 1960s there were a lot of first races in January and

February and finishes in October and November. It would be a shame to let the facts get in the way of a good story, but when it comes to the film and TV world, it is fair to say that truth is quite often an early casualty.

On the grid in Abu Dhabi I have often wished people "Merry Christmas" because as soon as the race ends everyone takes off in every possible direction and to a large extent you don't see them again before Christmas. Most people take the greeting in the spirit that it is intended and so we end the year with a smile, but when I tried it out on Mattia Binotto, the reaction was pretty much what I would have expected if I had called him "a boofhead" instead. It was somewhere between a scowl and daggers flying from his eyes like tracer bullets. I thought this rather odd, but was not going to let it ruin my good mood but on reflection, I concluded that either he was very tired and needed some time off (although he was not in Brazil), or that the stories that he might soon be replaced as team principal at Ferrari could possibly be true. Whatever the case, I felt that he has no great future as a Father Christmas, even if he is used to wearing red clothing and doling out jolly platitudes.

Prior to this interlude I had discounted the Ferrari upheaval story, on the basis that it sounded so ludicrous. Everyone (and their family pets) had denied that such a thing could be possible. Even Ronald McDonald denied he was in the running for the job, although I did hear that Ferrari sounded out the yachtsman Max Sirena, who has been leading the Luna Rossa Challenge team in the America's Cup in recent years. The company stated that the rumours about Binotto were all "totally without foundation" and once that was on the record it would be pretty hard to go ahead and guillotine the bloke without looking like a bunch of liars.

Who knows what will happen now? What we do know is that Abu Dhabi was a moment of farewell for a number of F1 folk: Sebastian Vettel drew much of the spotlight, but it was also farewell to Ross Brawn, although he has said goodbye before and then came back again. This time there was no song and dance. An even quieter farewell came from Formula 1 chairman, Chase Carey, who is expected to hang up his chair soon and retire. Chase stepped back from his role as CEO when Stefano Domenicali took over, but has remained as chairman. As far as I am concerned, Chase is a worker of miracles and his achievement will stand forever in the annals of the sport for convincing all the teams that a budget cap was a great idea. The result is that teams are now all worth upwards of $800 million (probably more) and that many of them will be posting profits when they get around to filing their returns. The sport should put up a statue to Carey for doing that, and add another for Sean Bratches for getting Netflix to undertake "Drive to Survive".

Formula 1 is now so popular in the United States that Liberty Media boss Greg Maffei last week told financial types that there are certainly rumours of a fourth race in the United States, in addition to Austin (which runs until at least 2026), Miami (2031) and Las Vegas (2032), and that the Mayor of New York Eric Adams had offered F1 the chance to host a race on Randalls and Wards Island. As the name suggests, this used to be two islands until someone filled in the waterway between them. It is now largely parkland although across the top of it runs a major motorway connection that links the Bronx, Brooklyn and Manhattan with what is still called the Triborough Bridge, although it has been named after Robert Kennedy for many years. Maffei said that the idea is "probably not our perfect venue" and that "it's hard to see that they're going to shut Central Park for us". He added that trying to get a race in New York was "a fight we don't need to have".

The message was fairly clear: "Mr Adams. Do you have a better offer?"

Meanwhile, down in Miami, the success of this year's race – even allowing for some teething problems – has resulted in an acceptance in Miami that the event is a "jolly good thing". The critics who opposed the race have melted quietly away as it has become clear that it was a huge success. Miami Dade County voted last week to raise the cap on the amount of money that can be given in grants to Hard Rock Stadium, partly because of the Grand Prix. The cap was originally set at $5 million per year over a 20-year period, although this has already increased by $1 million to recognise the success of the Miami Open tennis tournament. The County now says that it will make a grant of $4 million for each Grand Prix, each World Cup Final and each Super Bowl, with $3 million for other big events. The annual cap is now up to $7 million a year.

This has been done at a time when the County needs to find a new naming sponsor for the FTX Arena, where the Miami Heat basketball team play. This follows the collapse of FTX, which had agreed as $135 million naming rights deal for 19 years.

Elsewhere, Liberty Media has quietly announced that it is going to split to the Atlanta Braves baseball team from the group and create a new unit called Liberty Live. This came about because some investors argued that the value of the Braves was being held back because of the complex structure of shares and various cross-holdings within Liberty Media. They even argued that F1 might gain in value if it was an independent unit, but it remains tied for the moment to the Xfinity media operation. The split off will mean that none of the three Liberty units will hold shares in the others.

The driver market in Abu Dhabi offered no real surprises as Haas confirmed Nico Hulkenberg and Williams Logan Sargeant, Daniel Ricciardo will become Red Bull reserve driver and if he wants the job, Mick Schumacher will become the Mercedes reserve driver. Things should now be quiet on the driver front until Fernando Alonso falls out with Aston Martin early next year.

The big story of the next few weeks (Ferrari eruptions aside) is that there is unlikely to be a Chinese Grand Prix in 2023 and thus F1 must decide what to do about the one-month gap that will appear in the calendar between Australia on April 1 and Baku on April 30. The logical thing would be for Baku to move forward a week and take place on April 23, which would then get rid of the difficult Baku-Miami back-to-back that was being planned. Baku does not want to move, arguing that the weather will not be great, but it is an easy race to move because few spectators attend. And if Baku does not want to go on hosting a Grand Prix, F1 might not be too upset because although the fees from Azerbaijan are high, the strategic value of the race is somewhat limited.

The Chinese have been hoping that they might find a gap in the F1 calendar in the autumn but there is no sign of that happening although the recent shenanigans about beer and the FIFA World Cup has done Qatar no good at all, as changing the policy about alcohol sales two days before an event begins is not necessarily the best way to win friends and influence people. It will cause major legal headaches for Qatar, FIFA and Budweiser. Money may smooth over some of the pain, but a settlement will not come cheap. The other thing that this will do is to make other sporting bodies very, very, wary of doing deals with Qatar and such behaviour will mean that the country will need to pay much higher rights fees to attract tournaments in the future. I doubt this will impact much on F1 because the sport is not obviously keen on promoting alcohol, but you never know...

The other announcement of note in Abu Dhabi was no big surprise as F1 gave details of its plans for an all-women series which it will help to fund. The Formula 1 Academy will feature five Formula 2 and Formula 3 teams, each running three Academy Formula 4 cars, at seven events (each with three races). These races will be held on Formula 1 tracks but only one will be held in conjunction with a Grand Prix. The logic in this is that what the girls need more than anything is track time and the aim will be to get women from this series into Formula 3 within a couple of years. Formula 1 says that it will pay €150,000 towards the budget of each car, with the drivers required to provide another €150,000, with the teams providing the rest. This is rather different from the W Series, which ran into financial trouble this year.

The only other story that reared its ugly head in Abu Dhabi was surrounding Red Bull's order to Max Verstappen to move over and let Sergio Perez get back ahead on the last lap of the Brazilian race. Max refused and made it clear that there was a very good reason for his actions and the team knew exactly why it happened. This was obviously about some gripe that Verstappen had with Perez and there were soon reports claiming that this was because Sergio had deliberately crashed in qualifying in Monaco and deprived Max of his chance to take pole position (and therefore win). The team jumped in to try to stamp out fires but made things worse by saying that all of its discussions were private and that it was not anyone's business why it had all happened. This simply fanned the flames because there was no reason to keep secrets unless, of course, admitting things might have caused all kinds of other problems.

The whole thing petered out as the FIA showed little interest because while one can prove from data that a crash was suspicious, one cannot prove an intent to crash and one dare not punish a team and damage its reputation if the evidence is not 100 percent certain. So, I guess that we can expect a new rule at some point which will stop drivers benefiting from crashes on the last lap in qualifying. In the interim, Perez came out of this one smelling like a fish market and Red Bull's attempt to divert attention by trying to turn the whole story into a campaign against nasty social media, looked like someone trying to get past a security man by pointing in the sky, looking shocked and crying "Wow! A flying elephant".

You can call us F1 observers cynical, but over time we have seen a lot of tricks with smoke and mirrors, and off-stage flashes and bangs to try to disguise sleight of hand.

In the words of the song: "I saw a peanut stand, heard a rubber band, I saw a needle that winked its eye. But I think I will have seen everything, when I see an elephant fly…"

Sorry, Red Bull folks, but that was a major fail…

And now, some more sleep…

From Poitiers

29 November 2022

Jean le Bon might sound like a rock star, but he wasn't. He was just a king, and not a very good one, although for reasons now lost in time he earned his name, which means John the Good.

Medieval kings make Vladimir Putin seem like a decent and reasonable fellow. They were basically murderous thugs, constantly fighting for land so that their kingdom could be bigger than the one next door, which belonged to some psychopathic cousin. Wars were profitable for individuals if one plundered enough stuff. The kings told everyone that they had God on their side and if you didn't agree with them they would string you up from a tree, if you were lucky. We won't go into too much detail about what happened if you were unlucky, suffice to say that it was a grisly way to depart this earth.

The reason I mention Jean le Bon is that I happened to be passing by Poitiers the other day. It was there in 1356 that Edward the Black Prince (named presumably after his Johnny Cash-style fashion choices, rather than his genetic make-up) defeated Jean le Bon in so devastating a fashion that Jean was captured and ransomed by the English for an astonishing three million crowns, which was equivalent to the English royal revenues for five years. It was probably the most significant victory of the 100 Years War, although Crecy and Agincourt always seem to get the glory and Henry V had better PR than The Black Prince. Mind you, history is a funny thing because if you ask the average Englishman about the significance of Formigny or Castillon (two battles that they lost) they will most likely reply: "Don't they play for Chelsea?"

The F1 season may be over but normal life must now catch up and so it is a time to visit long-neglected relatives and other similar activities. This involved a trip through rain storms and rainbows to Aquitaine, by way of Le Mans and then the A10 autoroute. This modern road has little to offer, but the old RN10, which runs parallel to the motorway was the Mother Road of global motorsport, down which the early races thundered until 1903 when no fewer than 261 automobiles set off to race from Paris to Madrid. The performance of these frail and often dubious feats of engineering was diverse. The development was then moving so fast that the most advanced machines were capable of 100 mph, a concept which spectators struggled to comprehend. The dusty roads made vision almost impossible for the drivers and huge crowds were largely uncontrolled.

It was a recipe for disaster.

Even today, the exact total number of accidents and casualties is not really known. There were over a dozen crashes involving fatalities, often multiple, to both the racing crews and bystanders and a total of 40 dead is not an unreasonable estimate. One of them was Marcel Renault, who ran off the main road just south of Poitiers, while passing a rival at high speed, having failed to see the corner ahead. The Renault went off over a ditch and rolled, the driver suffered head and neck injuries. There were no medics, of course, and so the competitors who arrived at the scene did what they could. Leon Thery found a bicycle and went in search of a doctor, while Maurice Farman organised for Renault and his riding mechanic to be carried 200 metres to a farm in the hamlet of Bourdevay, just off the main road. Marcel died there two days later.

The race was called off at the end of that appalling first day and city-to-city racing died with it. Thereafter races were held on circuits.

Passing Le Mans earlier in the trip reminded me that the city is not just about the celebrated 24 Hour race, for which it is best known today. Le Mans also served as the venue for the very first Grand Prix, which took place three years after the Paris-Madrid disaster, on a large circuit was laid out on a triangle of country roads to the east of city, running from Champagné to a hairpin on the way towards Le Mans which sent the racers off to the east to Saint-Calais, then north to Vibraye and La Ferté-Bernard, and then south-west back to Champagné.

This was won by a Renault, driven by a mechanic called Ferenc Szisz, or Szisz Ferenc if one hails from his native Hungary.

The 1906 race is not the only link that Le Mans has with Grand Prix racing because after World War I a different track, to the south of the city, was used for the first major motor race to take place after the war. This would be the basis of the circuit used for the 24 Hours of Le Mans and, much to the chagrin of the French, the event was won by America's Jimmy Murphy, driving a white Duesenberg.

When you look at the history of the place and the geographical location of Le Mans, within easy reach of Paris by car or train, with a tramway that runs right into the middle of the circuit, one can only wonder why France has struggled to find a venue for Formula 1 for so many years. There is even a short version of the Le Mans track, known as the Bugatti circuit, which runs through the sandy, pine-covered area south of the impressive pits, grandstands and paddock. This hosted one Grand Prix, back in 1967, but it was not considered a very good circuit at the time (not surprising given its rivals Reims and Rouen) and few spectators turned up. That mean that the Automobile Club de l'Ouest, which runs the track, turned its back on F1 and continues to look down on F1 to this day, there is no doubt that if a race was held there today, it would be a great success and would give Le Mans a more valid claim to be the racing capital of the world.

But club presidents quite often do not see the wood from the trees and so Le Mans steers clear of Formula 1. Liberty Media isn't really bothered about France, despite the country's history as the birthplace of motorsport, and probably views Le Mans as a provincial city of little interest, rather than being "a destination city". It is a shame...

Not many people know that there is a direct link between Alpine, which today waves the French flag in Formula 1, and those early days of the sport. One of the Renault mechanics in those days, who sat alongside Szisz on several occasions, was a fellow called Emile Rédélé, who was a pal of the company boss Louis Renault. After the war, as Renault began expanding into a mass market car company, Louis sent Rédélé to Dieppe to open one of the earliest Renault dealerships. Emile's son Jean grew up as a mad racing fan but Renault showed little interest in the sport and so Jean Rédélé began converting 4CVs into racing machines in the late 1940s. These were quite successful and, in 1951, he set up Automobiles Alpine and began producing roadgoing versions of the cars. They were sexy and successful Renaults.

Later Rédélé took Alpine into single-seater races and won in Formula 3, Formula 2 and at Le Mans, in addition to being successful in international rallying with wins on the Monte Carlo Rally and World Rally Championship success.. Alpine even built the first prototype for Renault's F1 turbo programme in the 1970s but in the years that followed after Renault bought the brand it was left to fade away and was not revived until Malaysian aviation magnate Tony Fernandes decided to expand into the car business and did a deal with Renault to revive the road car brand and provide the same basic car for his Caterham operation. When Fernandes ran out of money, Renault was left with a half-finished project and decided to go ahead and so Alpine began again and the F1 programme today is the next chapter in the story and a key part of Renault's strategy for the future.

Renault's progress has been slow but it is moving forwards and having overtaken McLaren this year in fourth place in the Constructors' Championship is now focussing on closing the gap to the big three: Mercedes, Red Bull and Ferrari. It is an epic challenge but in F1, empires rise and fall and one never knows who will get it right. Mercedes had a tough year in 2022, while Red Bull Racing flew away with the titles, while Ferrari should have done a great deal better than it did. This is the big story at the moment as Ferrari decides what to do for the future.

While there is no question that mistakes were made in 2022, both by the team and by the drivers, the idea that a change of management is a good idea is probably not the smartest thing to do, as it will mean another period of getting things in whatever order the new incumbent thinks is best and then seeing if it works. By the time all of that is done, it will be halfway through the 2023 season and there are no guarantees that the result will be any better than in 2022. A new person will also probably want his own people around him and that will take time. If you look back in history Jean Todt took control of the team in July 1993 but Ferrari did not win a World Championship until 1999. If anything the cycles of F1 success are these days longer than they used to be and so changing a lot is not a good idea, unless the new person concludes there is no choice. Mattia Binotto may not be Toto Wolff, but he has overseen an upshift in Ferrari performance thanks to providing stability and a culture in which people are willing to take risks and come up with new ideas.

Binotto was fortunate (probably) to survive the cataclysmic 2020 season – the team's worst for 40 years – which was the result of the secret deal that was struck with the FIA regarding the Ferrari engine, after the controversies at the tail end of 2019. He was probably saved by the fact that there was an interregnum following the unexpected retirement of chief executive officer Louis Camillieri and the long wait before Benedetto Vigna took over nine months later. Vigna, who has no background in racing, is now 15 months into his time as CEO and one can only hope that this is not his decision because 15 months in F1 is not sufficient to understand how it all works. And, as many executives have learned over time, it is not like any other business and those who think it is, usually end up with omelettes on their heads. Binotto has been around the block enough times to avoid the obvious pitfalls and the last couple of months have been pretty unpleasant to watch as the bullets have landed closer and closer to his dancing feet.

It has felt like some strange modern version of the auto-da-fé, a ritual process used by the Inquisition centuries ago during which getting rid of heretics became a sort of public entertainment, which included a mass, a procession, the reading of the sentences and then finally the punishment, including the ultimate sanction, which was to be burned at the stake.

As to what happens after the Binotto's funeral pyre burns out, we will have to see. The only people who seem to want the job are people who are not qualified to do it. There have been some pretty wild rumours which I think probably reflects Ferrari's struggle to find a suitable replacement. It is a poisoned chalice, with far more chance of failure than success, unless the chosen one is given complete freedom and the high-ups at Ferrari are kept out of the equation. Todt did it by insisting that he be left alone and was able to develop the right atmosphere within the team. I cannot see why those who have been there before would want to go back and reprise the roles they had 30 years ago. An outsider is unlikely to work because it will take years for a newcomer to understand the politics that goes on down there. Perhaps the best chance is to have someone with some industry clout, who will take the flak and let the team get on doing what it is doing. Obviously there do need to be some changes because the mistakes made have often been repeated... which is never a good sign.

In the interim, the other F1 teams will continue to accelerate away, racing one another and sniggering quietly at Ferrari's misfortunes... Still, a massive failure can be a good source of motivation. In the end, the departure of Binotto can only be seen as the result of the top management thinking they know best. Binotto would not have left if he had felt protected from on high. Clearly he did not.

In order to have any success in Formula 1, a team must feel that it is a team. It is ultimately irrelevant whether Binotto was fired or resigned because the cause is the same.

The next chapter of Ferrari history will judge not only whoever drinks from the chalice that is offered, but also the people who offer it.

From Bexhill-on-Sea

8 December 2022

Bexhill-on-Sea is a nice enough seaside resort on the south coast of England, between Hastings and Eastbourne. It is a place where the average age is eight years above the national average. In some parts of the town, as many as 44 percent of the population is over 65. It is a place for peace and quiet. It is off the major roads and railways. It has a vague feeling of gentility, with its well-tended gardens and its greensward, with shelters in case of sudden storms. It has a shingle beach, with sand at low tide. There are wooden breakwaters and beach huts. Bexhill-on-Sea plods along in a cheerful English kind of way, although the holidaymakers are fewer these days. If one looks at the numbers, it is an impressive change with Britons making 6.7 million foreign trips in 1971, but 93 million by 2019. The pandemic and Brexit may change that, but Bexhill-on-Sea and other seaside resorts have been suffering for years.

The 7th Earl de la Warr, once the local landowner, would not be very happy as it was his idea to turn the place into something a bit more glamorous than the marshy scrubland it once was. In the late 1700s, physicians began to argue in favour of the restorative properties of fresh air and sea water, and so aristocrats started going to the seaside.

The south coast had fewer sandy beaches but more sunshine and once the railways were built, it was easier to get there. Earl de la Warr owned a large stretch of the coastline and decided it had potential and so he paid for the construction of a sea wall and planned a whole new district around the promenade he had created, including the imposing Sackville Hotel (Sackville being his family name). This was all back in the 1880s.

But you may be surprised to know that Bexhill-on-Sea was the birthplace of British motor racing... No, I'm not kidding.

It is a story that begins, I suppose, with a violent storm in the Irish Sea in 1890 when Lionel Sackville, the Viscount Cantelupe, the 7th Earl's eldest son, was drowned when his yacht Frania was blown on to rocks in the Lough of Belfast. He was just 22.

His younger brother Gilbert thus became Viscount Cantelupe and heir to the family fortune. He was like many rich young men at the time, a sportsman and something of an adventurer. He was a big fan of cycling and being a modern sort of chap, he was also investing in new technology and owned shares and sat on the board of the Dunlop Pneumatic Tyre Company.

He inherited the family estates in 1896 when the Earl went off to the big seaside resort in the sky. By then, the construction of Bexhill-on-Sea was largely completed and the new Earl went off to fight in the Boer War and was wounded at the Battle of Scheepersnek. When he came back, he got himself into a messy and rather scandalous divorce but found time to write some cheques for the construction of "a bicycle boulevard" along the seafront from the Sackville Hotel to Galley Hill, to the east. This was designed to promote the resort and at the same time to spread the word about the wonders of Dunlop tyres. In 1902, as a further piece of promotion, the Earl converted his boulevard into an automobile track. He had seen an event along similar lines in France but knew it was very difficult in Britain because of the country's daft speed limit of 12mph on all public roads, which meant that all racing had to be done either abroad, or on private land.

Bexhill-on-Sea was private land.

Thus, the Whitsuntide Motor Races took place on Monday May 19, 1902, a bank holiday, and more than 200 machines of various kinds were entered and tens of thousands of people arrived by train to watch the big event. The racing proved to be a big success with the French driver Léon Serpollet winning in one of his steam-powered cars, which recorded the highest speed of 54mph.

There would be further races in 1904 and 1906, despite some local opposition, before the construction of Brooklands in 1907 created a permanent motor racing venue for the sport and Bexhill-on-Sea dropped off the map.

It was all forgotten until the 1980s when the town, keen to attract more visitors, started publicising its history and the road signs began to read: "the birthplace of British motor racing".

This has nothing much to do with modern motorsport but I mention it because I went there, while killing time before catching the overnight ferry from Newhaven to Dieppe, having popped over to England to see some folk and attend the Autosport Awards, the annual motorsport industry shindig at the Grosvenor House Hotel in London. The Awards was busy as usual with many of the usual faces, although F1 was not represented in any massive way. Red Bull had a few tables with Christian Horner and Adrian Newey showing up to pick up prizes, while elsewhere there were a few folks from other teams. Given that seven of the 10 Formula 1 teams are based in UK it was not a huge turnout, which is no great surprise given that a lot of F1 folk need time off for good behaviour, while the factories are busy churning out new car bits for 2023. The major topic of conversation, inevitably, was Ferrari, but no-one seemed to know a great deal about the axes swinging in Maranello, although Christian Horner did mention that he heard it was coming as long ago as September. I didn't ask if he found out because Ferrari approached him to take the job, but I assumed that Christian is smart enough not to have ambitions to try to turn Ferrari around.

When you boil it all down, were it not for Jean Todt and the gang of people he built around him at Maranello, the team would look pretty terrible in the modern era of Formula 1. In the Todt era, there were six Drivers' and eight Constructors' Championships, a total of 14 titles. Before that, there was a 15-year period without a championship and now we have just finished the 14th year since the last championship. There have been four team principals since Todt: Stefano Domenicali (2006-2014), Marco Mattiacci (2014), Maurizio Arrivabene (2014-2019) and Mattia Binotto (2019-2022). If you look elsewhere in F1, you can see that stability pays: Horner has been at Red Bull since 2005 (as has Franz Tost at Scuderia AlphaTauri). Toto Wolff has run Mercedes since 2013. Amazing though it may seem, Gunther Steiner is now the fourth longest-serving team principal, having run Haas since 2014 (although the team did not start racing until 2016). Fred Vasseur arrived at Sauber in 2017, Andreas Seidl (McLaren) and Binotto were appointed in 2019, Jost Capito (Williams) in 2020, while Otmar Szafnauer (Alpine) and Mike Krack (Aston Martin) took on their current roles in 2022. Ferrari will now reset to zero with whoever is chosen to lead the team and it is clear that there are some areas at Maranello that need to be changed, although car design does not seem to be the problem.

What is the problem? Well, if the Italians knew that they would probably be able to fix it, wouldn't they? Instability is one thing that must be considered. The main Ferrari company currently has a chairman who has been in charge only a couple of years and the CEO has only been there since the middle of 2021. Neither has any pedigree in motor racing. Car manufacturer bosses have long had problems with F1 because they all underestimate the scale of the challenge. It is not "like any other business" as one occasionally hears them say. It's harder. Having sufficient money (which Ferrari always does) is no guarantee and there are plenty of examples of vast sums of money being wasted in F1 because the people involved did not understand the task.

But that is probably not the main problem at Ferrari. The problem seems to be that, because Ferrari is seen as a national asset and a source of pride for all Italians, there is always media coverage, often of a slightly hysterical nature, particularly if things are not going well. This impacts on the leadership, which puts pressure on the team bosses. The people who work in Ferrari F1 are, to a large extent, competent at what they do. Some are brilliant. Others less so.

Like many companies, there is a danger that the so-called Peter Principle will kick in. This is the paradoxical idea that competent people will be promoted until they get to a position where they are incompetent and then they will stay there, which means that in time, in theory, every position will eventually be filled by employees who are not fully competent in the roles they have.

There is also the question of the blame culture. When things go wrong, a healthy business needs to face up to the reality and fix the problems highlighted. If that does not happen, or if the staff blame one another, things go wrong. When this happens, people are reluctant to accept responsibility for failures and try to move the blame on to others. This creates a climate of fear, which then means that fewer risks are taken and risky decisions are not made, for fear that they will be deemed as mistakes and everyone is fearful that errors will lead to dismissal. This means that people do not feel safe in their roles and so become protective of what they have and reluctant to accept responsibility for their actions and their mistakes.

A new boss at Ferrari will have his or her own views about what needs to change and this will not help the situation. It will probably mean other new people who will need to be integrated into the Ferrari system, who need to learn who is who and who is to be trusted. A change incites more politics rather than less. At the end of the day, however, a leader can only do so much if the top bosses are getting involved.

The ultimate responsibility for all of this rests with the Ferrari chairman John Elkann and the chief executive officer Benedetto Vigna. Vigna has been at Ferrari for only 15 months. His background is in technology. He has no history of motorsport. Elkann is the scion of the Agnelli empire and has other problems that need to be solved. He is the chairman of Stellantis (the merged Peugeot-Fiat), he is CEO of Exor and chairman of its parent company Giovanni Agnelli BV. These two entities control stakes in a wide variety of businesses, including Stellantis, Ferrari, the publishing companies GEDI Gruppo Editoriale (La Repubblica, La Stampa and various other regional newspapers in Italy) plus The Economist. Most significantly at the moment is the ownership of the Juventus football team, which has just fallen into a major scandal, with the entire board of directors resigning as the result of a police investigation into alleged irregularities with the team's transfers. The club has been accused of presenting false accounts to investors and producing invoices for non-existent transactions. It is not what one wants. Caught up in all of this is not only Elkann's cousin Andrea Agnelli, who has run Juventus for the last 12 years (and is a non-executive director of Stellantis) but also former Ferrari team principal Maurizio Arrivabene, who is the managing-director of the team.

No-one was paying much attention to other stories kicking around. F1 folks would be happy without a replacement race for China. The fact that McLaren has named IndyCar driver Alex Palou as the reserve driver for all Grands Prix that do not clash with his commitments in the US is an interesting development, but only if something happens to Lando Norris or Oscar Piastri. In the longer term, it is expected that Palou will join the McLaren IndyCar operation but he obviously still has F1 ambitions. Who knows?

The consensus in F1 seems to be that Daniel Ricciardo could well be a replacement one day for Sergio Perez at Red Bull if the Australian can get back some of his confidence. Daniel has shown that he is a winner and may or may not be a better bet than Perez, who is usually a way off Max Verstappen's pace. If Ricciardo seems to be a better bet one can see him making a comeback as the next generation of Red Bull youngsters is still some way away from knocking on the door in Milton Keynes. Having said that, Red Bull has been beefing up its Formula 2 army with Barbadian driver, Zane Maloney and Enzo Fittipaldi joining Norway's Dennis Hauger, Japan's Ayumu Iwasa and India's Jehan Daruvala. There are also expected to be France's Isack Hadjar and American Jak Crawford in Formula 2 but whether all seven drivers will run in Red Bull colours remains to be seen. Still, Nyck deVries and Yuki Tsonoda are going to be under pressure to deliver more in F1...

It was interesting to see that the 2024 Tour de France will be finishing in Nice, the first time that this has happened in the 119-year history of the event. Officially, this is because the Paris Olympics will start a few days after the bicycle race ends, but one can imagine that Nice has spent a lot of money to land the right (money which probably would have been spent on the French Grand Prix, if there was one). You can bet also that the Amaury Sport Organisation, which runs the Tour, will be looking at other solutions for 2025 onwards because there will always be somebody willing to pay for the start and the finish of the Tour. The ASO likes money, as has been proven in recent years with its decision to run the Dakar Rally in Saudi Arabia. One of the longer speeches at the Autosport Awards was made by Prince Khaled Al-Faisal, the man who has organised the Saudi Arabian Grand Prix in Jeddah. The fact that Saudi was named by Autosport as the inaugural Motorsport Presenter of the Year was an interesting choice, although the Mexican Grand Prix was probably not delighted as it won the last five Race Promoter Trophies, offered by Formula One and presented at the FIA Prizegiving Gala. That award stopped in 2021, which was interesting as it allowed Autosport to slip in there and grab the idea.

It was also quite amusing to see Zak Brown presenting the Award for the Racing Car of the Year to Red Bull Racing's crew and rather sweet that Sebastian Vettel asked for his Gregor Grant Award to be presented by Autosport's F1 reporter Luke Smith (a man from Bexhill-on-Sea, by the way).

Vettel has always been a popular fellow, but he is not in the league of the really big dogs of popularity in F1: Lewis Hamilton and Guenther Steiner. The Haas boss is so popular that tee-shirts bearing his mug have been selling like hot cakes. There is probably even a Guenther Steiner merchandising after-market. I suppose we should now expect to see a range of Steiner stuff... For those who are enamoured by Guenther, there is a book, chronicling his adventures in 2022. This will be called "Surviving to Drive" and has been ghostwritten by a non-F1 journalist. It will be fun to see how it turns out.

When I got back to France, in the early hours of Tuesday, the Dieppe area was wreathed in the worst kind of fog, too thick to see through with normal headlights, and reflecting back the light of the high beams in a blinding fashion. To add to the pain it was thicker in some places than in others and even at that strange hour there is always some idiot who wants to sit on your tail and cannot see what the conditions are like ahead.

It struck me, as I was going through the village of La Chapelle-du-Bourgay, that nearly 100 years ago (in September 1923) a 20-year-old chauffeur called William Grover was going down the very same road in very similar conditions, at the wheel of a Rolls-Royce Silver Ghost, owned by the artist Sir William Orpen. The car was making a strange noise and Grover had a fellow chauffeur with him to try to figure out the problem. In the back were two friends of the chauffeur. Just after La Chapelle-du-Bourgay, as the road curved downhill into the valley of the Varenne, they ran into a bank of fog and Willy lost his bearings. The car went off the road and hit a tree. They were all thrown out and when he came too it was in pitch darkness and only one of the others replied to his calls. They stumbled around in the woods for several hours before finding a farm in Torcy-le-Grand, in the valley below. When dawn came they went back to the crash site and found the other two passengers dead. It was a traumatic moment but despite the crash, Willy still wanted to somehow break into racing, although he had no money.

Probably as a way of avoiding anyone making the connection with the accident, he chose to race under the name "W Williams". Five years later he won the first Monaco Grand Prix, although little was known of him and his story remained a mystery for many years afterwards.

I went very carefully down the hill...

Wherever we go, we are never far from history, whether one is by the seaside, or in the fogs of Normandy...

– Joe Saward's 2022 Green Notebook –

Onwards...

15 December 2022

And so we come to the end of another season in Formula 1. It is hard to believe that I have been doing this job for 40 years, my entire working life. When one puts that number on paper it sound rather a long time, but things moves quickly when you love what you do. Time is elastic. When we are young we have endless afternoons, when time stands still as we play our games and dream our dreams. Life plods along slowly at a linear pace, day after day, week after week. We are keen for it move faster so that we can be "grown-ups".

As we get older and realise that being a kid is great, it feels like everything is rushing by, even if we know that it cannot possibly be the case. When one is young, 20 years is an unfathomably long time. When one is older, what happened 20 years ago seems like just yesterday.

Some may say that I have seen some golden ages in the sport, but if we are forever looking backwards, we do not always appreciate what we have now. Today we can do things that our grandparents only dreamed of doing. How lucky we are. The sport has been able to progress for a period of more than 70 years during which time Europe has been at peace and we have been able to do much as we pleased. Racing has become an industry in which one can make a living, rather than being a hobby for the rich.

For now, the action is over and I am at home, in a forest, deep in the French countryside, about an hour from the nearest city of any size. As I sit at my desk I can hear nothing. The house overlooks a marsh. The local wildlife may not seem fascinating when compared to the world of Formula 1, but it provides a perfect antidote. And in a few short weeks we will be off, doing it all again.

– Joe Saward's 2022 Green Notebook –

– Joe Saward's 2022 Green Notebook –

www.ingramcontent.com/pod-product-compliance
Lightning Source LLC
Chambersburg PA
CBHW050030090426
42735CB00021B/3441